Security Studies Today

Security Studies Today

*Terry Terriff, Stuart Croft, Lucy James
and Patrick M. Morgan*

Polity Press

First published in 1999 by Polity Press in association with Blackwell Publishers Ltd.

Editorial office:
Polity Press
65 Bridge Street
Cambridge CB2 1UR, UK

Marketing and production:
Blackwell Publishers Ltd
108 Cowley Road
Oxford OX4 1JF, UK

Published in the USA by
Blackwell Publishers Inc.
Commerce Place
350 Main Street
Malden, MA 02148, USA

ISBN 0-7456-1772-7
ISBN 0-7456-1773-5 (pbk)

A catalogue record for this book is available from the British Library and has been applied for from the Library of Congress.

Typeset in 10½ on 12½ pt Palatino
by York House Typographic Ltd, London.
Printed in Great Britain by MPG Books, Bodmin, Cornwall.

This book is printed on acid-free paper.

Contents

Introduction

The study of security is central to the study of international relations. Security – being or feeling safe from harm or danger – is usually a condition that is held to be of great value. Political actors in the international system are often willing to exert considerable effort and devote considerable resources to ensuring that they are protected from harm. In thinking about security most of us probably would equate it with the safety of the state from attack, with the possibility of war, and with questions relating to the threat, actual use and management of military force. These issues are indeed important considerations in the study and practice of security, and during the Cold War these issues came to dominate the study and practice largely to the exclusion of other perspectives. Security, however, is more complex than this relatively straightforward interpretation would suggest.

The central problem in the study of security in the post-Cold War era is, simply, that there is no agreement on what constitutes security. Barry Buzan, drawing on W.B. Gallie, has argued that security is an essentially contested concept.[1] Buzan lists twelve different definitions of security that important analysts have produced: the effect, as Buzan desired, is to demonstrate the enormous breadth of approaches that underlie the range of work on definitions of security studies. For Buzan himself, 'the nature of security defies pursuit of an agreed definition.'[2] David Baldwin and Helen Milner have gone so far as to claim that 'The concept of national security is one of the most ambiguous and value-laden terms in social science.'[3] The inherent problem, as Patrick Morgan has neatly summed up, is that 'Security is a condition, like health or status, which defies easy definition and analysis.'[4]

The complexity involved in trying to come to grips with how security should be defined arises for two reasons. First, security studies is a sub-field of international relations, and as will be seen below, the discipline of international relations is deeply divided about its core theoretical ideas. Second, at the core of the concept of security are normative elements that mean that analysts and policy-makers cannot agree upon a definition through an examination of empirical data. Indeed, as will be seen later, one important group of international relations theorists (the post-positivists) deny that empiricism is a valid tool.

The lack of an agreed definition and varied theoretical approaches to examining security raises the question of how one defines security. There is, as Morgan has suggested, no easy answer to this. The act of providing a definition includes some things and excludes others. Yet it is precisely this issue, that is, what should and should not be included, that much of the discussion and debate about security since the end of the Cold War has been about. How, then, are we to make sense of security?

Although the literature that addresses or at least relates to the issue of how security should be conceived or practised is quite disparate, even seemingly divergent approaches do have some common characteristics. What is in dispute is not so much the concept of security *per se* as the sorts of specification that are made about security. Arnold Wolfers, in an article first published in 1952 titled '"National Security" as an Ambiguous Symbol', argued that 'It would be an exaggeration to claim that the symbol of national security is nothing but a stimulus to semantic confusion, though closer analysis will show that if used without specifications it leaves room for more confusion than sound political counsel or scientific usage can afford.'[5] Wolfers's point is that, though security can be characterized as being 'the absence of threats to acquired values',[6] the meaning of security, in terms of what the policy objective is and the means by which this aim is achieved, depends on the specifications made about the concept. Baldwin, drawing on Wolfers's work, has argued that there are essentially seven main types of specification that need to or should be made to impart more precise meaning to the concept of security.[7]

How we understand security, how we can make sense of it, thus depends on the sorts of specification that are made. Much of the recent debate centres on two critical questions.[8] First, who or what should be the focus of our interest in security? Should it be states, groups based on nationality or gender, or individuals? Must we prioritize one level of analysis over another? Second, who or what threatens security? Is it states and the policies of decision-makers? Or are there functional threats, emanating from the environment, or non-state actors such as drug traffickers and transnational criminal organizations? There are also two additional important questions that are closely linked to, and follow from, these key questions: who provides for security, and what methods may or should be undertaken to provide for security? How one answers these latter two questions depends directly on how one answers the first two, and provides a foundation for developing policy designed to achieve 'security'.

With so many questions, it is difficult for students of security to know where to start. Indeed, these questions stretch to the very name of the area that we are trying to investigate. Should we talk of *strategic studies* or *security studies*? Or should we refer to *international security* or, as Barry Buzan would prefer, a theory of *international security studies*?[9]

This book is not going to offer answers to all of these questions. Given the fractured nature of the debate about security, to do so would simply be to assert the hegemony of one set of theoretical assumptions over others. Rather, what we seek to do is to illustrate the range of choice that is available to the analyst when thinking about security issues.

The confusion over what constitutes security is a condition that has been exacerbated by the end of the Cold War. For Kolodziej, the failure of those in the security studies field to predict the end of the Cold War and the collapse of the Soviet state is important, in that it demonstrates that security studies during the Cold War was too narrow.[10] With the collapse of the bipolar confrontation between capitalism and communism, between the United States and the Soviet Union, the heart of the traditional conception of security has been removed. This has had at least four implications.[11] First, there is no longer any consensus about who constitutes the enemy (even though there was always dispute about this). This is a product not only of the collapse of Cold War structures but also, as will be seen below, of the collapse of the hegemony of the realist paradigm in international relations. Second, the officials of states, policy-makers in international organizations such as NATO and the UN, and those who work in non-governmental organizations as well as academics have all sought new definitions of security. That is, more people from more different perspectives have sought to redefine 'security' in the period since 1989–91 than ever before. Third, this has raised in importance the relevance of domestic factors in security issues. Factors such as ethnic strife within the borders of individual states and migration for economic reasons point to the importance of the economic, political and societal strength of a state. Fourth, it is increasingly clear that domestic factors have an impact far beyond national borders. Thus, Germans are concerned about the implications of economic and political stability in Poland for Germany; transnational criminal organizations undermine state authority in nations as diverse as Colombia, Russia, Italy and Myanmar; and so on.

However, as important as the end of the Cold War is for the debate over the meaning of security, it is vital to realize that disagreement over what constitutes security was not created by that end. Of the above four factors, all were present to some degree before 1989. The prominence of realism in theorizing about international relations during the Cold War era was repeatedly contested. Many in the West argued that the Soviet Union was not a threat, and some in the East argued that the West was not a threat. Not all decision-makers were happy with notions of security bipolarity even in the United States, while especially in the non-governmental organizations (NGOs), analysts sought a much broader notion of security. Analysts focusing on Third World security had, from the late 1970s, been focusing not only on domestic sources of insecurity. And transnationalists had widened the focus beyond state action in the early 1970s. Thus, in terms of the meaning of 'security', the division between 1989–91 and that which went before must not be overdrawn. The four factors outlined here were seen to be more significant more widely in the 1990s than earlier; the growth in the amount of interest in security is thus a product of psychology at least as much as it is of geopolitics. One of the problems of contemporary international relations (IR) is that there is a lack of coherent theories of change; thus, when change occurs, there is a tendency to over-emphasize the new and under-emphasize the old. Dramatic change is not unusual, nor is it unique to the late twentieth century. As Jan Aart Scholte notes:

> who in tenth century Europe would have predicted that the Universal Church would subsequently yield to the primacy of the nation state? Who in fifteenth century Africa would have foretold a world steeped in racial discrimination several hundred years later? Who in eighteenth century matrilineal Minangkabau villages on Sumatra would have envisioned the move to a male dominated society? Who amongst the peaceful Eskimos in an earlier epoch would have imagined the present century of total war?[12]

The upsurge in interest in what constitutes security in the post-Cold War period means that there is greater contention on this issue, and hence that there is a much wider range of perspectives on offer. What is the range of thinking on security? Even a brief survey of the literature makes clear that there is a quite broad range of perspectives about how we should think about and analyse security. Unfortunately, given the breadth of the discussion, it is not possible to examine each and every perspective. The spectrum we present should not be seen as being inclusive of all possibilities. There are any number of arguments, many focused narrowly on the question of what precisely is meant by security, that we have not specifically examined. That we have not addressed these does not mean that we judge that they lack validity or are not useful.

The Structure of the Book

The approach we adopt is to examine the main schools of thought in order to elucidate the foundations of the main perspectives, and hence of the main differences, in the debate about security. We seek to explicate how each of these main perspectives conceives security. This task involves identifying the various specifications made about security, and we focus on the two that are most fundamental to understanding what is meant by security: what is being secured (or what is the referent for security), and what is being secured against? What we are concerned with in each chapter is how these two questions are answered and why they are answered in the way they are.

We begin the book with an overview of security and IR in order to delineate the main schools of thought about or approaches to defining security as they are situated in the wider debate on theorizing about the international system. We survey the relationship between the study of IR and the study of security, and examine how other bodies of literature that are predominantly policy-oriented delineate the referent for security and how they analyse what constitutes a threat. From this survey we have identified seven categories of thought that structure the approach taken in the rest of the book: realism, neo-realism, neo-liberalism, peace studies, feminism, post-positivism, and transnational challenges.

Broadly speaking, the book can be divided into two parts. The first examines those bodies of thought whose approach to questions of security is determined by their epistemological and theoretical perspective. The second part examines those bodies which are more pragmatic in their approach, in that they are policy-oriented and concerned with developing new understandings of what we should be secure from.

Chapter 2 explores the realists and neo-realists and the neo-liberalist approach. They define security studies fundamentally in terms of conflictual military relations between states. Born of states' competition for power and a concomitant insecurity, they vehemently oppose broadening the notion of security. One of the strongest realist critiques comes from Stephen Walt, for whom broadening the concept of security threatens to 'destroy its intellectual coherence and make it more difficult to devise solutions to any of these important problems'.[13] Neo-liberals emphasize the role of institutions in minimizing conflict, and suggest that empirically IR is normally peaceful.

Chapter 3 focuses on peace studies, stressing the importance of co-operation between states. Peace studies analysts also see security studies as concerned with co-operative relations between states, but press for a more positivist, prescriptive role for the analyst. Chapter 4 examines the complex and sophisticated feminist literature, with a particular emphasis on feminist perspectives that are grounded in positivist or empirical social science. The fifth chapter examines post-positivist approaches. While the above approaches examine the referent point for security studies and the relevant threats, the post-positivists examine the meaning of security. The similarities in the positivist approaches stand out when compared with post-modernist and critical theory perspectives.

The last two chapters examine several bodies of argument that do not stem from a particular theoretical or epistemological perspective, but rather focus on particular factors or processes which can affect security. These analyses seek to broaden relevant threats to include non-military ones and in doing so shift the referent point for security. Included in this group are those analysts who argue that environmental challenges are of central importance, and those who focus on other transnational challenges such as economic well-being, transnational criminal organizations and the mass movement of peoples

The structure outlined above for this book seems to us to be the most useful, but it reveals certain values and assumptions and, as a consequence, is vulnerable to criticism. First, chapters 2–7 look like a modified version of White's 'Three Rs' conception of IR: realists (Machiavellians), rationalists (Grotians) and revolutionists (Kantians); or of Michael Banks's realism, pluralism and structuralism.[14] Many others have used a similar approach to describe the nature of IR, and thus it may not seem controversial.[15] However, there are dangers in picturing IR and security studies in this way, for it encourages us to ignore other legitimate perspectives and theoretical concerns.[16] As Steve Smith puts it, 'where, for example, is class, or ethnicity, or gender … ? Where are the concerns of developing countries … ? It is, in fact, a Western/white/male/conservative view of international theory.'[17] Hence, we seek to broaden the 'Three Rs' approach by including a range of quite different epistemological and pragmatic perspectives, and within each chapter an attempt is also made to consider a range of perspectives.

The second potential problem is that some analysts may argue that by *beginning* with categories of realist thought as we do, we are necessarily *privileging* it. This is not the aim. However, we argue that since realists and neo-realists have provided the dominant theoretical approach in IR, much of the theoretical debate has been constructed in terms of criticizing realism, and this has also been true in security studies. We seek to identify and illustrate a range of approaches to security, believing that some perspectives have been ignored for too long (feminist arguments) and are struggling to be seen as legitimate (post-positivism). We seek to outline a spectrum of traditions rather than choose between them, and we do not seek to provide a way for the reader to choose between them. There is no independent basis for choosing between the rival claims, and trying to do so asserts the hegemony of one theoretical perspective. We aim to provide a comprehensive picture of views in security studies while taking into account that there is more literature on some perspectives than others.

We do recognize that realism is on stronger ground in the security field than in other parts of IR. This has led to suggestions that neo-realism be applied to security issues and neo-liberalism, for example, to international political economy, where co-operation is the norm. However, this means ignoring insistent claims that neo-liberalism can be readily applied to security,[18] and we seek to open the security field to perspectives other than realist ones.

Finally, why do we write a book which seems to reassert the centrality of security in debates on international politics? Does this illustrate a longing for the certainties of the Cold War, or a desire to re-establish the hegemony of strategic studies? No, our belief is that security is important because everyone else agrees that something called security is important. We are well aware that 'those strategists who do not attempt to be a part of the solution will undoubtedly become an increasingly important part of the problem',[19] and that 'when all is sweetness and light, harmony and fraternity, the security specialist should either take a well-earned rest ... or else do the rounds pointing out where everything might still come apart. In doing so care should be taken not to aggravate matters by exaggerating dangers. That is in itself a threat to security.'[20] Still, the end of the Cold War does not mean that all is sweetness and light; it depends on one's perspective on security.

There is nobody in the IR debate who would argue that security concerns are irrelevant, but there is little consensus beyond that. As seen above, many argue that traditional security issues, which focus on the security of states against other states, are much less relevant to the majority of humanity, and certainly to the lives of the poor and a large number of women, than IR has allowed. Part of the logic is that we study what we are. As Ken Booth has put it, 'the explanation of who got what in world politics, as told ... by white male Anglo-American professors of international relations, looked very different from that which would have been told (had we had the chance to hear it) by, say, a genitally mutilated, child-worn, hungry young woman from a war-torn part of Africa.'[21] This is a very important warning, especially for three white, Anglo-American-Canadian male analysts and one white, Anglo female analyst writing on the nature of security; we recognize that we are giving a partial view. But this is true of all publications in security studies, in IR and in the whole of the social sciences.

1 | International Relations and Security Studies

This first chapter seeks to set the context for our examination of security. It does so through two sections. The first examines the relationship between the study of security and the study of international relations, tracing the development of the discipline of international relations (IR). Security, and war, were at the heart of IR in the self-conscious formation of the discipline during the twentieth century. The vehicle for planting security at the heart of IR was the long domination of realist theory in both IR and the sub-field of security. The second section examines how others define the referent point for security and, consequently, how they have analysed the nature of threats.

International Relations and Security

The origin of thinking about IR is much debated. Among the many suggested starting dates for the discipline, three are outlined here. In each, the rise of thinking about IR is associated with the nature of, and conclusion to, a war – the Peloponnesian War, the Thirty Years War and the First World War. In other words, war, peace and security have been absolutely central to the nature of IR's development.

One view, identified with realists such as E.H. Carr,[1] suggests that IR began with Thucydides and the conflict amongst the Greek city-states two and a half thousand years ago. Thucydides wrote that 'the strong do what they have the power to do and the weak accept what they have to accept.'[2] Echoing this deliberately, Carr wrote in *The Twenty Years' Crisis, 1919–1939* that 'The majority rules because it is stronger, the minority submits because it is weaker.'[3] Under this argument, the bloody Peloponnesian War displayed the core theoretical parameters for the nature of IR, by highlighting violent conflict between sovereign entities in a condition of anarchy.

An alternative origin of IR theorizing is the late Middle Ages, symbolized by the Peace of Westphalia. Kal Holsti, in his sweeping *Peace and War: Armed Conflicts and International Order 1648–1989*, notes that 'there is a consensus amongst scholars of international relations that a single states system, or society of states, has existed since the treaties of Westphalia.'[4] Torbjörn Knutsen agrees, suggesting that the origin of IR theory 'largely coincides with the long sixteenth century'.[5] By this time, the concepts of sovereignty, notional equality of states, international law, legitimacy and international society had emerged along with the practice of diplomacy and the balance of power.[6] In this perspective, IR was created by theorists and leaders of states seeking to understand the military, political and normative limits that constrained violent conflict.

A third possibility is that academic enquiry into IR 'began in Aberystwyth [UK] in 1919'.[7] The level of violence associated with the Great War was such that many felt that it was important not only to analyse the origins and conduct of war but to prescribe means of preventing it. This led to considerable investment in the study of war and IR. Academic chairs and departments were established in the United Kingdom and the United States, as were research institutes such as the Royal Institute of International Affairs in London, and the Council on Foreign Relations in New York, and major new journals such as *International Affairs* in Britain and *Foreign Affairs* in the US.

The central point is that within each of these three views, the starting point for the field is *insecurity*, the experience and implications of war and resulting fears for the viability of new structures of peace. Thus, the Peloponnesian War, the Thirty Years War and the Great War have traditionally been taken as instigating and then shaping our theoretical approaches to IR. It is not surprising that security is the 'preeminent concept of international relations. . . . No other concept in international relations packs the metaphysical punch, or commands the disciplinary power, of "security".[8]

For some, IR is a sub-field of security. For example, Jervis tells us that 'we are accustomed to thinking of *international relations* in terms of deterrence and compellance', core concepts of a security studies that focuses on military relations between states.[9] From a different perspective and, indeed, a different discipline, Michael Mann has argued that what is really sought from IR 'is substantive theory on its most important issue of all: the question of war and peace'.[10]

We certainly do not go this far. Security studies is presented in this book as a sub-field of IR. This means that an approach to security ought to be defined by the central theoretical perspective on IR that is being employed. However, this immediately presents a problem, for the discipline of IR is fragmented into highly contending perspectives.

That the origin of thinking about IR is contested will not surprise readers, given that the IR debate had, by the late 1980s, become deeply fractured. Major analysts cannot agree on even the most basic issues. Bachrach and Baratz argued over thirty years ago that force is not the same concept as power.[11] Hammond tells us that the use of armed force means a failure of policy in terms of power, for a power relationship is psychological and aims to achieve goals without the use of force.[12] However, Freedman suggests that 'this does not require a distinction between power and brute force. Force is not something different, merely the most extreme case when recognition of . . . power becomes inescapable.'[13] And in Morgenthau's most famous work, 'power' and 'force' are used interchangeably.[14]

The presence of a significant debate over the nature of IR for the entire twentieth century is of great importance. That IR needs theoretical grounding is not controversial; whether it *has* a theoretical grounding is. A first-year undergraduate in political science may take a course which introduces the rich tradition in political theory. All too often, a student taking a degree in IR will enter the programme expecting to study current events and takes an introductory course that does not cover the heritage of theorizing in the field.

The reluctance of the IR community to emphasize its intellectual roots, heightened by the post-positivist attack on those roots, weakens identification of IR as a discipline worthy of study. Of course this is nothing new, Martin Wight having voiced these concerns in 1966 with his question 'why is there no international theory?'[15] But that timidity has led to an under-emphasis on the changing nature of theorizing about IR, and has weakened our ability to account fully for the relationship of security issues to IR.

There are three broad traditions in the study of IR.[16] The first draws on political theory and social scientific theorizing, seeks to generate prediction and models of explanation, and has been very influential in the United States. The second works in the tradition of the historian, is usually termed 'contemporary history' in the IR literature, and has been very influential in the United Kingdom. The third is international law and has been particularly powerful in the development of IR in continental Western Europe.

Many have struggled to break free from these intellectual roots. Political scientists criticize the discipline for lacking theoretical sophistication. Historians criticize it for being no more than a commentary on contemporary events, its practitioners being at worst mere 'journalists'. International lawyers see it as soft, lacking legal rigour. Most obviously missing as an intellectual root is sociology, an oversight that did not begin to be corrected until the late 1980s.

Much of the discussion since the late 1980s has been characterized as a 'third debate'. According to the usual chronology, the first great debate occurred between the utopians, who dominated the profession after the Great War, and the realists, who became dominant in the late 1930s. The utopians were allegedly concerned with improving the world, particularly through the abolition of war (how the world *should* be), while realists were concerned with the state of the world (how the world *is*). The second great debate arose in the 1960s, most notoriously in the argument between Bull and Northedge on one side, and Kaplan and Rosenau on the other.[17] For the former, an understanding of history and good judgement were central, while their opponents stressed the need to develop a scientific (behaviouralist) approach focused on quantification. The 'Great Debate' threatened to pull the discipline apart. Although it did not, theoretical pluralism did expand with the emergence of a transnationalist challenge to realism in the

1970s. This led to the third debate in which we are now involved.

However, there is a problem here because there are really three 'third debates' now taking place.[18] The first is between neo-realism and neo-liberalism; the second includes the structuralists in what Michael Banks has called the inter-paradigm debate; and the third involves the post-positivists. We review them in order here according to their relative prominence.

First, the debate between neo-realism and neo-liberalism. Many argue that 'Since the publication of Kenneth Waltz's *Theory of International Politics* in 1979, neo-realism has become a dominant school in international relations.'[19] In the 1980s, it was challenged by a new variant of liberalism.[20] Both accept anarchy as the starting point. For neo-liberals, anarchy inhibits co-operation among states because it offers incentives to cheat; thus, if institutions can ameliorate this problem, co-operation can flourish. Realists hold that under anarchy there is no superior authority to provide protection against defection or cheating and institutions cannot fundamentally change this.[21] However, the points of contention between the two seem very narrow – being focused on whether states must be preoccupied by relative gains or can settle for absolute gains – leading to the possibility of what Wæver calls a 'neo-neo' synthesis.[22]

The second version of the 'third debate' is put forward by Michael Banks, who argues that there are three paradigms: realism, pluralism and structuralism. Realism embraces both classic and neo forms; pluralism refers to variants of liberalism; and structuralism involves analysts who focus on socio-economic structure. The structuralists – or globalists – see world politics in terms of globalized economic forces. An example is Immanuel Wallerstein, who explores international politics in terms of a single world system which changes over time. The current capitalist world system is four hundred years old, is based on the global-scale division of labour, and is guided by capital accumulation. Similar structuralist views are put forward by dependency theorists – who argue that the South, or periphery, is structurally prevented from developing by the North, or core – and by neo-Marxists such as Halliday and Rosenberg.[23] Halliday, for example, argues:

> yet it is precisely the globalizing dynamic of capitalism which

explains the growth of the whole international system, since Columbus set sail in 1492, and which explains how and why the West prevailed over the communist world in the Cold War: as a thwarted development project communism was a product of the tensions of capitalist society, socially, ideologically and internationally, but it was in the end destroyed by it.[24]

Each paradigm is internally coherent, but contradicts the others in terms of actors (states; states plus other actors; classes, respectively), variables, concepts, and so on.[25]

The final 'third debate' is suggested by Yosef Lapid. In his conception, the first debate was between realism and idealism in the 1940s and 1950s; the second between behaviouralism and traditionalism in the 1960s; and the third is a discourse about the nature of analytical frameworks (positivism against post-positivism).[26] Neo-realism, neo-liberalism and structuralism are all in the positivist camp, now opposed by post-positivists as in critical theory and postmodernism.

The distinctions between these 'third debates' are important, for they emphasize different perspectives. The neo-neo debate ignores structuralism and (usually) post-positivism.[27] Banks sees the third debate as including the structuralists, but not post-positivists; Lapid sees it as involving the post-structuralists, but puts all 'traditional' forms of IR into one category.

The variant of the third debate to which Lapid refers is rather different, for he includes post-positivists. But what is the positivism that this group attacks? 'Simply and briefly put, the positivist believes that knowledge can only be gained from sensory experience, that complex ideas (or facts) about the world are arrived at by combining simpler ideas but that all complex ideas ultimately can be traced back to component simpler ideas acquired by sensory experience.'[28] The post-positivists come in a variety of forms – postmodernists and critical theorists to mention a couple – but are united by the belief that the world is socially, not objectively, constructed. Consider an example from authors who would not label themselves 'post-positivist'. Smoke and Harman argue that 'the widespread absence of this belief in [the] real possibility [of real peace] is one of the most important hindrances to actual progress toward these goals.'[29] That is, if more people believe real peace is possible, it automatically becomes more possible:

social constructions (beliefs) are more important than geopolitical ones. A classic version is provided by Alexander Wendt,
who argues that there is no independent reality to international anarchy; rather, 'anarchy is what states make of it.'[30]

A central component of social construction is identity. It is
clearly important to the way we think. In one sense this is not
controversial: most people would agree that international politics revolves around an identity we call nationality. The power
of identity in social, economic and political relations is clear. To
be black in the southern United States in the period before the
Civil Rights movement, or in South Africa before the fall of
apartheid, was to have a social, political and economic position
imposed regardless of one's choice, abilities and willingness to
work hard. Post-positivists take this much further. A central
insight is that we all have *multiple* identities, that sometimes
these identities conflict, and that at times one (or more) of them
are suppressed. Examples abound: to be Jewish and German in
Nazi Germany; a kulak and a Russian under Stalin; a middle-
class professional and a Cambodian under Pol Pot; in each of
these extreme cases, one identity was violently suppressed.

It is in considering identity that conceptual space is provided
for the extensive literature on feminism. 'Just as realists centre
their expectations on the hierarchical relations between states
and Marxists on unequal class relations, feminism can bring to
light gender hierarchies embedded in the theories and practices of world politics and allow us to see the extent to which all
these systems of domination are interrelated.'[31] All feminist
analysts agree with realists and others that power is important;
but feminists argue that analysts:

> have under-estimated the amount and varieties of power at
> work. It has taken power to deprive women of land titles and
> leave them little choice but to sexually service soldiers and
> banana workers. It has taken power to keep women out of their
> countries' diplomatic corps and out of the upper reaches of the
> World Bank. It has taken power to keep questions of inequity
> between local men and women off the agendas of many nation-
> alist movements in industrialized as well as agrarian
> societies.[32]

In IR, women are invisible. One can see this in titles like
Waltz's *Man, the State and War*, which many feminists see as

symbolizing all that is wrong in the way in which the study of IR is constructed,[33] as with Kenneth Thompson's *Masters of International Thought* and *Fathers of International Thought*.[34] Is it the case that only men have had anything of note to say about IR, and if so, what does this say about the position of women within IR?

In security, feminists emphasize the gender-specific nature of violence. In addition, feminists argue that security must be seen in a broad fashion. 'Feminist perspectives on security would assume that violence, whether it be in the international, national, or family realm, is interconnected. Family violence must be seen in the context of wider power relations; it occurs within a gendered society in which male power dominates at all levels.'[35]

We can conclude this brief overview of the development of IR and the role of security studies within it with a final observation. The chronology of the development of IR does not mean there has been an evolution, in the sense that ideas/ theories have become more complex and sophisticated. Ideas have changed and theories have sometimes interacted, but there has not necessarily been intellectual progress, or a dialectic advance. What has been traced above is, in essence, a chronology of dominant conceptions of IR and challenges to them. Inevitably, there are a number of silences in examining IR in this way. A feminist analysis of the development of thinking about IR and security studies would produce different insights.[36] We do not seek to delegitimize such approaches; rather, we seek to start from the traditional core of security studies and then work through alternative notions of security.

Conceptions of Security

In this theoretical competition, it is inevitable that there are multiple conceptions of security, and in this section, we outline the range of different approaches. And it is very extensive. Jack Levy cites 441 different authorities who have made a contribution to the theoretical or empirical study of war.[37] And his study is partial, limited by being the work of only one scholar and by Levy's decision to include only works in the English language.

This section proceeds in four parts. The first two draw on the two central questions posed in the introduction: should the referent point for security be states, peoples, or individuals, and what range of threats should be considered? The third part probes whether insecurity and war can play any useful role in international relations. The final part considers the meaning of peace and whether it can be attained.

The Referent Point for Security

In realist conceptions of security the clear referent point is the state. Buzan defines threats to states in three senses: to the idea of the state (nationalism); to the physical base of the state (population and resources); and to the institutional expression of the state (political system).[38] However, there is debate over whether one definition suffices for the entire world or whether different parts of it require different notions of security. In the former camp are most neo-realists, who, seeing the system as dominant, necessarily suggest that security anywhere is derived from the system's anarchic nature.

In the latter camp are those who argue that Third World states are so different from those in the developed world that different notions of security must be applied. There are significant differences, however. Some make the state the referent point and stress the fragility and comparative infancy of the Third World state. Ayoob, for example, argues that Third World security refers to 'vulnerabilities – both internal and external – that threaten or have the potential to bring down or weaken state structures, both territorial and institutional, and governing regimes'.[39] As a consequence 'the demands of the state-making process and the societal responses that [such vulnerabilities] generate put a tremendous load on the institutional machinery of the state, a load which the state is usually unable to handle effectively', so that 'the Third World state's lack of control over its international environment and, even more importantly, its inability to insulate its state-making process from international systemic pressure' combine to produce an 'all-pervading security problem that is basically insoluble'.[40] Hence security is a political condition, in which Third World states can have external threats, but are also internally threatened, often primarily, by the political impact of a low level of social cohesion and the lack of regime legitimacy.[41] But for others, such as Nicole Ball, it is not Third World states but ruling regimes that are the key referent point. Regime security is central in this literature because in some Third World states it is clear that the purpose of government policy is not to make citizens secure but to safeguard the elite's grip on power.[42]

In Buzan's *People, States and Fear* the referent object is the state. However, in one of his later books society is raised to an equal level with the state while the threat to a state is to its sovereignty; for a society the threat is to its identity. Societal security is about 'the sustainability, within acceptable conditions for evolution, of traditional patterns of language, culture, association, and religious and national identity and custom'.[43]

This is one of just several ways of widening the referent point beyond the state. Kolodziej would push the analysis beyond the state level so that 'security policy may be defined as the pursuit by groups and states to influence and determine the overall structure of the international security system or the component parts in preferred ways'.[44] Some go further and argue for a people-centred approach, rather than one that privileges the state. Within this, Booth suggests that 'feminist perspectives are integral to any people-centred subject.'[45] Feminists deny:

> the separability of gendered insecurities from those describable in military, economic, and ecological terms; such problems cannot be fully resolved without also overcoming the domination and exploitation of women that takes place in each of these domains. Such a conception of security is based on the assumption that social justice, including gender justice, is necessary for an enduring peace.[46]

Other analysts argue that the referent point should be the security of individuals. This view takes seriously such threats as starvation, disease, disablement and 'all sorts of other hazards – from bankruptcy to unemployment'.[47] Ken Booth argues 'emancipation is the freeing of people (as individuals and groups) from the physical and human constraints which stop them carrying out what they would freely choose to do ... Emancipation, not power and order, produces true security. Emancipation, theoretically, is security.'[48]

Thus, there is no consensus on the referent point. As Job puts it:

> in principle, four or more distinct securities may be at issue simultaneously: the security of the individual citizen, the security of the nation, the security of the regime, and the security of the state. For a society composed of communal groups, with distinctive ethnic or religious identifications, their perceived securities may also be at stake, making the interplay and competition among the various players even more complex and unresolvable.[49]

We may lack agreement on the referent point but there is no shortage of choices!

The Nature of Security Threats

In the same way, there is widespread disagreement over what constitutes a threat. A general analysis of threats must begin with war in its traditional sense: military conflict between states. As noted above, war was at the heart of the academic study of IR, whenever one thinks it began. But there is no agreement on what is meant by the threat of war. Hobbes argued:

> that in the nature of man, we find three principal causes of quarrel. First, competition; secondly, diffidence; thirdly, glory. The first, maketh man invade for gain; the second, for safety; and the third, for reputation ... Hereby it is manifest, that during the time men live without a common power to keep them all in awe, they are in that condition which is called war; and such a war, as is of every man, against every man.[50]

This view is the classic realist analysis – human beings unconstrained by government and law (anarchy) display motives and behaviour that lead to war and hence to threats and insecurity.[51]

Once we anticipate war due to anarchy, then preparations for war, the realm of strategy, become crucial. War as a threat is the possibility of being forcibly subject to others. In the words of Karl von Clausewitz: 'War is nothing but a duel on a larger scale. Countless duels go to make up war, but a picture of it as a whole can be formed by imagining a pair of wrestlers. Each tries through physical force to compel the other to do his will ... Force ... is thus the *means* of war; to impose our will on the enemy is its *object*.'[52]

Other realists – notably Gilpin – may also argue that economic inequality is the root of threats. 'As a consequence of this tendency for uneven growth, the functioning of the world economy has major consequences for international security. In transforming the international balance of economic and military power, it makes some states more secure while it increases the insecurity of some others.'[53]

But there are a number of other threats that analysts contend should be included in security studies. Buzan suggests that 'the security of human collectivities is affected by factors in five major sectors: military, political, economic, societal and environmental', with threats of each sort (military, political, etc.) having to be confronted.[54] Developing this theme, Richard Ullman defined threats as follows:

> A threat to national security is an action or sequence of events that (1) threatens drastically and over a relatively brief span of time to degrade the quality of life for the inhabitants of the state, or (2) threatens significantly to narrow the range of policy choices available to the government of a state or to private nongovernmental entities (persons, groups, corporations) within the state.[55]

This certainly broadens the notion of what can threaten (while maintaining that what is threatened is the state).

Some analysts worry that military issues impinge upon security at other levels. Adler argues that the overwhelming security threat is nuclear war, and the costs – especially environmental and economic costs – that would result should such a war ever occur. Hence, 'progress in international security will take place only when avoiding nuclear war does not come at the expense of human welfare and human rights.'[56]

There is a range of possible threats once we move beyond the military sphere. Caroline Thomas, for example, suggests that when examining Third World security one must consider 'nation-building, the search for secure systems of food, health, money and trade, as well as the search for security through nuclear weapons.'[57] This gives us poverty, poor health care and lack of education as security issues. This was part of the thinking of the Brandt Report: 'while hunger rules peace cannot prevail. He who wants to ban war must also ban mass poverty.'[58] Others include environmental issues: 'it is deceptive imagery to pretend that the "environment crisis" is something "out there" which threatens us all. The environmental or planetary situation is as much a product of state policies as is the danger of war.'[59]

In a sense, none of this is new. Peace studies made a vital contribution to security discussions in the late 1960s when these analysts first introduced the concept of structural violence, including consideration of the harm done to the life expectancy and health of individuals and groups through certain economic and political processes.[60]

Those in a post-positivist vein argue that there is a problem with the notion of threat. Constructing 'threats' is part of constructing the 'other'; an identity imbued with characteristics we like to think are opposite to our own. Rather than looking 'out there', we should concern ourselves with the problems and threats we cause. If 'ozone holes are a threat, is the enemy us?'[61] Ken Booth goes further: 'some analysts argue that one of our problems in dealing with the future is that we presently lack an easily identifiable enemy ... This is misconceived. We do have an enemy, and an enemy of global proportions at that. The enemy is us. Western consumerist democracy ... is the problem.'[62]

The Utility of War

It may seem redundant to ask whether war can play any useful role. After all, is war not inevitable? As Carr argued, war 'lurks in the background of international politics just as revolution lurks in the background of domestic politics'.[63] Hedley Bull also argues that war is a central institution: 'War and the threat of war are not the only determinants of the shape of the international system; but they are so basic that even the terms we use to describe the system – great powers and small powers, alliances and spheres of influence, balances of power and hegemony – are scarcely intelligible except in relation to war and the threat of war.'[64] And not just realists and those in the English School hold that violent conflict is inevitable. For historical materialists:

> the central concern of International Relations becomes not security, and the actions of the nation-state directed to defending and enhancing it, but rather conflict, and the ways in which this is generated, conducted, and resolved. Underlying the myriad events of international affairs lies social conflict, within and across frontiers, the pursuit of wealth and economic power as the source of these manifold events.[65]

But if conflict is inherent, this is not an entirely negative view. For Waltz, the best we can hope for is not peace but long periods of systemic stability, which he defines as the absence not of war, but of system-wide war. Like Bull, Waltz sees war as playing a useful function, with systemic stability enhanced and the chances of a great war reduced when there are a relatively low number of powers in the system. Thus, a bipolar structure is the most stable.[66] For some analysts in this tradition, Gilpin for example, war has been the key engine of change in the international system.[67]

Wars between all the great powers, which are termed system-transforming (or system-convulsing) in nature, 'are cataclysms through which a coalition of challengers to the prevailing hegemonic power has overturned the preexisting rank order of states. These wars and the hierarchical reorderings that follow in their aftermath have occurred at fairly regular intervals.'[68] War and conflict, for these authors, are therefore both inherent and useful. So how can we talk of peace?

The Possibility of Peace

This seems to suggest that threats are inescapable, and conflict inevitable. But is this so? Stoessinger argues that:

> whereas aggression may be inherent [in human nature], war is learned behaviour, and as such can be unlearned and ultimately selected out entirely. Humans have dispensed with other habits

that previously seemed impossible to shed. For example, during the Ice Age, when people lived in caves, incest was perfectly
acceptable, whereas today incest is almost universally taboo ...
Like slavery and cannibalism, war too can be eliminated from
humankind's arsenal of horrors.[69]

And Jan Aart Scholte points to cases where 'organized group
killing has been absent from a number of social contexts, e.g.
amongst the Shoshone of the Great Basin, the Lepchas of
Sikkim and others'.[70] An excellent example is provided by Neta
Crawford in an examination of the League of the Iroquois in
pre-colonial North America, which prevented warfare
between the indigenous nations for over three hundred
years.[71]

This has led analysts to argue that war can be overcome; they
therefore disagree fundamentally with the realists, neo-realists
and neo-Marxists. As Lynn Miller put it:

we are now confronted with a realistic possibility for ending for
the first time in human history large-scale warfare among
advanced states ... we have come to a point in world development at which we begin to see that true greatness for societies
will increasingly be measured in terms, not of the empires or
military resources they command, but in the extent and quality
of their socioeconomic relationships.[72]

Inspiration for these views is often taken explicitly from Kant's
Perpetual Peace.[73]

There are several important bodies of thought here: those
who argue for the abolition of anarchy; liberals who argue that
the benefits of commerce will overcome the will to fight; and
democratic peace theorists, who suggest that anarchy does not
lead to war between democracies. In the first group are those
who contend that only centralized authority – eliminating
anarchy – can lead to a peaceful world. Clark and Sohn argued
in favour of the creation of a system of world law, with world
tribunals and a world police force, to eliminate war.[74] Silviu
Brucan argues for the transfer of power to a world authority –
not a world government, for the abolition of states is not
envisaged – in order (in part) to entrench peace and abolish
war.[75] These analysts agree with the realists that anarchy leads
to war; they disagree with the realists in believing it is possible
to go beyond anarchy.

Liberal capitalists have argued that 'commerce was essentially peaceful, the pursuit of rational men following their own interests. By contrast, they regarded war as an irrational anachronism.'[76] Norman Angell put this forward at the beginning of the twentieth century, suggesting that war would eventually end because it was not profitable. It only continued because leaders did not understand this and thus the key task was to convince them.[77] Neo-Marxists disagree with this, as they see the expansion of capitalism leading to more voracious capital accumulation and resulting conflict.

Finally, democratic peace theory suggests that democratic states do not go to war with each other. The more democracies in the world, the greater the zones of peace. One such theorist is Francis Fukuyama, who argues that an expanding number of democratic states will continue to change fundamentally the nature of the international system, overcoming the conflictual nature of anarchy.[78] However, Mann disagrees. In his view the 'civil society militarism' of liberal states resulted in the genocide of the Carib people and the population of Tasmania, while the native peoples of the Americas and Australia were reduced by 90 per cent from their initial levels.[79] He also points to Doyle's evidence that in the twentieth century liberal states have been more likely than authoritarian ones to commit aggression against non-European peoples.[80]

But what is this 'peace' that is being discussed? 'Peace' may be used in two analytically distinct senses. As Burton put it:

> the first describes a 'non-war' condition; strategy, armaments, alliances and collective security arrangements are designed to prevent war, to maintain a non-war or a 'neither-peace-nor-war' situation ... The second meaning of 'peace' as a goal in International Relations theory relates to those processes of the system which do not rest upon deterrence or enforcement by any agent.[81]

The discussion so far has rested upon a meaning of 'peace' that derives from the second definition; what of conceptions derived from the first, which focus on the possibility of international co-operation minimizing the resort to violence? Three perspectives will be discussed, relating to collective security, a security community, and a security regime.

The most popularly discussed variant for minimizing

conflict is collective security, an approach that has been of continuing interest since early in the twentieth century. 'Under collective security, states agree to abide by certain rules and norms to maintain stability and, when necessary, band together to stop aggression. Stability – the absence of major war – is the product of cooperation.'[82] The central idea is that 'the governments of all states would join together to prevent any of their number from using coercion to gain advantage, especially conquering another. Thus, no government could with impunity undertake forceful policies that would funda-mentally disturb peace and security.'[83] The key elements here are first, as for the realists, that the focus of security studies is on states but second, where realists would disagree, that inter-national aggression is *morally* unacceptable and preventable.[84]

One can trace early notions of the concept of collective security to Rousseau's work on the thought of the Abbé de Saint-Pierre. Rousseau wrote:

> if we are to form a solid and lasting Confederation, we must have put all the members of it in a state of such mutual dependence that no one of them is singly in a position to overbear all the others, and that separate leagues capable of thwarting the general League, shall meet with obstacles formi-dable enough to hinder their formation . . . such a Federation, so far from ending in mere vain discussions to be set at defiance with impunity, would on the contrary give birth to an effective Power, capable of forcing any ambitious rulers to observe the terms of the general treaty which he has joined with others to set up.[85]

However, although he agreed with the Abbé that such a League would be beneficial and was rational, Rousseau did not see a way to attain construction of the League.[86] In this sense Rousseau and the realists share a common perspective; both see collective security as rational and peaceful but neither believes it can be brought about.

A second perspective is the concept of the 'security commu-nity', developed by Karl Deutsch. In a security community not only is force not used over long periods but it is impossible to conceive of violence among its members.[87] The security com-munity is both more and less than collective security; more, because it relies not just on the fear of global revenge to prevent conflict, but on the development of values of community; less, because, being based on values, it can only be regional at best. A variant of this is the notion of a Kantian core of developed nations among which conflict is inconceivable, and a Hobbesian periphery in which inter- and intra-state violence is the norm. But the focus is the key. Even if it is accepted that inter-state violence is lower in the 'core' than the 'periphery', it does not necessarily automatically follow that there is less overt violence there. Street violence in Los Angeles measures up very well against that in Rio or Lagos. Obviously, the concern in such approaches is still with inter-state relations and not internal security.

The third variant emerges more fully from neo-liberal notions of co-operation. Whereas realists assert that anarchy forces states to be constantly aware of threats to their survival, some neo-liberals argue that no such automatic awareness exists. In his analysis of the Prisoner's Dilemma, Axelrod argues that 'there is no way to eliminate the other player or run away from the interaction. Therefore each player retains the ability to cooperate or defect on each move.'[88] This generates a role for international co-operation, the voluntary adjustment of policies by states in order to manage differences and reach a mutually beneficial outcome.[89] From co-operation develop regular patterns and norms, in security as in any other field, leading to the emergence of regimes. As Jervis explains it, 'By a security regime, I mean . . . those principles, rules, and norms that permit nations to be restrained in their behaviour in the belief that others will reciprocate. This concept implies not only norms and expectations that facilitate cooperation, but a form of cooperation that is more than the following of short-run self-interest.'[90]

Thus, we have yet another fundamental division. There is no agreement on the referent point for security, on what constitutes a threat to security, and on whether war plays a role in IR or peace is possible. In fact, we even lack agreement that security is a valid end. It may well be that security – and thereby, peace? – is preferable to insecurity or conflict. However, as Wæver powerfully argues, this does not mean that security is the only value. There is no such thing as absolute security; conflictual relations can only be resolved politically. Thus the desired end-point should not be *security* but a *desecuritization* of relations, moving conflicts into civil political society, the realm in which problems may be resolved and there is space for non-state actors to play important roles.[91] As Buzan describes this view, 'The ideal world is not one in which everyone successfully achieves security, but one in which there is no longer any need to talk about security.'[92]

There is, as indicated in the overview presented in this chapter, a considerable range of approaches to the study of international relations. There is much argumentation and dispute in the field about the relative merits of the various approaches. The study of international relations is deeply divided, and so is the study of security as a consequence. This book will now proceed to examine in turn the major categories of thought on security studies.

2 Traditional Views of Security in International Politics

The dominant schools of thought about international relations in the second half of the twentieth century have been realism and neo-realism. Realism dominated theory and practice after the Second World War when an influential group, including Morgenthau, Aron, Neibuhr, Kennan, Herz and Wight, produced major texts.[1] They styled themselves as 'realists', willing to look at the world as it was rather than as they would like it to be. Beginning in the late 1960s, the theoretical foundations of realism were subjected to critical questioning on a number of grounds and neo-realism emerged in part as an outgrowth of this. In 1979, in an attempt to identify and elaborate a scientific basis for the study of international relations, Kenneth Waltz published *Theory of International Relations*, in which he developed a structural explanation for the logic of power politics. In the 1980s Waltz's book generated a critical literature and attempts by others to apply his theory so as to develop and refine his ideas. Neo-realism has greatly expanded since then in influence and today is seen by many as the dominant theoretical paradigm. Mearsheimer goes so far as to argue that it is the only theory of international relations with significant explanatory power.[2]

Realism and neo-realism are related yet different. Waltz accepts that he is a neo-realist but would object to being characterized as a realist, for he sought to distance himself from the older traditions of realism, what many now term 'classical realism'. There are also some clear similarities between realism and neo-realism, especially in many of their key assumptions. Neo-realism can be seen as an important contribution to a coherent tradition of thought going back through Hobbes and Machiavelli to Thucydides. Classical realism and neo-realism are not the only ones to claim this distinguished lineage. In the 1990s a number of writers have put forward an alternative to these two 'realisms' in the form of 'structural realism'.[3] Nor do these perspectives encompass all the variations which can legitimately lay claim to the realist tradition. When one includes its variations, realism is a broad theoretical church, quite ecumenical in scope and detail.

In this chapter, we focus on realism and neo-realism[4] and address neo-liberalism/neo-institutionalism. We do not, however, try to identify and sharpen their distinguishing features; rather we try to blend realist and neo-realist perspectives in order to emphasize what they have in common. In conflating the two perspectives we can be accused of oversimplification, of glossing over important distinguishing features and nuances. But our purpose is not to explain and elaborate fully the two perspectives and how they can be used. Our concern is security and what these perspectives indicate about this concept. Both perspectives have security as their primary concern, and their approach to security derives ultimately from their common assumptions about the world, from what we call the 'realist world'.

The Nature of Realism and Neo-Realism

Classical realism arose from the effort of a number of writers to develop a theory of international relations that would explain state behaviour. They recognized that the study of history could usefully illuminate how political actors behaved. The point of their historical inquiry was to delineate the important determinants of political behaviour in the past which were not situation-dependent, that is, which could be seen to have applied throughout history. They ultimately identified a number of perennial factors; in particular they isolated and focused on 'power' as a key variable in political behaviour and central in the development of international relations.[5]

The starting point of realism is the nature of the international system. Political groupings – tribes, city-states, kingdoms, empires or states – exist and interact in an international system that can be characterized as anarchic. 'Anarchy' in its common usage implies chaos and disorder, but this is not what is meant when analysts label the international system as anarchic; rather it is that there is no overriding authority or government to discipline the interaction of its constituent parts. Each constituent unit – in the modern era the state – is autonomous, exercising sovereign authority over its own affairs. In this sense, the international system is quite different from typical domestic political systems where the state, whatever its nature, regulates – with the power to enforce those regulations – the interaction of individuals and domestic groupings. The international system has no governing system with enforcement power to regulate the behaviour of states.

The fact that the international system is anarchic has significant implications. To say that each state is autonomous or sovereign is not to say that states can do as they please, that they are free of others' influence or that they are able to get what they want. States are constrained, particularly in their external behaviour, by the effects of other states' actions. To say that each state is autonomous, or sovereign, is to say that it is the final arbiter of what constitutes its interests and decides for itself how best to achieve those interests, how best to cope with the internal and external problems it confronts. Each state, then, is free to pursue its internal and external ends as it sees fit.

In pursuing these, however, a state's actions may conflict with the objectives of another state. In an anarchic system by definition there exists no reliable process of reconciling conflicting interests, as there is no overarching authority with the power of enforcement. A state may negotiate a solution to such conflicts, or seek accommodation, but it may also resort to force to secure its interests. The requirements for state action are imposed by the circumstances in which all states exist, that is, the lack of security given via law and institutions, so all states are faced with the constant possibility that any state may, at any time, use force to achieve its ends. The possibility that force will be used when states' interests conflict looms always as a threat, if only in the background. As a consequence, if they are to be secure all states must be constantly ready to counter force with force. Wars and the constant possibility of wars make the anarchic international system, as Hobbes put it, a 'war of all against all'.[6]

That political groups or states often have conflicting national objectives, which might lead to war due to the nature of the system, is an important precept underpinning realism. Realism assumes that there is no essential harmony of interest amongst states. Realism also asserts that, unlike a domestic system where groups can resort to a higher authority to resolve conflicts, the international system is characterized by self-help;[7] states ultimately can only rely on their own efforts to keep safe. Because any state may resort to force, all states must be prepared to do so; otherwise they are at the mercy of militarily stronger neighbours. As a consequence, the capabilities of states for using force are crucial to the outcome of international conflicts and for one state's ability to influence another state's behaviour. It is not the intentions of other political actors which are important, for actors may not know themselves what their intentions are or may readily change them, but the capabilities for force they have at their disposal. Thus, for realists, the key independent variable in shaping, and thus for understanding, international relations is the notion of capabilities, or power, particularly military and militarily relevant power.[8]

Realism further assumes that certain largely immutable factors such as geography and human nature affect international conduct. Realists generally agree that a state's location affects its national capabilities and its foreign policy orientation. Owing to geography some states are more vulnerable to attack and occupy more strategically important areas than others. Geography also affects the resources readily available to states, as position determines climate, the ability to grow crops, and the natural resources which can be transformed into economic and military capability. Hence, geographic, demographic, resource and geopolitical factors are central to realist theory.[9]

Another central factor is human nature. Realism assumes that human nature is constant or at least not easily altered. The propensity to engage in conflict cannot be changed, and the task of the statesman[10] is to fashion a political framework within which it can be contained. But the frameworks and associated resources to contain conflict found in domestic politics are largely unavailable. As a consequence, realists emphasize distinctive international regulatory mechanisms, particularly a balance of power, as the primary means of minimizing conflict and war.[11]

Realists further assume that moral principles in the abstract cannot be applied to international political actions, because moral principles are artefacts of an established political framework and supporting authority structure. The criterion for judging a particular policy in international relations is whether its political consequences serve and preserve the needs and interests of the state. Pursuit of national interest is therefore governed by a morality quite different from that for individuals in personal relationships. The primary responsibility of statesmen is the survival of the state, and to confuse individual morality with a state's morality is to court disaster. Realists do not insist a state's policy cannot be moral, only that notions of morality understood as applying to individuals must be subordinate to the survival of the state and its people and the furtherance of the national interest.[12]

Power is the central notion that informs realist thought. Robert Stausz-Hupe perceived international relations as being 'dominated by the quest for power' and that 'at any given period of known history, there were several states locked in deadly conflict, all desiring the augmentation or preservation of their power'.[13] Frederick Schuman argued that each nation-state 'necessarily seeks safety by relying on its own power and viewing with alarm the power of its neighbours'.[14] Hans Morgenthau defined international politics, like all politics, as a 'struggle for power'. He further conceptualized power as both a means and an end; states use power to secure their interests, so their primary interest is to secure more power.[15] If states depend on power for their existence, and achieve their national objectives through the application of power, then the management of power is the main problem to be solved in international affairs, which is why realism is often characterized as being about power politics.

The foregoing explanation is, in some ways, a simplification. There are many differences amongst realists regarding the details of realist theory and its implications. But realists agree on the central assumptions that inform classical realism.

Neo-realists argue that earlier theories used notions such as environment, situation, context and milieu which were too vague and variable to be useful. Realist theory, as originally conceived, was inadequately scientific. To put international relations on a sounder theoretical basis, neo-realists focus on system structure, defined by the arrangement or ordering of the parts of the system. Structure is concerned with how units (states) stand in relation to each other, how they are arranged or positioned, not on how they interact. Kenneth Waltz argued that focusing on the structure of the system was the most fruitful basis for constructing theory. Emphasizing structure permits abstracting from, or leaving aside, the characteristics of units, their motivations and their interactions. Waltz delineated a three-tiered definition of structure: the organizing principle of the international system; plus the functional differentiation of units; plus the distribution of capabilities across units.[16]

The first question to answer in determining structure in a system is: what is the principle by which the parts are arranged? Domestic systems are hierarchically ordered in that units in domestic political activity, institutions and agencies, stand in relation to each other in a superior or subordinate manner. The international system is not hierarchically ordered; it is anarchic. The key to understanding this anarchic system is recognition that each state can, in the end, depend only on itself to ensure its survival. The aims of states are endlessly varied but survival is a prerequisite for attaining any of them. This does not preclude the possibility that some states may value something higher than survival, and states may act with imperfect knowledge; but they can be expected to act to ensure their survival, or act in ways that do not endanger it. Structure is not an existential force; a structure that rewards behaviour that conforms to what is required in an anarchic system emerges out of the interaction of the constituent units as they take steps to ensure this and punish that which does not contribute to survival. Simply put, the environment is determined by the fact that states prefer survival over any other goal and act relatively efficiently to achieve it.

The second question is: what are the units of the system and their characteristics? In neo-realism the units of interest are states, for states are the dominant actors and it is their interaction which establishes the structure of the international system within which other actors function. States vary widely in wealth, power, size and form, yet they are characterized by sameness, or being 'like' units. This is because all states, despite variations, perform essentially the same functions and seek more or less the same ends. They are functionally alike, whatever their form, ideology, peacefulness, and so forth, and can be treated as having the same attributes.[17]

The third question is: what accounts for variation across the system in terms of structure and outcomes? The answer is that states, though functionally undifferentiated, have quite varied capabilities. This is significant because a structural approach focuses on how states stand in relation to each other, and states are positioned with respect to each other by their power (the ultimate capability). The distribution of power amongst states, measured by comparing the capabilities of a number of individual units, is a systemwide concept. System structure is composed of the most powerful states, for only these determine whether the system is bipolar, multipolar, and so on. Variation in the distribution of power across the system introduces variation in structure. Capabilities, or power, strongly influence the success or failure of a state in its interactions with other, often competing, states; those with greater power are more likely to achieve their ends. The nature of the power relationship amongst states affects their expectations of success or failure. Thus, large changes in relative power across the system constitute a change in the structure, which affects the expectation of how states will behave and of the outcomes their actions will produce.[18]

The foregoing is a simplified version of the key elements of neo-realist thought. Subsequent work by Waltz and other analysts has refined neo realism and has resulted in sophisticated analyses.[19] Nevertheless, the foundation is in the theoretical framework described by critical elements, which may be used to generate other assumptions that help in examining and describing state behaviour. The organizing principle can only change if the international system shifts from anarchic to hierarchic, while key characteristics of the system's units – states – are unchanged as long as the system remains anarchic. In spite of greater interdependence, the growth of international organizations, and a significant increase in the number and influence of transnational non-state actors, the international system remains more or less anarchic. In other words, the ordering principle and the characteristics remain more or less fixed. Thus, for neo-realists, the key determinant for analysing the international system and the interaction of states within that system is the distribution of capabilities or power across the system, and changes in structure can stem only from changes in this distribution.

Realism and neo-realism are part of the same continuum of political theorizing about international politics. Both have identified two variables – the anarchic nature of the international system and capability or power – as critical to any theory about international affairs, though they vary in how they utilize these variables to develop a theory. In spite of obvious distinctions, they have much in common.

Realists and neo-realists agree, as do other approaches, that the international system is anarchic and that this has important implications for state behaviour. The key to the impact of anarchy is that 'good' behaviour by states and statesmen is never guaranteed. No state can be certain that all other states will behave in a highly pacific fashion and not resort to force, or the threat of force, to have their way.[20] The history of international relations makes clear that states can be and frequently are dangerous to each other, are quite capable of inflicting deliberate physical harm on each other, for whatever reason. States cannot be certain that others will be constrained from resorting to force, and indeed states resist attempts to limit their freedom to act as they see fit.

The result is that states continue to live in an anarchical international system. Indeed, they arguably have reasons to prefer it that way. Even though any state might be willing, under ideal conditions, to curb anarchy in some fashion, in the world as states find it they must live with anarchy and will sometimes go further and take steps that reproduce or sustain the continued existence of anarchy. For example, we might expect that powerful states are more satisfied with anarchy than less powerful or very weak states, because they are better able to fend for themselves and enjoy the fruits of autonomy, and – with some exceptions – this is true. So they behave accordingly, doing little or nothing to erode anarchy. Or, states find that they cannot trust each other enough in trying to agree on co-operative arrangements for many important matters, so they never give up much autonomy – anarchy forces them to be too suspicious to give it up. Hence, the attractions of anarchy (in terms of the autonomy that is its hallmark) are reinforced, in the sense of promoting its continued existence, by the self-sustaining nature of anarchy in terms of the behaviour it strongly encourages or actually imposes on states. Actions taken in response to, or for coping with, anarchy can undermine efforts at doing away with it.

From a realist perspective, what are the responses to anarchy that have this effect? One is that states are preoccupied with maintaining autonomy, fending off restrictions on their freedom of action, particularly with respect to ensuring their security. States want as much freedom as possible to avoid being drawn into circumstances that could cause them great harm. They want as much freedom as possible to take the actions necessary to keep safe. They suspect that collusion with others on these matters might be dangerous because those others will, out of a desire for autonomy, be reluctant to restrict their freedom of action sufficiently, especially in a crunch.

Another response to anarchy is a preoccupation with the accumulation of power, particularly the capacity to use force. Since power is relative, and considered vital for security, states constantly attend to their relative power with respect to other states.[21] In doing so, of course, they reinforce anarchy. Still another response to anarchy is the active contemplation of using force on behalf of the state's purposes should circumstances require it, taking advantage of the lack of constraints on the use of force under anarchy, and being aware that others are also likely to try to take forceful advantage of this condition for their own purposes. Finally, on some occasions states actually use force to achieve their goals.

They do all these things because they live under anarchy in a system where they have significant capabilities for doing physical harm and there are insufficient restraints on using them. If all states were basically weak, their security would not really be much of a problem. The problem is acute because there is an uneven distribution of capabilities within the system; some states have more power than others, sometimes considerably more, which they can use at the expense of the less powerful. And states have no guaranteed assistance if they are threatened or attacked. Hence, anarchy means that, in response, states must do as much as they are able *on their own* to advance their purposes or to keep safe.

As well as concurring on the implications of anarchy, realism and neo-realism also hold a number of assumptions in common about political life:

1 The most important actors are groups rather than individuals, especially conflictual groups (tribe, city state, kingdom, empire), it being widely accepted today that the most important group in world politics is the nation-state.
2 International affairs are essentially conflictual.
3 The prime motivation in political life is power (in that states seek power and calculate their interests in terms of power) and security.[22]

These assumptions form the basis of the realist tradition, provide the foundations of what can be called the 'realist world'.

Security in the Realist World

In the view of realists/neo-realists, international relations is fundamentally about power and security in the relations among states.[23] The core of the subject is states, their power and, given the implications of anarchy, their insecurity. All realists hold that the manifestations and impact of power and insecurity are what give international politics, and the field of study devoted to it, a distinctive identity.[24] The many other aspects of international relations are regarded as of lesser importance and relevance. It was to assert that this conception most closely accorded with the activity being studied that the label 'realist' was first adopted.

The crux of international politics, indeed its defining characteristic, is *insecurity*. This is what makes it different from other sorts of politics, worthy of separate intellectual understanding. Domestic politics can be fraught with insecurity too but only when this politics is seriously distorted or has deteriorated into an inadequate condition; international politics, however, is normally and consistently insecure. This is the essence of the matter, because nothing else is so important or affects states' behaviour so deeply. A modicum of security (which is always tenuous) is a prerequisite for everything else that states and societies might wish to pursue.[25]

To realists power is conceived, at bottom, as resting on the capacity to do physical harm to others, whilst insecurity is defined primarily as being vulnerable to being seriously harmed by others' deliberate use of force.[26] Other capabilities are important only in so far as they contribute to the capacity to do physical harm. Assessments of power begin with military capabilities, and only then turn to other capabilities that contribute directly to maintaining and applying military capabilities, then to factors that more indirectly make such a contribution, and so on. The most powerful actors, therefore, are those with the greatest military strength.[27]

States are the key actors in the realist world because they represent the greatest concentrations of power, especially in having the greatest capacity to use military force to do harm. States are insecure because they often come into conflict, sometimes very intensively, and because they can harm each other in very serious ways. Their power, and the insecurity it produces, dominates their relations. The result is that security is their constant preoccupation.

A possible implication is that states and analysts should give primary attention to determining the causes of conflicts and finding ways to keep them from arising, as the best means to enhance security and reduce the role of power in international politics. Indeed, seeking to understand the causes of war has received much attention. Contributions to this understanding have come from a wide range of fields, from biology (animal behaviourists) through anthropology, psychology, economics, sociology and history to political philosophy. The findings have shed valuable light on why peoples fight. Though the root causes of war are, in the end, extraordinarily complex, they can be clustered into three main categories: the nature of humankind; the nature of the state; and the nature of the international system.[28]

To realists, however, trying to eliminate war by uncovering its origins is not a promising way to proceed. Political conflict is ubiquitous and cannot be eliminated. The analyst should just assume the existence of serious political conflicts amongst states and proceed from there. But must political conflict periodically result in war, or could warfare be eliminated? As argued in the previous chapter, realists are deeply sceptical about eliminating war. They note that in the long history of relations amongst actors in anarchical systems – states, empires, tribes, city states – war is a persistent and prominent phenomenon.

What about limitations or constraints on states' ability to do harm to each other? Even if serious political conflicts remained, insecurity would be greatly eased or eliminated if states' capacities and/or willingness to harm each other were seriously, and permanently, curbed. Relations would not then be dominated by competition for, and about the distribution of, power. To realists and neo-realists, however, the available constraints are weak and unlikely to become stronger. They cannot come from human nature. Realists hold that human nature is either constant and hence unalterable to any significant degree, or is a universal background condition and thus cannot explain variation in human behaviour. As a consequence, it can be ignored. This leaves perhaps three possible types of constraint. One has to do with the domestic nature of states and their societies. Another involves states having a propensity or willingness to adhere strongly to norms of behaviour that would make doing harm to each other quite unacceptable. The third would be the existence of a higher authority with the legitimacy and/or capacity to promote and/or enforce peaceful relations. Realists/neo-realists hold that none of these constraints can be expected to work very well, and certainly not consistently.

On the Nature of States and Societies as a Possible Constraint

The first possibility is that states might be naturally peaceful in their outlook and behaviour and so not inclined to war and violent quarrels with each other. If the nature of states and societies was such that they were most unlikely ever to do grave harm to each other (that is, if they were basically pacific communities), they would hardly pose a threat even though they possessed great military power (of course, such communities would be highly unlikely to maintain large military capabilities in the first place). Many analyses of international politics, past and present, make suggestions to this effect, asserting that democracies or communal states or societies with market economies, etc., are inherently more pacific than others.[29]

The realists' rejection of this possibility begins with the historical record, which provides abundant evidence that states and state-like entities have frequently engaged in war and have even more regularly conducted their relations in such a hostile, competitive fashion that war was consistently plausible, no matter what their nature.[30] States and societies of all sorts have behaved as if war was always a realistic concern. Realists and neo-realists see few examples in history of truly successful co-operation to prevent wars, and even fewer examples when co-operation of this sort was durable, no matter what kinds of state and society were involved.

If we accept this view, then we might just end the discussion at this point. Given the way states behave, international relations is a violence-prone, dangerous arena and thus a realm of pervasive insecurity. It is what it is and we must take it that way, which is what states do. There is no real alternative to worrying about security; analysis must therefore focus on how states manage the problem of insecurity and on how their traditional methods can be better employed.

Much more interesting is to ask *why* states behave as they do. Realists often seem to 'black box' this matter, settling for the assumption that conflict is ubiquitous, but over the years a number of different answers have been offered within the realist perspective or seem implicit in it. A classic view is that power in its various forms, including the capacity to do harm, is its own reward, is something human beings care deeply about and which some will strive mightily to possess.[31] A closely related view is that power is so attractive because it is a currency which can be readily employed to acquire many other things of great value. In a world of scarcity, there is only so much power, and only so much of other things that power can be used to get, and thus strong conflicts arise.

In any domestic political community politics is therefore a fractious, competitive process. Struggle arises over control of the state, over the power that comes with such control. Political struggle may also arise out of the efforts of those who do not control the state to evade or at least to weaken its power as it would apply to them. Conflict over power in the domestic realm is often peaceful, constrained by institutional procedures that regulate the struggle for control of the state, but it can at times be violent and dangerous, as can the application of political power once it is attained. The power of the state can be, therefore, both an objective of competition and a means for keeping the process of political competition within bounds as part of providing the basis for sustaining a community. Politics within the international system is simply more of the same in a different arena; international relations is about the distribution of power amongst the main actors in the international system, and at times this politics can be conflictual to the point of violence.

There are other, more elaborate, explanations as to why states behave as they do, but these all lead to the same conclusion, and realists can normally be found subscribing to at least one of them. One explanation is that since human beings are interested in and highly competitive about power, the states they create and operate merely reflect this.[32] A second explanation is that though all human beings are not driven to seek power, those who are drawn to politics are innately interested in and competitive about power, and these are the people who end up managing states. A third possibility is that individuals enter into politics with a wide variety of motivations but are soon socialized by their political experiences to be preoccupied with power, and this in turn affects the way they operate states. Which of these three explanations applies is not that important to realists, who hold that they lead to the same result: states in their international relations are singularly interested in and strongly competitive about power and other things of great value that power can be used to obtain.

As a consequence, states and statesmen naturally and inevitably seek to gain and exercise additional power in their dealings with each other. Power is relative; a state can make gains only at the expense of the power of other states. This zero-sum calculus produces competition and strife. There being no equivalent in international relations of a state or higher authority that is able to keep this competition within bounds, it takes the most extreme forms and involves deliberately organized violence. Ultimately, this line of analysis invites the conclusion that states will not consistently be constrained by their domestic natures to forgo violence. The lure of power acts to shape the politics of all states, and operates on all states in the international arena.

Closely related to power, the other side of that coin, is *autonomy*. From a realist perspective autonomy is best seen as not being subject to the power of others. Autonomy is therefore widely considered to be its own reward, something of great value in politics. It is related to power in that power can create autonomy, and the desire to maintain or achieve autonomy can be a prime reason for the pursuit of power.[33] (Power and autonomy are not exactly the same thing, since a community could consist of people with a high level of autonomy because they have little power over each other and no powerful state either.) Domestic societies are characterized in part by resistance to the power of the state in favour of the autonomy of the individual or group – the tension between state power and individual or group autonomy is what much of politics is made of.

Given the importance of autonomy, international relations is not hard to explain. Autonomy in the system is its own reward and is pursued by states and statesmen accordingly. Just as in domestic affairs, power can be used to create and sustain autonomy, and the power of other states is feared because it can be used to cancel one's autonomy. The only way ultimately to guarantee one's autonomy would be to have more power than anyone else, either individually or collectively. The ultimate in loss of autonomy is to be subject to the coercion of others, being killed or seriously harmed or being controlled by the threat of harm. Hence strife, competition for power, and insecurity as states strive for the power to enhance autonomy and ward off threats to it are ubiquitous in international politics. In this regard, too, the domestic nature of states does not act as a constraint; the desire for autonomy acts on all states.

Although the realist tradition focuses on states, realists/neo-realists readily embrace the idea that in pursuing autonomy, states often reflect the deepest wishes of their populations, that the desire for autonomy is not simply an artefact of state power. The state is often seen as an expression of the national or ethnic community; its autonomy embodies the nation's freedom from rule by 'others' who are not a part of it. This makes the preoccupation with autonomy something a state does not just for itself but for those it rules and represents. The lure of autonomy runs deep, and in all sorts of states and societies.

Realists do make one concession to the idea that the nature of states can make a difference. They frequently suggest that a state's behaviour is tempered by whether it is primarily seeking to sustain the status quo or alter it sharply, and a desire to alter it sharply can sometimes be traced to domestic factors and not just the nature of the international environment or a generalized desire for power.[34] A collection of states satisfied with the status quo is less preoccupied with gaining power and less fearful about security, allowing more opportunities for co-operation on security and other matters.

On International Norms as a Possible Constraint

International norms or customary standards of behaviour are often perceived as another possible way in which states may be constrained.[35] In the realist perspective, the constant desire for power and autonomy makes international norms insufficient constraints. Power and autonomy make states and statesmen naturally and inevitably resist such norms when they are inconvenient and seriously constraining. Scarcity reinforces this tendency. If states are engaged in competition for scarce values of great importance, universally held norms of behaviour that effectively and consistently restrain the competition are unlikely to emerge, and those that do emerge and occasionally act as constraints will not command universal adherence all the time, for what is at stake is too vital. Politics and power are always partially about who gets to determine the norms, to determine which norms take precedence, to determine when and how they apply, and to have the ability to evade them when they are inconvenient. In the absence of any compelling, universally accepted means to arrive at decisions on these things (an effective political process), politics and power too often culminate in struggle and strife, even about norms.

The relationship between norms and power is complex. If politics and power are about who gets to determine the norms, then the pursuit of power and its exercise can often be facilitated, not simply constrained, by norms.[36] Constraining the power of some can have the effect of enhancing the power of others. Even if norms constrain all states equally, those with greater power will always have more ability to establish norms that they like. Those which perceive norms as benefiting others more than themselves will chafe at the constraints. They will seek to change such norms, and those which benefit from them will resist. This dynamic has commonly operated down through the history of international politics. Thus, while the struggle for power may seem antithetical to the establishment of norms and their operation, in many ways it also occurs as a struggle for norms, making them an additional target of competition and strife and an additional source of insecurity for those that lose.

Autonomy seems particularly difficult to reconcile with norms. Norms constrain autonomy. More important, norms of real consequence are those that proscribe states from resorting to force. This makes the development of truly functional norms difficult, for sovereign states have always conceived of autonomy as including the right to use force. One cornerstone of sovereignty has been the control by a state over a particular area and the people within it *by force if necessary*, and legitimately so. A core element of the definition of the state is that within its society it has or can claim a monopoly on the legitimate use of force. In international relations states also claim the right to use force in self-defence, to avoid harm and to preserve autonomy. And they claim the right to decide when forceful self-defence is necessary, and, as part of autonomy, the right to acquire the means to self-defence they deem necessary. It is but a small step to the further claim by the state that it has the right to use force outside its boundaries to protect its other interests. (At one time states even claimed the right to use force whenever and however they wished but, though such a claim is still inherent to states, this is now uncommon.)

There are certainly many instances, frequent now but not unheard of in the past, of concerted attacks on the sovereignty of some states – insistence that they cannot just do anything they please domestically, cannot use an infinitely elastic conception of 'self-defence' to justify the use of force abroad, cannot acquire any means of self-defence with impunity; and insistence that when they go beyond certain limits, outside interference is justified. Such cases are not inconsistent with the realist perspective. States with great power can use allegedly universal norms, often of their own devising, to justify imposing constraints on others to get results that are in the powerful states' interests, and indeed, it is their power that produces much or all of the success that results. Such states are simply using norms as an extension of their power. What one expects to find, and does find, is that these states do not accept the universality of the norms to such an extent as to cancel *their own* autonomy.

Neo-liberal Institutionalism: On Higher Authority or International Institutions as a Possible Constraint

The third category of possible constraints on states concerns the establishment of a higher authority of some sort with the capacity to promote and enforce peaceful relations among states, or the establishment of supranational or international organizations or institutions in which states agree to abide by sets of rules that limit their freedom. In recent decades international organizations and institutions across the spectrum of state interests have increased dramatically in number. Indeed, expansion in the number of such international organizations is a central component of the neo-liberal institutionalist approach to international relations. The fact that states willingly become members of international organizations and institutions, that they co-operate under the auspices of such organizations and institutions, that states become party to limitations on their power and autonomy, is seen as evidence which challenges some tenets of realism. Whether institutions matter, whether they can mitigate the implications of anarchy, is the subject of considerable dispute between the neo-realist and neo-liberal institutionalist schools. The centrality of this argument makes it worthwhile to provide an overview of the debate between neo-realists and neo-liberal institutionalists.[37]

In realist thought, states interested in power and autonomy must regard steps towards such constraints, if they are to be carried very far, as unacceptable *in principle*. A supranational or higher authority would concentrate power in a new place at the expense of states' individual power, and would also subject states and societies to that power at the expense of their autonomy. Realists do not argue that such an authority can never exist. They maintain that states will submit to a higher authority only when it is unambiguously to their benefit, or when forced to do so. In other words, a state subordinates itself only if the benefits outweigh those of not doing so.[38]

There is another limitation, in a realist world, on raising a higher authority to impose peace and security. States will regard the prospect of this balefully not just out of considerations of power and autonomy in the abstract, but because there cannot be universal agreement on the values the higher authority is to embody or on who should exercise such authority, and when, and how. Disagreement on just such matters is a critical element of politics and the origin of much political competition and strife. And it is not being subject to higher authority that makes peoples, and states, cherish autonomy, because they must fear that without it the values embodied and acted upon by the higher authority could be ones they would not choose themselves (either in the abstract or in terms of their application at any one time).

Another possible constraint on state behaviour could be international institutions. Institutions can be defined as sets of rules that establish the ways states should co-operate and compete with each other,[39] prescribing acceptable kinds and proscribing unacceptable forms of behaviour. States negotiate these rules, which entails a mutual acceptance of norms or 'standards of behavior defined in terms of rights and obligations'.[40] Institutions or sets of rules are frequently formalized in international agreements and incorporated into an international organization. Such organizations, however, do not constitute a higher supranational power with the authority and means to compel member states to obey. Rather, they embody the 'decentralized co-operation of individual sovereign states, without any effective mechanism of command'.[41] Members abide by the rules because they choose to, not because they are forced to.

It would seem only common sense that states co-operate either to pool their capacities to resist the power of other, especially more powerful states, or to achieve greater benefits than they can achieve acting alone. Moreover, if states can co-operate when it is beneficial, this might provide the basis for mitigating the conflictual nature of international politics. Yet, in spite of the proliferation of international and even supranational organizations, realists doubt that co-operation will stop states from pursuing their interests as they see fit. It is on this point – whether institutions matter – that neo-realists and neo-liberal institutionalists disagree.

In the IR debate, the terms 'neo-liberal' and 'realist' are misleading. This is not a replay of the first great debate in international relations theory between idealism (or utopianism) and realism in the 1930s and 1940s.[42] The debate between realism and utopianism was between two paradigms, offering alternative conceptions of the international system. Neo-realism and neo-liberal institutionalism do not, however, offer an inter-paradigm debate. Realism/neo-realism and neo-liberal institutionalism, as Caporaso notes, share a rationalist approach, viewing states as 'conscious goal-seeking agents pursuing their interests within an external environment characterized by anarchy and the power of other states. The paradigmatic question is how they pursue their goals given the constraints under which they operate.'[43] Thus they share the same starting point for their analysis of the world.[44]

Neo-liberal institutionalism developed from theories of interdependence and international regimes, and gained credence as a coherent body of theory in the mid-1980s. The central concern of neo-liberal institutionalism is 'how institutions affect incentives facing states'.[45] The starting point is, as Keohane and Martin state, that 'liberal institutionalists treat states as rational egoists operating in a framework in which agreements cannot be hierarchically enforced, and that institutionalists only expect interstate co-operation to occur if states have significant interests.'[46] In other words, they accept, like realists, that states exist in anarchy, are insecure, behave in a self-interested manner, and must rely on themselves.

There are a number of main issue areas on which realists/ neo-realists and neo-liberal institutionalists disagree: the nature and consequences of anarchy; the ease and likelihood of international co-operation; the importance of relative versus absolute gains; the priority of state goals; the relative importance of intentions versus capabilities; and, finally, whether international institutions mitigate the constraining effects of anarchy.[47] The core issue is whether, as neo-liberal institutionalists contend, international institutions 'have become significant in world politics' in that they 'have a role in changing conceptions of self-interest'.[48]

Both sides concur that the anarchic nature of the international system affects the likelihood of co-operation between states. Both do not expect co-operation to occur if states do not foresee that it will benefit them. Realists agree that states may attempt to co-operate when they have common interests and that it sometimes works, for a time. They argue, however, that co-operation is difficult and potentially perilous for a state because it can be counter-productive to its interests and survival, and hence it is hard if not impossible to sustain. Neo-liberal institutionalists contend that when states jointly benefit from co-operation they can and do create institutions which facilitate and sustain it. Institutions can mitigate the constraints imposed by anarchy because they provide information, reduce transaction costs, make commitments more credible,[49] establish focal points for co-ordination, and facilitate reciprocity in state actions.[50]

If it is to succeed and be sustained co-operation must overcome two major barriers imposed by anarchy: state concerns first about cheating and second about relative gains from cheating.[51] Concern about cheating is endemic in any co-operation but it is acute in the realm of security. The nature of military weaponry, especially modern weaponry, makes sudden shifts in the balance of power possible. States have to be concerned that if a state defects from a co-operative security agreement, it can – if it cheats before defecting – have a military superiority that allows it to threaten others or inflict serious harm on them via an attack. States must always worry about non-compliance and try to hedge against cheating,[52] and this limits co-operation.

Neo-liberal institutionalists argue that institutions ameliorate concerns about cheating in a number of ways. First, rules increase the amount of information available to states engaged in co-operation so that it is easier to monitor what other states are doing. This increases the likelihood that cheaters will be caught and furnishes potential victims with early warning of non-compliance, enabling them to take preventative or protective measures before being harmed. Second, rules tend to increase the number of transactions.[53] This institutionalized iteration increases the future gains which a potential cheater stands to lose if caught, reducing cheating and lowering fear of cheating as well. Iterative transactions further permit victims to engage in a tit-for-tat strategy to punish a cheater. Finally, iterative transactions reward states that develop a reputation for faithful adherence to agreements and penalize, through exclusion, states that do not.[54] Third, institutionalized rules facilitate linking together interactions between states in different issue areas, enhancing interdependence. Issue linkage can discourage wayward states because of the prospect that the victim (and perhaps third-party states) will retaliate in other issue areas, raising the costs of non-adherence.[55] Fourth, institutions can reduce the transaction costs of individual agreements, that is, the time and effort involved in negotiating deals, if states do less negotiating and monitoring of agreements and developing of hedges against non-compliance. The costs of co-operation are lower and the profitability higher.[56]

Realists/neo-realists accept that institutions centred on economic interactions may discourage cheating or at least reduce state concerns about the prospect and ramifications of cheating. However, they are dubious about whether institutions have more than a limited effect in security interactions. Realists argue that neo-liberal institutionalists assume that states are simply interested in absolute gains over the long term. The primary interest of states is survival. Improving their individual well-being is important but not crucial.[57] In the realm of security, states must fear that another's quick defection could result in their own devastating military defeat and even their disappearance.[58] In international economic affairs the prospect of retaliation can constrain cheating because the victim is harmed but will still be around to retaliate. However, a state cannot assume, given the destructive power of modern weapons, that it will survive a sudden defection and be able to retaliate. Hence, on security matters a state will not be willing to place its faith in institutions. The fear of cheating is much greater when security could be at risk and institutions cannot overcome this.

The second obstacle to co-operation mentioned above has to

do with relative gains. Realists/neo-realists argue that states are most interested in relative, not absolute, gains. States fear other states which may pose a threat to their power and autonomy. Thus they worry that others will make gains that improve their relative power.[59] A state has to be careful that others do not, through mutual co-operation, make relatively greater gains, because the increasingly powerful partners of today could easily become dangerous foes in the future.[60]

Neo-liberal institutionalists agree that states have to be mindful of relative gains when co-operating with other states, and ask two important questions. First, under what conditions is the issue of relative gains significant? Second, what is the role and impact of institutions when relative gains are at stake? Liberal institutionalist theory suggests that the importance of relative gains is shaped by at least two factors. One is the number of major actors in the system. In situations in which there are only two states with conflicting interests, relative gains matter a great deal and co-operation is very difficult. In situations in which there are a number of small states of more or less equal power, the states will not worry much about relative gains because they have more opportunities for forming coalitions for protection.[61] A second factor is whether in military affairs the offence dominates the defence. When there is little prospect that military force will be used to resolve disputes (that is, when the defence dominates offence and hence the threat of war is low), relative gains considerations do not matter much because they do not translate into a greater military advantage, so co-operation is easier.[62]

Realists/neo-realists concur that in such conditions relative gains considerations may not have much impact. They point out, however, that these two conditions are largely hypothetical, not empirically illustrated with historical examples. Mearsheimer argues that multipolar international systems have usually consisted of three to six great powers, with more power than the rest of the states, and with significant asymmetries in power amongst themselves. Systems with a large number of roughly equal small powers are rare exceptions that prove the rule. Realists/neo-realists are sceptical about the possibility of a world in which the military advantage lies with the defence and states are completely convinced of this. It is notoriously difficult to distinguish between offensive and defensive weapons. A state may adhere to a purely defensive strategy, but the weapons it procures and deploys will be likely to have some offensive capacity, and other states will assume that they might be attacked unless they protect against this possibility.[63] On balance the realist/neo-realist position is that in the real world, given potentially very serious consequences, states have to be concerned about relative gains.

Neo-liberal institutionalists argue that institutions can mitigate state concerns about relative gains in co-operation. First, institutions provide a framework within which disagreements about gains, which can serve as an obstacle to co-operation, can be resolved. In each potential co-operation arrangement there are multiple options with different distributions of gains and so states will have different preferences. Institutions provide a co-ordinating mechanism that permits states to make trade-offs to develop a stable co-operative outcome. Individual states may achieve greater relative gains in one arrangement by accepting this for others in other matters, resulting in a rough overall balance. Second, and more important, institutions provide information about other states, including information about the distribution of gains and the ends to which they are being put. This information can alert a state if others are making significant and worrisome relative gains, and the mechanisms provided by the institution may offer a means to redress this imbalance.[64]

Realists/neo-realists remain unconvinced. They acknowledge that institutions may have an impact on the problem, for states do at times settle for absolute economic gains. At the same time, even in their international economic relations states will constantly seek to adjust mutually beneficial agreements if they perceive others as benefiting more than themselves.[65] Realists/neo-realists seriously question whether institutions can and will have an impact in the realm of security, where the problem of relative gains is most severe because the consequences can be quite disastrous. Realists/neo-realists maintain that co-operation is conditional; states may see it as beneficial, but they will still want to constrain it sharply in time or scope, or leave themselves ways to escape from it should this become 'necessary'. Thus, in co-operative ventures the constraints on the ability of the state to pursue its interests will rest very lightly and the state has the option of defecting if its interests dictate this.

The debate between the realists/neo-realists and neo-liberal institutionalists does not obviate the underlying problem, namely that anarchy leads to state behaviour that makes co-operation difficult. The promise of institutions is that they might alleviate insecurity and lead states to change their notions of self-interest. A great many analysts believe in this and a great many policy-makers have been willing to invest considerable effort and resources in building international institutions. Yet as Keohane and Martin acknowledge, while international institutions are likely to be a component of any enduring peace, this 'does not mean that they are always valuable, much less that they operate without respect to power and interests, constitute a panacea for violent conflict, or always reduce the likelihood of war'.[66] Conceptions of self-interest may some day be changed sufficiently for states to act with restraint, but until then who cannot be absolutely certain others will be constrained from resorting to force. Nor can a state be certain that some sort of higher authority, if established, would not be used to do it serious harm in the future. Therefore, states must be sceptical about both the idea of a higher authority and the feasibility of creating it. Thus, they will continue to be wary of constraints on their sovereign authority and are likely even in co-operation always to reserve the right to defect if they deem it in their best interest to do so.

The Results

Whether states are inherently dangerous and conflictual because of the behaviour fostered by the nature of the inter-national environment or because of the nature of states and human beings, both views converge in a common description of the results. From either point of view, international relations has certain necessary characteristics:

1 the unconstrained or insufficiently constrained competition of states for power (and other values obtained via power), leading to pervasive insecurity;
2 the pursuit of security on a self-help basis to the extent

possible (because of the absence of effective norms or higher authority or the uncertainty about getting serious assistance from other states);

3 the necessity to rely on the use of force and threats in numerous instances (the competition for power and the need to act on a self-help basis call for using one's elbows to get ahead), which promotes insecurity;

4 the very limited application of canons of morality (because of the tenuous nature of international norms), which gives rise to insecurity as well because of the unpredictability of the behaviour of others;

5 the existence of security dilemmas – each state's self-help measures erode others' sense of security, thereby reinforcing insecurity. The more capabilities a state acquires to ensure its security, the greater the perceived or real threat it poses to the others, and the greater the likelihood that they in turn will acquire similar capabilities to ensure their security, which will be perceived as threatening to the first state.

These characteristics are so compelling, so central to states' experience in the realist view, that they colour all other aspects of international politics and have more to do with shaping state behaviour than any other considerations. Reduced to essentials, international relations is a security-driven competition for the various components of power, with war always a distinct possibility.

An additional characteristic of international politics, in view of all that has been discussed thus far, is great power domination. Having the largest concentrations of capabilities, especially the ability to hurt others, the great powers inevitably dominate the system. The relative distribution and concentration of these capabilities give the international system its central character and structure. The patterns in great power relationships that flow from this structure, and the structure itself, significantly affect all other actors, constraining and shaping their behaviour.

The place to start analysis of the behaviour of the members of any international system, therefore, is with an examination of the distribution of power and an identification of the most powerful members. There are three primary systemic power structures. In a unipolar system, one state is much more powerful than the others. It may overwhelmingly dominate, with no likely combination of states able to equal its power; or it may be sufficiently powerful to dominate but could be balanced by some combination of other states. In either case, the relationships between the dominant state and others determines the structure of the system, with the dominant state exercising a degree of hegemony.

The second system structure is bipolar, with two concentrations of power significantly greater than any others and with capabilities exceeding those of any other state by a wide margin. The relationship between the two great powers, or poles, is the dominant pattern which influences all other states and their behaviour. Each pole seeks to ensure its survival and its autonomy from the threat posed by the other's power. Central to a bipolar system is a balancing between the two giants, either through their internal efforts or through the maintenance of alliances and co-operation with lesser powers.

The third structure is multipolar, where the main concentrations of power can be found in three or more major states. Behaviour patterns in a multipolar system are more complex, and depend on the number of states considered great powers and whether their capabilities are relatively equal or somewhat unequal. Although several of these states may act in concert to dominate the system, more often there are temporary and shifting coalitions. If one state increases its relative power through self-help or an alliance, others are likely to react by balancing it through co-operation or an alliance against it. Thus the great powers often align with each other, plus lesser powers, producing two or more alignments of states. In such circumstances, the defection of an ally, especially a great power, from an alignment can destabilize the power distribution and set off realignments.

States must cope with the environment in which they exist as best they can, yet their menu of serious options is limited. They have little choice but to act within international relations as they find it, and realist perspectives depict them as forced to be preoccupied with power and autonomy. There are a number of options available, but they are all, at bottom, variants of the general strategy of acquiring and maintaining power to offset the power of others.

An obvious option, particularly when there is a bipolar or multipolar distribution of power, is to produce and maintain a 'balance of power' in the system. The concept of a 'balance of power' is central to realist/neo-realist thought, particularly in connection with notions of system stability.[67] The concept did not originate with realists, but realists/neo-realists have considerably elaborated it and analysis as to why and how states balance.

Although the concept is widely known, the term has many definitions and is used in many different ways. Ernst B. Haas found at least eight different definitions or usages: (1) any distribution of power; (2) an equilibrium or balancing process; (3) hegemony or the search for hegemony; (4) stability and peace in a concert of power; (5) instability and war; (6) power politics in general; (7) a universal law of history; and (8) a system for and guide to policy-makers.[68] The concept of balance of power can simultaneously be taken as an objective condition, a tactic in state behaviour, and a mode of system maintenance characteristic of certain international systems. All three meanings are used by realists. Of primary concern are the last two: a guide for policy-makers who would, rationally and with constant vigilance, respond to the power of other states and the threat it poses, ever ready to form countervailing coalitions against states which seek to change the current equilibrium of power in the system; and a kind of multinational society in which the essential actors seek to preserve their identity, integrity and autonomy through a balancing process.[69]

States engage in balance-of-power behaviour because of their preoccupation with power and autonomy. The purpose of developing and/or sustaining a balance is to: prevent the establishment of a regional or global hegemony; preserve the current system and its constituent elements (that is, states); ensure stability and security in the system; and deter war by confronting an aggressor or potential aggressor with a countervailing coalition. Thus, states engage in balancing to preserve their security and autonomy from the depredations of other states or to preserve the prevailing balance which lends itself to their being able to sustain their security and autonomy. There are a number of methods for maintaining or restoring a balance of power: (1) a policy of divide and rule, to diminish the power advantage of the stronger by aligning with the weaker; (2) territorial compensation after a war to offset gains by the winner; (3) creation of buffer states; (4) formation of alliances; (5) maintainance of spheres of influence; (6) intervention; (7) diplomatic bargaining; (8) settling disputes through legal and peaceful means; (9) reducing armaments or engaging in arms races; and (10) waging war, to maintain or restore a preferred balance. All have been practised by states concerned about preserving security and autonomy and are the essence of security as traditionally conceived.

In the modern world, balancing often takes the form of alliances, formal military agreements and arrangements between two or more states through which they seek either to protect themselves or to collude in expanding their power at other states' expense. Such arrangements can be effective but even if they are institutionalized and a permanent organization is created, such as in the North Atlantic Treaty Organization (NATO), the co-operation can be limited or fluctuating. Alliances can readily evoke counter-alliances, and in a realist view are likely to do so, raising the prospect of confrontations between even greater concentrations of power and thus not alleviating insecurity. Alliances themselves impose constraints on autonomy and create patterns of dependency, and are thus uncomfortable for states in various ways. They are often beset by mistrust arising from serious or residual competition among the members and the effects of anarchy, and they are unreliable or uncertain in duration and effectiveness. Each ally must consider the possibility that the others may defect from the agreement if it looks as if they would be better off doing so, and this breeds suspicion and mistrust. Moreover, always looking out for oneself makes allies constantly try to push the burden of the alliance onto their partners, to free-ride as much as possible, which is not a good basis for harmonious and lasting co-operation. Other co-operative security associations states sometimes use – such as the United Nations – are beset with the same problems to an even greater degree. With all this in mind, realists are the foremost champions of the view that alliances are marriages of convenience and readily subject to divorce.

As a consequence, states are usually loath to rely solely on such alliances and other co-operative arrangements for security. They will often either back-stop such strategies by, or reject them in favour of, balancing the power and threat of others through their individual efforts. Or a state may eschew working with other states and seek to increase its power and security on its own.

States often try to expand their power by enlarging and better exploiting their domestic resources. This approach can be fruitful for states with significant extractable natural resources within their boundaries or under their control, particularly when they have the population, knowledge and technology needed to exploit them. However, this strategy is of only marginal utility to those with limited domestic resources, particularly to a state directly in competition with one state much better endowed in this regard. This approach is also apt to be quite expensive and can be very slow in adjusting a state's relative power. Another option is to squeeze more resources out of the society for the state's purposes abroad – drafting more citizens into the armed forces, imposing higher taxes, etc. Of course, in poor societies there is not much to be squeezed. Moreover, extracting more resources is politically difficult, even dangerous, and can have serious consequences in terms of political unrest or damaging the economy.

States can also try to acquire additional resources through trade. The exchange of its surplus resources for resources it lacks can contribute to the development of a state's capabilities. This is also apt to be slow. Thus, states often try to improve their capability more directly by securing arms from others. This can be much quicker than developing one's own arms production but it is rarely cheap and can be very dangerous. Buying arms can incite the concern and antagonism of other states and hence become a source, not just an effect, of insecurity. It also raises the possibility of an erosion of autonomy, for getting arms from other states (for payments or as a gift) can create dependence by granting suppliers undue influence, which is another form of insecurity.

Alternatively, states can try to seize additional resources or use force to damage the power of rivals, including going to war to enhance their security. This can be quick and offers the possibility of a permanent enhancement of power and autonomy. But it is very dangerous. War is uncertain and unreliable in outcome, and failure means a relative loss of power. Even if the war is successful, the long-term consequences may increase insecurity. The defeated state may vigorously attempt to recover its position, acquiring arms and other capabilities which breed insecurity for the victor in the long term. Other states may be sufficiently alarmed about the victor's increased power to move to oppose or offset these gains, adding to the insecurity. The victor, though now much stronger than the state it defeated, may have expended so many resources or suffered so much damage that it is vulnerable to attack by others. Thus, to employ force in pursuit of security is fraught with risks.

All such steps are variants of trying to arrange a 'satisfactory' distribution of power for a state, either in relation to another state (or states) or in relation to the system as a whole. The underlying basis for the security these steps provide can always be traced to deterrence, based on threats of serious harm, or war. Security is sought through the ability to deter and defend or (in a war) through the ability to ignore or overcome others' ability to deter and defend. The only real change in this over time has been that deterrence has been assigned a greatly increased weight in the search for security, in comparison with war or outright defence, because of great increases in the destructiveness of war. Thus, from a realist perspective it is the confrontation and containment of power with power that is needed to make states behave prudently and cautiously. Nuclear deterrence is the ultimate in this, because it compels an extremely high level of prudence and caution.

As other possible constraints on states' capacities to do serious harm are inadequate, it is vital to employ power in this way. The 'satisfactory' distribution of power for a state might be one of superiority *vis-à-vis* certain other states or other coalitions of states, or some relatively even level of power *vis-à-vis* those others, or even an 'acceptable' level of inferiority that appears to offer enough constraint. It will depend on the circumstances, in particular on the degree and intensity of the threat that a state feels it must confront.

The same is true for the system as a whole. The satisfactory distribution of power for the system, to minimize the outbreak of violent conflict and contain insecurity, could be seen by states as superiority for one particular concentration of power in the system (hegemony for one state or a set of co-operating states), or a relatively even distribution of power among the major states or sets of associated states, or for many states an acceptable level of inferiority, one that leaves them rather costly and dangerous to tackle. As to how this proper distribution is achieved, some realists believe it arises automatically – an anarchical system tends toward the kind of equilibrium appropriate to its distribution of power. Other observers think the proper power distribution is episodic, arising from a confluence of factors not readily manipulated by states, or that it can be deliberately created via successful strategic manipulation by states (individually or collectively). Thus hegemony, bipolarity or multipolarity are readily understandable in realist terms as options that states might seek, or accept, or adapt to, but the underlying principle is the same – security is shaped by the distribution of power in the system.

In the same way, all three are subject to the same realist analysis in detecting their limitations. Arranging for, or counting on, a satisfactory distribution of power is:

1 expensive, and anything expensive is unevenly available both across states and, for any one state, over time;
2 dangerous – the distribution of power can readily be misjudged, leaving a state more vulnerable than expected and a system more fragile than it appears;
3 less than universally acceptable – whatever the distribution there are winners and losers, and thus it is not likely to be stable over the long run;
4 intrinsically unstable because the relative strength of states shifts over time in uneven and unpredictable ways due to uneven rates of growth, technological change, domestic political instability, and other factors.

Ultimately, seeking security via a satisfactory distribution of power is simply the controlled application of the core elements of insecurity, that is, the capacities and willingness of states to do serious harm to each other. The search for security is best thought of as *the management of insecurity* rather than its elimination.[70] Hence international relations is intrinsically the realm of insecurity.

An example will show how all of these elements come

together. In the second half of the twentieth century the ultimate method of constraining powerful states through a
satisfactory distribution of power was nuclear deterrence, and
it clearly displayed all of the features just discussed. Several
states accumulated nuclear weapons to gain a capacity for
overwhelming destruction so that they could block, by threat
of a devastating punitive response, any contemplation by other
states of using force against them. A state that gained such
weapons was seeking a satisfactory distribution of destructive
capacities between itself and any other state in the system, one
that would ensure its autonomy and survival.[71] Some of these
states sought nuclear superiority, some were willing to accept
rough nuclear equality, and several were willing to settle for an
acceptable nuclear inferiority. Building nuclear weapons was
particularly pursued by each of the 'great powers', the foremost centres of power in the system. Eventually, a systematic
body of theory and related practices was developed to indicate
the ways in which the distribution of nuclear weapons could
produce a satisfactory distribution of power in the system, one
that sustained stability and order. Hence, both by the individ
ual competitive efforts of states and by some attempts at
deliberate design, nuclear deterrence contributed centrally to
the structure of the system. The high level of competition
among the major states that gave rise to nuclear weapons, and
the weapons themselves, became dominant facts of life for the
other states in the system to which adjustments had to be
made.

The arrangements for individual states and for the system
as a whole turned out to be:

1 *expensive.* It was expensive to acquire nuclear weapons and
suitable delivery vehicles. It was expensive to keep up with the
competition. It was expensive to maintain non-nuclear capabilities necessitated by the uncertain willingness of nuclear
powers ever to use such weapons and the uncertain credibility
of their alliance guarantees to use these weapons to defend
other states. The NATO allies, for example, maintained very
large and expensive conventional forces despite the massive
nuclear arsenal of the US. This expense made for great variations in the security states could afford to purchase.
2 *dangerous.* The distribution of power could readily be mis-

judged – nuclear-armed states might be more vulnerable to a first strike aimed to disarm their capacity to retaliate than they realized, the system might be more unstable due to accidents, misjudgements or irrationality than it seemed, or states depending on nuclear-armed protectors might find themselves exposed as their guardians proved unwilling to risk nuclear war.

3 *not universally acceptable.* States without nuclear weapons resented being inferior, feared being vulnerable, disliked being at the mercy of decisions made by the great powers, and disliked the dependence they experienced on great power allies. States in such a position might, as have India and Pakistan, develop and deploy nuclear arms.

4 *intrinsically unstable.*[72] Three of the five nuclear-armed great powers – France, China and the Soviet Union – experienced enough internal political disarray to have caused the conceivable collapse of their political systems. One – the Soviet Union – was undone to some extent by a poor rate of growth which could be traced in part to the enormous national security expenditures of the government. In US–Soviet relations, technological change consistently raised the possibility that nuclear deterrence would be undermined.

Ultimately nuclear deterrence was a form of security for individual states in which every state and society was vulnerable to being completely destroyed at almost any time should deterrence ever collapse and bring on a general war. It was security via maintenance of a stable international system which was always poised on the edge of possible destruction. It was the height of controlled insecurity.

Realism and Security

Both forms of realism focus on the state and its interaction with other states in an anarchic system. The state is the most important political group and hence the referent of security in realist/neo-realist conceptions. What the state is being protected from is efforts by other states to get their way and threaten external interests the state sees as important to its welfare and survival. What is meant by security, then, is the state's capacity to protect its territorial boundaries and its sovereign ability to act as it sees fit.

Both forms of realism acknowledge that while international relations is conflictual states are not always in conflict. Conflict arises when one state's pursuit of its interests, which are primarily power and security, clash with the interests of others. Thus, in the realist/neo-realist view, threat stems from the interaction of states within an anarchic system. The degree to which a state is threatened by others, whether as a consequence of its own or other states' actions, depends on its ability to impose its will or to resist efforts by other states to impose their will on it. This capacity rests on its relative power, or capability, *vis-à-vis* others.

As noted earlier, the concept of power is the subject of debate.[73] A simple and usable definition is that power is 'the ability to move others or to get them to do what one wants them to do and not to do what one does not want them to do'.[74] It is often perceived as synonymous with military might, which is certainly an extremely important element of power and has been the focus of much realist-based analysis. The notion of capabilities, or power, however, is not synonymous with force levels; it has military and non-military components. Power also includes levels of technology, population, natural resources, geographical factors, forms of government, political leadership and ideology, among others. Because of this, measuring power is very difficult for leaders and how best to do it is debated by analysts.

Nevertheless, a key element is military capability. In the realist world the possibility of violence is pervasive; in the realist world the central threat to security is the threat or actual use of force. Other factors can be important when thinking about security, and are ignored only at some risk. But these are usually perceived by realists/neo-realists as significant only in so far as they contribute to or hinder the development of military capabilities or the ability of the state to wield the military capabilities it has available. Thus, a strong economy determines how much military capability a state can build and maintain; geography determines the natural resources available to transform into military capability and has an impact on how vulnerable to or protected from military attack a state is; form of government affects how well a state can mobilize its citizens for military purposes; political leadership can determine how appropriately and even how wisely military force is used; and so on. In a very real sense, then, the traditional approach to security is that everything may affect security, but security is not about everything.[75] The study and practice of security have centred on the threat and actual use of force and how the state should manage this fundamental source of insecurity.

3 | Peace Studies

The realist/neo-realist paradigm has influenced and often defined the way that security has been interpreted in the post-Second World War period, but it was not the only interpretation. An alternative strand of thought founded on a different intellectual tradition, known as peace studies, evolved in tandem with the realist-based interpretation. Traditionally, peace has been of little significance to the strategist – the focus has been on the threat, employment and control of military force. Peace is the antithesis of warfare, logically the end result of successful strategy, but largely unexplored as a security issue or a goal in its own right. Moreover, because of the dominance of the realist paradigm after 1945, peace research was marginalized, viewed as 'essentially an intellectual protest movement',[1] often dismissed as the remit of bearded, sandal-wearing, bleeding-heart liberals rather than as a serious research area. Yet while often caricatured as utopian, peace studies has evolved over time and it remains anything but a unitary discipline, embracing as it does 'a family of discourse' from the Kantian idealist tradition to the hard-nosed scientism of Kenneth Boulding.[2]

This variety will emerge as we examine the development of peace studies. This chapter charts the development of peace studies, identifying five distinct periods of its history. The first section looks at peace studies and its roots in the idealism of the post-First World War era, reified in the League of Nations and Woodrow Wilson's fourteen points. After idealism's apparent discrediting by the Second World War, peace studies adopted the scientism that was *de rigueur* in the social science of the 1950s; this phase was characterized by a fairly narrow approach, and a concern with conflict resolution, arms control, game theory and disarmament. The third section will examine the impact of a more radical social science in the 1960s–70s, which challenged the assumed objectivity of traditional methods, and instead focused on inequalities within the spheres of political economy, social injustice and social conflict. In the 1980s this broader, politicized approach continued, but was somewhat overshadowed by (while contributing to) the burst of popular protest against nuclear weapons and superpower nuclear policy, which formed the main arena for peace research at that time and is the focus of the fourth section. The chapter concludes by looking at the significance and potential role for peace studies in a post-Cold War world, where ideas of critical security seem to overlap with much of the peace studies agenda.

Inter-War Idealism

The roots of peace studies are closely linked with the origins of IR as an autonomous area of research and study in the early part of the twentieth century. After 1918, attempts were made to ensure that there would never again be such a total and destructive war; means were sought – through processes and institutions, to mediate and control relations between states – to prevent war from ever reoccurring. These attempts took shape in US President Woodrow Wilson's fourteen points, which called for (among other things) free trade, an end to secret diplomacy, arms cutbacks to a minimum level, and national self-determination. Wilson also proposed the establishment of a collective security system, the League of Nations, and called for the perpetuation of democratic systems within states (under the assumption that democratically accountable state leaders are less likely to go to war).

So the main thrust of inter-war idealism was to prevent wars (perceived as irrational and excessively costly in resources and lives) by imposing effective institutions, structures and processes to allow for rational, measured negotiation; in this way, peace was to be a product of 'reason'. Peace as an end-point and something to work towards rationally amounted to an absence of war, a negative construct. Instead of focusing on peace positively, as a state of social justice and harmony (as later writers did), the inter-war idealists defined it as the situation that exists when there is no formal state of war.[3]

Different writers focused on different strategies – for example, a world government with powers of enforcement,[4] an international police force, or disarmament. A common theme was that supranational structures would be adopted, so some state sovereignty would have to be surrendered.[5] There was a shared belief in the Kantian rationalist argument that people are perfectible and institutions reformable, rejecting the realist claim that a Hobbesian state of nature is inevitable. Through the institutionalization of peaceful means of conflict resolution, and the consequent socialization of people and states into non-violent forms of interaction, it was believed that peace would be attainable.[6] Reason demanded 'a reformist commitment to perfecting the political organization of the world', which echoed the Kantian notion of the categorical imperative, presenting an external standard of 'the good' which, if applied, would bring about universal justice and perpetual peace.[7] This was embodied in the Kellogg–Briand Pact of 1928, which sought to outlaw war as a legitimate form of state policy.

Thus inter-war idealism focused on reducing wars and keeping wars limited, as well as on restructuring the world system by reducing the power and autonomy of states in the interest of greater systemic stability. Ostensibly, this was a very radical departure from the tenets of realism, but the policies proposed did not, epistemologically, differ radically from the realist agenda. To start with, the analysis was state-centric. In both discourses, states were the key units of analysis, reified as the main actors, and depicted as able to adapt their behaviour to the external environment. Second, this focus offered a hierarchical and militarized conception of power and security. Realism and idealism were concerned with hierarchical structures, with power exercised over others (for realists, more powerful states dominating within a balance of power; for idealists, supranational institutions imposing order). In neither was there scope for bringing in a broader range of actors or challenging the idea that security is achieved through dominance. Finally, realists and idealists envisioned security and peace as negative constructs, as entailing an absence of war rather than a more positive condition.

This sheds light on the weaknesses of inter-war idealism as a manifestation of peace studies. Like realism, it focused on symptoms – the immediate and observable phenomena of the international system, atomized into nation-states, and the use of warfare as a state tool – rather than the underlying causes of warfare and the structure of the system.[8] And the key products of this phase of idealism are now generally referred to as failures – for example, the League of Nations proved impotent against the Nazi move into Central and Eastern Europe, the Italian invasion of Abyssinia, and the Japanese march into China during the 1930s.

The concept of 'peace' in early peace studies is somewhat one-dimensional, ignoring any analysis of the underlying dynamics of structural violence and inequality that may be significant factors in the downward spiral that leads to war. 'Peace' fell within the domain of high politics, imposed on states by supranational institutions as the product of a hierarchical power relationship, and consonant with an external, categorical notion of 'the good' for international actors. With the perceived failures of the 1930s, this belief system was discredited. For the best part of forty years after the Second World War, the orthodoxy was realism, which defined itself in opposition to idealism. Writers such as E.H. Carr and Hans Morgenthau wrote in disdain of misplaced utopianism, and sought instead to depict the world as it is.[9]

Peace Studies Post-Second World War: Realism Resurgent

Carr and Morgenthau, among others, argued that violent conflict was inevitable and that history had disproved the key thesis of idealism, namely that people were rational and peace was possible via international institutions. Key policy-makers perceived the bipolar politics of the early Cold War as demonstrating the unavoidability of constant tension, expedient alliances, a balance of power, and a quest for dominance. Yet the notion of peace as achievable, and as a realistic goal of state policy, managed to survive, albeit at a low level.

The peace studies of the 1950s was shaped in relation to the pre-eminence of realism and to the social science positivism then emerging. Peace studies was characterized by defensiveness and an attempt to present a scientifically authentic and rigorous argument. The discipline moved away from idealism's normative rhetoric, focusing instead on the empirical and factual. This positivist slant was evident in the creation of the Centre for Research on Conflict Resolution at the University of Michigan and the Centre for Advanced Study in Behavioral Sciences at Stanford, California, with Anatol Rappaport and Kenneth Boulding. These research programmes merged perspectives from social psychology, economics and sociology with quantitative techniques in conducting the study of war. This research cloaked itself in science and was deliberately free of any explicit taint of ethics.[10] A key work was *A Study of War* by Quincy Wright, a quantitative analysis that attempted to determine scientifically the causes of war through history.[11]

In this way, peace research adapted to what was politically acceptable at the time – particularly what was acceptable in the US, the dominant power. It was only through 'scientific', 'value-free' analysis that peace research could attract funding and gain academic credibility. This American school held a fairly narrow conception of peace, claiming that war and peace could be separated from other social problems and explained quantitatively. It focused on observable and measurable institutions and processes, and the agenda was primarily practical, as befitted a technocratic approach.[12]

Outside the US, an alternative locus for peace studies was developed in Norway by Johan Galtung. Originally a mathematician and sociologist, Galtung shared the behaviourist slant of the American school and rejected the speculative, *a priori* tendencies of earlier idealism.[13] In the US the main focus was on conflict resolution, seeing conflict as inevitable to a certain extent, while Galtung was more concerned with peace *per se*. And he saw peace research as vocational, applying a necessary ethical code to the conduct and analysis of the international system, developing 'a scientific analysis of conflict which would provide the basis for developing peace proposals that would be free of the taint of ideology and national bias'.[14]

To some degree this school paralleled Boulding and

Rappaport in the US, in exploring deterrence, arms control and game theory, much like the military strategists of the day. But for the peace researchers, especially Galtung, the aim was not to help manage the status quo to the advantage of one side or the other, but to change it.[15] In terms of method, this particularly included empirical studies of attitudes to disarmament, statistical research on arms procurement, and so on. The key distinguishing features of the Scandinavian approach were the assumptions that humanity has a tendency towards empathy and solidarity, and that the nation-state was transitory and need not be the ultimate focus for research.[16]

These ideas were developed at the International Peace Research Institute in Oslo and propounded in its *Journal of Peace Studies*. In the first issue, Galtung laid out the premises on which he based peace research.[17] First came the empirical claims that humanity has the ability to empathize (countering the realist view that humanity is inherently evil) and that increasing levels of integration were unavoidable. Just as even warfare was constrained by established and accepted rules and limitations, so peace research must focus on this inherent potential for co-operation rather than on violent conflict. Next was the extension of the agenda to cover more than war and conflict, shifting away from the state-centric approach of idealists and the American school.[18] Instead of peace as an absence of war, Galtung construed it positively, as the pursuit of goals such as co-operation and integration, aiming for a 'better' world.

The Radicalization of Peace Research

Despite this normative bent, Galtung was very much within the traditional, positivist school. This made him a target of accusations from the newly energized left in the 1960s that he endorsed notions of objectivity that had the effect of reinforcing preservation of the existing system. The political turbulence of the late 1960s in the US and Europe had a considerable impact on the social sciences, which were seen as ripe for radicalization. With the development and widespread adoption of neo-Marxism and dependency theory in IR,[19] Galtung's notion of peace research came under sustained

criticism, particularly for its assumption of progressive integration and harmony and its view of the peace researcher as
science-bound rational technocrat. At a Peace Research Society
international conference on Vietnam in the US in 1969, a group
of European rebels argued that by focusing on levels of arms
and violent conflict, and so on, peace research amounted to
little more than a discussion of US strategy, implying its
legitimization. The critics of Galtung and Boulding called for
exposure of the global dynamics of exploitation and, if necessary, their resolution by revolution, a strategy that was
anathema to the process of rational transformation envisaged
by Galtung. Writers such as Krippendorff, Lars Dencik and
Gunder Frank identified capitalism as the key source of war
and violent conflict. The nation-state was a product of an
international capitalist system, and unless the class character of
the state changed, the dynamics of violence would continue.[20]
Traditional peace research was seen as embracing the dominant conception of power, presenting Western development as
the ideal model of progress, and doing little more than tweak-
ing the power balance underlying the status quo. It resulted in
abstract mathematical models rather than grounding peace
research in the reality of social relations. For the radicals, only
revolution and the overthrow of class society – not technocracy
and pacifism – would end systemic patterns of exploitation
and violence and bring about peace.[21]

Hence peace research began to shift away from its almost
exclusive concern with the strategic relationship of the superpowers and the logic of deterrence, towards the dynamics of
the North–South relationship. According to the neo-Marxist
perspective, the capitalist world market has systematically
disadvantaged Asia and Africa. Under the dominant division
of labour the South supplied raw materials in return for manufactured goods. This rendered the South dependent as raw
materials declined in relative value and the North dictated the
production and trade of commodities.[22] Thus, it was argued, a
dynamic of economic exploitation was established, reinforced
by institutions such as the International Monetary Fund (IMF).
Third World countries borrowed large amounts of capital in
the 1960s–70s in an attempt to industrialize and develop, but
the Organization of Petroleum Exporting Countries (OPEC)
crises in 1973 and 1979, heavy spending and costly pharaonic

projects, plus high levels of variable interest, combined to impoverish the poorest states of the South even further.[23] This was interpreted as a form of neo-colonialism: a structural economic version of imperialist control, oppression, and racism, denying autonomy and hence meaningful security to the colonized.[24] And these patterns of oppression are seen as replicated within states as well, for example by the development of the bourgeoisie in the South, who establish their own positions of power as agents of neo-colonialism. In this understanding, then, the focus of attention shifts away from simply the nation-state, to take on board the class and power dynamics at an intra-state and transnational level as well.

Recognition of a structural version of economic oppression and insecurity resulted in mainstream peace studies adopting a more radical political direction. This was best articulated in Galtung's article 'Violence, Peace and Peace Research' in 1969, where he developed the idea of structural violence.[25] This represented a radicalization of his peace research, rendering it an essentially critical activity replacing his positivist, analytical approach. While Kenneth Boulding saw such a shift as a damaging move away from the traditional focus on immediate, direct conflict and conflict resolution, it marked the development of a less immediately obvious and more conceptually imaginative notion of peace.[26]

In this seminal article, and some of his later work, Galtung expanded the ontology of peace research, distinguishing between direct and structural violence. Direct violence can be crudely defined as A physically assaulting B with the intention of causing harm, pain or suffering. Such a definition covers armed acts of war. However, violence need not involve a direct physical assault. There may be policies which deliberately or knowingly result in the deaths or suffering of others from starvation or disease. Such policies can be described as a form of structural violence, acting via the impact of unequal and oppressive power relations.[27] Structural violence is built into basic social structures and results in life expectancy of less than a human being's biological potential due to oppression, poverty, pollution, and so on.[28] Violence causes the difference between potential and actual life expectancy. When life expectation is low (for example, with a death from TB in the 1850s when there was little in the way of prevention or cure) there is no violence. If the harm was avoidable (for instance, a death from TB in a wealthy society today with high levels of medical effectiveness) then there is violence, as the death could have been prevented; and with this kind of violence there is, therefore, no peace.

According to this analysis, violence takes various forms, from physical – hurting to the point of killing – to psychological – for example, via brainwashing and indoctrination, limiting and diminishing mental potentialities – to structural. If people starve when this is avoidable, if life expectancy for the wealthy is more than twice as high as for the poor, then violence is occurring, even with no specific individuals carrying out an assault.[29] Traditionally in peace studies the focus has been on personal rather than structural violence: personal violence is obvious, sudden and dramatic whereas structural violence is static and hidden. A lack of personal violence is not a positive condition, but instead amounts to a negative peace (peace as an absence of direct violence). But the elimination of structural, latent violence creates positive peace in the form of social justice and a redistribution of power and resources. For Galtung, peace must mean more than the absence of intentional physical violence; otherwise many unacceptable social orders would be theoretically compatible with a state of peace.[30] For him, then, peace requires the elimination of patterns of structural domination.[31] Moreover, these two sorts of peace and violence are interdependent and can develop dialectically – for example, structures of violence may easily breed direct violence or a regime of social injustice may be maintained by force.[32]

This development of the concept of peace, beyond the absence of war, marked a shift away from the state-centrism that had dominated realist and idealist thought and post-1945 peace studies. By locating peace and war within exploitative and unequal socio-economic processes this approach depicted peace and security as holistic, multidimensional and indivisible concepts. Key issues of concern were the relationship between rich and poor states, and the rich and poor within states, the links between arms and underdevelopment and the recognition that, in terms of security for individuals, the relevance of arguments by nuclear strategists was often marginal at best, when the primary concern might be to get enough to eat to survive for another day. This suggested that the established mode of international politics – sovereign states operating in anarchy – was itself problematic, as it provided limited security and short-term peace.[33]

This, then, presents a very different concept of security from that provided by realism. A realist concept of security depends on the maximization of national power and/or security – that is, security is defined in terms of the capabilities (primarily military) of the nation-state unit, and its strategic position as regards the threatening capabilities of its neighbours. In contrast, in this later Galtungian notion of security, security is the result of a state of positive peace – that is, security is defined not in terms of nation-state might, but in terms of a holistic understanding that moves beyond the currency of military power, with states as key actors. Instead, economic and social processes are given greater prominence, and the analysis fully embraces individuals and communities, thereby qualitatively transforming the traditional nation-state approach. Another key divergence is the use of power here – while the notion of power is of central significance to both realism and peace studies (as it is in all fields of politics), it is clearly differently constructed in the two. For realists, power is a hierarchical model; and the objective is to be at the top of the pyramid, wielding power over others. For radical peace theorists, power is defined in terms of empowerment and enabling; and power and security depend on equality and justice, not superiority.

In this exploration of the concept of positive peace, and the elimination of structural violence, Galtung endorsed the view that differing rates in mortality were due to exploitation and social injustice. Yet he sought to draw a clear distinction between his ideas and those of a Marxist position.[34] He agreed with neo-Marxists that structural violence could be found in international economic relations that resulted in unequal power and life chances, but also argued that in socialist societies which were undemocratic and politically oppressive individuals could be crippled by a lack of freedom. The difference between potential and actual self-realization, achievement and freedom meant violence was at work.[35] Thus, for Galtung, peace embraced the left's goal of equality with the right's goal of freedom and personal growth – human rights were crucial to a positive understanding of peace and had to be accessible to everyone. As a consequence, peace studies is concerned with the liberation of individuals from *all* dynamics of violence, however insidious, and all impediments to self-realization, and the individual is a more significant unit of analysis than the state, a collectivity or a class.[36]

This interpretation had the effect of factionalizing the peace research movement during the 1960s–70s. Boulding and the more traditional American school continued to focus on disarmament and arms control, while others followed Galtung to focus on eradicating structural violence.[37] Then in the 1980s, the emphasis shifted again. Although the concept of peace as an academic tool was still undecided and there was increasing acceptance of Galtung's approach, in the 1980s international politics moved disarmament to centre stage and the anti-nuclear movement became the key focus.

Peace Studies and the Anti-Nuclearism of the 1980s

In the late 1970s–80s, the superpower arms race reached unprecedented levels of intensity and technical potency, and US–Soviet relations descended into a 'Second Cold War'. For the first time since the Cuban Missile Crisis, a nuclear war appeared imminent as new flexible weapons were deployed. On 12 December 1979, NATO decided to deploy ground-launched Cruise and Pershing II missiles in Europe, giving NATO a new medium-range strike capability, with nuclear forces based on land, at sea and in the air, giving the alliance a secure second-strike capability.[38] Meanwhile, the escalation of international tension, with the Soviet invasion of Afghanistan and the Iranian revolution in 1979, subversive US action in El Salvador and Nicaragua, and the election in 1980 of the strongly anti-commmunist Ronald Reagan, was almost tangible. Given this, the burgeoning of the peace movement was unsurprising. This was exacerbated by the commitment of many Western governments at the time to reducing public spending while strengthening defence – for example, as Britain developed Trident and its general defence posture, resources were diverted from public services into defence. Government policy prioritized national security, while the broader notion of economic and societal security was less important. By explicitly connecting these two levels of security – the strategic and the economic/social – the peace movement and peace studies broadened their agenda and the conception of 'peace'. The term was contextualized and deepened, and sited at individual, community and societal levels of analysis, rather than being limited to the more abstract level of nation-state power relations.

As a consequence of the high-risk, tension-ridden superpower nuclear politics of the 1980s, peace studies became more visible, vocal and significant. Fear of the likelihood of nuclear war – especially the possibility of Europe as a theatre for US and Soviet tactical strikes – meant that nuclear disarmament and nuclear freeze movements grew rapidly.[39] For many in the peace movement, the national nuclear arsenals were a threat to the citizens they were intended to protect[40] – mere possession of nuclear weapons held the possibility of accidents, massive radiation, or a pre-emptive strike from an opposing nuclear power, and represented a massive drain on domestic resources. For example, while the Thatcher government saw the primary threat to Britain as the Soviet Union, the peace movement felt that a far greater threat was the nuclear build-up itself: the government saw its nuclear policy as a defensive measure, while the peace movement argued that individuals might well survive foreign occupation but not a nuclear war.

The peace movement may have had little electoral impact, but it had some resonance, simply by raising the level of debate and boosting popular awareness of the nuclear threat. The key argument of peace theorists was that by adding 'nuclear' to strategy, rationality was abandoned – they claimed that 'nuclear war' and 'nuclear strategy' were paradoxical and meaningless terms because they implied national suicide rather than the apparently rational, Clausewitzian pursuit of policy by other means.[41] By continuing to focus solely on weapons and defence of the state, strategic understandings of security failed to deal with the destructive power of nuclear weapons, which ultimately transcended nation-state boundaries. For the peace protestors, as destructive power increased, overall security – at the state and other levels – was diminished.

During the 1980s, the peace movement expanded both in numbers of people involved and in the range of issues and concerns addressed. Before the 1980s, apart from selected academics, much of the energy in the Western peace movement came either from committed pacifists with a strongly moral stand or from communist sympathizers who saw the Soviet Union as a force for peace. The two groups did not fit easily together and in terms of practical protest; the movement largely consisted of small active groups rather than an all-embracing, potent organization.[42] But in the 1980s, a range of other groups and interests joined the movement, such as women's groups, environmentalists and specific professions (for example, physicians against the bomb who would present clear descriptions of the medical consequences of nuclear war; or lawyers against the bomb who focused on the illegality of nuclear possession). This opened up the debate and range of interests represented by the peace movement and peace studies to the importation of feminist arguments on the patriarchal nature of nuclear strategic thinking or to environmentalists' calls for a focus on the well-being of the planet.[43]

One branch developed the notion of 'alternative defence', of defence without nuclear weapons.[44] This started from the premise that security is indivisible – any attempt to improve the security of one nation-state at the expense of another merely accelerated the arms race via the security dilemma (whereby even defensive actions may be interpreted as offensive and threatening). A possible solution, it was argued, would be to base national strategy and security solely on explicitly defensive premises, to reduce the possibility that another state posed a threat.[45] Mainstream security theorists saw Europe as secure since 1945 because of the superpower nuclear umbrella. However, this ignored the particular destructiveness of nuclear weapons, and assumed deterrence to be fail-safe. Traditional strategists took conflict in international politics as a given, instead of seeing it as a factor that promoted insecurity by institutionalizing military tension and distorting perceptions.[46] And this concept treats security as an end product, the consequence of no war, rather than as a process on various levels, from the individual to the systemic. Alternative defence theorists refused to accept the nuclear stalemate status quo, and took a long-term approach, considering other possibilities and highlighting the threats to security that the possession of nuclear weapons posed (such as that to the environment).[47]

A central argument of peace campaigners and alternative defence theorists during the 1980s was that insecurity was largely a matter of perception and an inability to accept difference. It was argued that an awareness of this would transform the nature of defence policy and IR as a whole. Offensive weapons and nuclear weapons can be seen as a threat because of their potential for destruction; and they invite pre-emption, generating endemic instability and insecurity.[48] This line of thought mostly developed outside established government institutions and processes, but an important exposition of some elements was the report of the Palme Commission (1982), which called for 'common security'[49] and contended that since 'all nations would be united in destruction if nuclear war were to occur', avoiding war was a shared responsibility.[50]

With the end of the Cold War this focus on nuclear disarmament largely dissipated, but peace research continued. Without the intensity and drama of Soviet–US relations and the immediacy of the nuclear threat, the popularity of peace campaigning subsided. Some might argue that in an increasingly interdependent world, where large-scale military force and traditional strategic thinking have minimal utility, where economic transactions take priority and where integration is a global trend, peace studies is redundant. Without the immediate threat of war, ongoing arms races, or the dominance of nationalistic military thinking, why bother with peace studies any more? In a sense the pacifists have won, as the Cold War ended without massive conflict or violence.

The Galtungian notions of positive peace and the elimination of structural violence remain powerful critiques of dominant economic patterns and their impact on security in the Third World.[51] Even though parts of the Third World have rapidly developed, a substantial swathe (especially in Africa and parts of South Asia) remains tied down by massive international debt. In addition, strands of anti-nuclear arguments that surfaced in the 1980s, such as the feminist and environmental arguments, are now pursued and developed independent of peace studies, expanding the subject's ontological agenda and challenging traditional epistemological assumptions.[52] Most importantly, idealist notions of collective security, and Galtung's recognition of human rights as a requisite to peace, have been reactivated in various forms, from the New World Order of the 1991 Gulf War through UN peacekeeping forces in Bosnia to the West's (admittedly sporadic) references to the significance of human rights in foreign policy, which extend the security agenda beyond the integrity of states to take on board the freedom and security of individuals. These examples suggest that the peace studies agenda continues to be pertinent for the security challenges and the developing security discourse of today. Indeed, at times it seems that most of our thinking about security now is more in line with the agenda of peace studies than with strategic studies. The classical realist focus on the nation-state can be seen as somewhat anachronistic and inflexible in a globalizing, interdependent world. The breadth and range of peace studies, its shift away from state-centric and institutionalist 'solutions', its recognition of the holistic and indivisible nature of security, and its development of a positive concept of peace have many links with the post-Cold War security agenda currently being developed.

Peace Studies: The New Agenda

As is evident from other chapters in this volume, the concept of security, and the discipline of security studies, have changed substantively. There appears to be a converging of agendas among security studies, IR and peace studies. The new contributions of critical theorists, postmodernists and feminists have challenged the traditional ontological assumptions of IR. As a consequence, there is a much wider range of argument about what issues and questions should be included in the meaning of security, many of which have been advocated by peace studies. These issues and questions include environmental security, gender-aware security, Third World security and the development of critical security, the ideas of structural violence, the incorporation of non-state actors, the recognition of multiple levels of security which incorporate the political and societal, and ideas of individual emancipation and positive peace.

The end of the Cold War has opened up the concept of security: the preoccupation with being armed to the teeth against an 'enemy' is now challenged, and oppositional structures based on demonization of the 'other' are questioned, with alternative perspectives gaining in credibility.[53] The continuing significance of conflict resolution and positivist peace studies (for example, as explored in the *Journal of Conflict Resolution*) can be seen as being played out in practical terms in the increasingly interventionist and mediatory policies of the UN. Indeed, to a certain extent even such traditional security concerns as NATO and armed international intervention have dramatically changed in terms of their agenda and character. The notion of NATO as a tightly bound, defensive structure in opposition to an aggressive Soviet empire has been disintegrated by the process of expansion and inclusion, depicting instead a dynamic of holistic rather than relative security. That is, the idea of security being promoted has more in common with that developed within peace studies than the security of realism; in fact, it can even be seen as containing echoes of the early idealist project of collective security. More contemporary, social constructivist ideas of NATO take this on board – that in the post-Cold War world, the character of NATO has changed, to one concerned with issues of belonging and identity as well as the more obvious ones of military defence. Feminist perspectives looking at human relationships and needs rather than institutions and organizations, and at kinship rather than hierarchical organization, can present an alternative, inter-relational, web-like notion of power and security.[54] A neo-Marxist or Coxian interpretation of structural violence can be used as a means of understanding problems of security in the Third World where economics appears to be the primary determinant of who has security and who does not.[55]

Because of the broad range and diverse history of peace studies, it is difficult to come up with a simple definition of its key referent object, and its key agent of threat. Whereas this is relatively straightforward for realists (the referent is the state, and the threat is other states' capabilities), for peace studies it depends on your starting point. For the inter-war idealists, for example, a state-centric analysis remained pre-eminent; in the scientific approach of Boulding, this continued, with the threat defined in military terms. It was only with the radicalization of the peace studies agenda that the focus of analysis really began to be opened up. For neo-Marxists, the referents to be secured were the victims of unequal and oppressive class relations, against national and international capitalism. Galtung developed this further: his unit became the individual, to be protected against direct violence (from the state or individuals) and structural violence. This in turn can be developed into Booth's neo-Kantian view of security as emancipation – a development of the Galtungian idea of peace as freedom from physical, structural, political and psychological violence or oppression.

As in other areas of security studies, the positivist tradition of peace studies has been challenged by the newly fluid nature of the post-Cold War world. Old bipolar oppositions and identities are being deconstructed, which, it might be argued, leaves peace studies with less to address now. But while the positivist tradition none the less continues, the state-centric arguments and positivist number-crunching of post-1945 peace studies have less hold. The 'factual' correctness of this tradition's findings was undermined by examples such as Galtung's assertion in 1984 that the most 'secure' countries in Europe included Yugoslavia and Albania, while the most at risk were in NATO and the General Agreement on Tariffs and Trade (GATT).[56] The idea that 'security' and 'peace' are observable, quantifiable, measurable units according to objective, generalizable laws is under assault from the post-positivists. Security theory increasingly recognizes the significance of perception, and the elimination of fluid, insidious dynamics of violence which may be inter-state, or intra-state, inter- or even intra-personal. The shifting agenda of peace studies reflects (and to a certain extent predetermines) this agenda, with its early introduction of new and different actors, and its more complex and holistic notion of threat and hence security.

4 | The Impact of Gender on Security

At first glance, gender may appear to have little to contribute to security studies. Yet the injection of gender promises to open up two key areas of understanding and research that are new. It locates women as a group within security studies, and by giving this gender awareness a political edge, in the form of feminism, it challenges our fundamental understanding of 'security', a conceptual shift opening the field to ideas traditionally associated with the female (such as the emotive, the interpersonal, the spontaneous and the unstructured).

This chapter has four main topics: first, a look at the general contribution feminist analysis can make; second, the need for a gender-aware analysis; third, specifically feminist security concerns; and finally, a feminist understanding of security studies.

Feminism's Contribution

The feminist re-visioning of academic disciplines through a gender-aware lens can be widely observed in everything from literary analysis and sociology to medicine, biology and law.[1] The intent is to expose underlying structures and practices which, feminists argue, are taken as given and endow our overall understanding with a patriarchal tilt.

In addition to challenging and deconstructing the status quo, feminism is increasingly engaged in a project to build something new: redefining the nature of the disciplines themselves, by recognizing and revealing the dimension of gender that is implicit in all constructions of knowledge and under-standings of power. In doing so, this approach uses a core set of feminist values and principles as an analytical tool in the construction of knowledge.[2]

Feminism is unique in security studies in its focus on gender as the defining factor in all relations, domestic or political. Some view this as a weakness, obscuring other significant relationships and imbalances. Feminists argue that without giving weight to the underlying dimension of gender, which determines not only the position of women as a group within relationships but the hierarchical structure of all relationships, our understanding can only be partial. Essentialist feminists categorize gender as biologically determined, seeing certain male/female characteristics as inherent and immutable (such as violence in men and nurturing in women). Non-essentialist feminists see gender as a social construct, and believe that male and female roles are flexible and open to change. For both types, it is necessary to locate and recognize the gender divi-sion in order to contextualize and make sense of everything else. Such an emphasis challenges the traditional approach which relegates gender issues to the private sphere, a view which takes as given the division of issues and people into public–private and masculine–feminine, instead of addressing this initial process of segregation as well.

Security and Gender

As discussed in previous chapters, security studies is tradition-ally realist, focusing on states as the key actors and as the main source of conflict and violence; a security issue is concerned with direct, inter-state conflict. Over the past decade, this realist view has been increasingly challenged as constricted and anachronistic. For example, realism may be inadequate in helping us understand the end of the Cold War, as factors such as international co-operation and interaction need to be accounted for.[3] In its place, a 'broad' understanding of security studies has developed, which sees as relevant the internal workings of states, not just the purely state-centric level of analysis; it is this understanding of 'security' that is most compatible with feminism.

Writers in this broad school, such as Buzan and Thomas, apply the general definition of security (absence of threat of violence, or use of force) to other actors besides states.[4] Whereas the realist focus on states amounts to their reification, to the extent that politics is virtually depersonalized and the human, socio-cultural dimension inherently involved in any decision-making process is abstracted, broad-school theorists maintain that security as a concept is not bound by nation-state borders and the parameters of rational thought. For example, ecological concerns are increasingly viewed as fundamental to a state's survival; moreover, they are indicative of our growing international interdependence and the need for co-operation and multilateralism as the full, global impact of any action is realized.[5]

Intra-state issues are also security concerns: as Thomas points out, contemporary violent conflicts which threaten to disrupt the international system tend to be intra-state and anti-regime rather than caused by external physical threats and geopolitics. This means that military issues are rendered less crucial, as the security threat posed by states is outweighed by other factors that undermine the survival of the state, its citizens, and the international system as a whole.[6] Poverty and starvation affect citizens' survival, and their ability to serve and defend the state; if the well-being of individuals is threatened by economic collapse, political oppression, scarcity, ecological damage or crime, then their survival and, ultimately, that of the state and the stability of the international system are at risk, whether or not their neighbours' intentions are malevolent.[7]

The narrower, realist school purports to explain the world as it is, seeing the status quo as the best the world can do. In fact, no explanation can be fully value-free, and any theory helps to define what are taken as 'facts'. Realism as a tool of analysis uses concepts such as power and national sovereignty to judge and assess the viability of policy and outcome. It sees states and wars as central and significant, and it assumes the existence of warring states or enemies, postulating polarized relationships from the start. It limits its construction of reality by excluding so much (for example, sexuality, masculinity, ethnicity) from its analysis that it never entertains the idea that such factors could be relevant to the causation or operation of war/insecurity.[8] In contrast, the broad school is explicitly value-laden and idealistic, actively seeking solutions and looking beyond purely inter-state dynamics. A broad-school security policy is thus aspirational and morally grounded, attuned to the requirements of long-term interdependence rather than short-term gain.[9]

Yet while the work of broad-school theorists is invaluable in challenging the abstract assumptions of traditional security thinkers, and in helping us recognize that international security can only be understood as a totality, from an individual to a systemic level, its challenge to established political parameters only goes so far. The level of gender tends to be overlooked (apart from Thomas's passing reference to the transnational tendency to discriminate against women when doling out scarce rations).[10] Thus, from a feminist perspective the broad school of security can provide a partial understanding of security issues, and needs to be supplemented by an analysis that acknowledges both the specific concerns of women as a group that is relevant to international security, and the general conceptual tendencies that betray a gender bias in the discipline.[11] In this way, a feminist analysis of broad-school theory extends even further than the broad school's own challenge to the dominant conceptual slant of traditional security studies.

The broad school embraces notions of structural as well as direct violence in its understanding of security, opening up a dimension of power relations that tend to be insidious, and which feminists also seek to expose. Direct violence can be defined crudely as A physically assaulting B, with the intention of causing harm, pain or suffering. In strategic studies, this means armed acts of war. However, violence need not involve a direct physical assault. There may be policies of violence, for example those which deliberately or knowingly result in the deaths or suffering of others from starvation or disease. Such policies can be described as a form of structural violence inflicted via the indirect operation of unequal and oppressive power relations.[12] In IR, this takes account of the North–South divide, whereby the flows of trade, massive debt repayments, and colonial exploitation condemn many to death through

poverty. From a gender-aware perspective, women are particular victims of structural violence, with female children often
unwanted at birth and hence fed less, and women are dis-
criminated against economically, legally and culturally. These
patterns of indirect violence, and consequent insecurity for
women, are explored in the next section.

Thus to a certain extent, the broad school does challenge the
established masculine conceptual bias of traditional security
studies, such as the narrow focus on state actors, military
defence, and power as a polarized, zero-sum concept. And
writers such as Booth adopt an approach consistent with a
more feminist focus on individuals, relationships, broader
political change and constructive, creative co-operation, call-
ing for empathy rather than ethnocentrism and human rather
than state-centred strategies.[13] In 'Security and Emancipation'
Booth argues that 'feminist perspectives are integral to any
people-centred subject'.[14] In this way, a truly broad understanding of security includes what are traditionally termed
'soft', women's concerns, in family/health/education. They
are crucial to individual-level security and play an increasingly
central role in contemporary government policy, as macro/
military concerns decline.[15] However, the impact of feminism
on security studies remains limited. For example, while broad-
school theorists call for the extension of liberal democracy to
minimize war or conflict, such concepts of democracy are
highly gendered, as most polities were designated liberal
democracies well before granting female suffrage, and sexual
discrimination is still rife. If we now shift the focus to feminist
literature, we develop a clearer idea of the impact of analytical
interplay between gender and security.

Specific Feminist Security Concerns

A gender-aware analysis opens up security studies in two
ways: first by looking at the position of women and how their
immediate security is violated; and second by focusing on the
patriarchal philosophy behind this reification and violence,
and how this relates to security studies.

On the first, an exhaustive survey of the literature is difficult.
It appears that the majority of feminist work so far is concerned

with cataloguing the misfortunes and oppression of women. In doing so, it attempts to compensate for the gender bias in most forms of analytical narrative as well as making the political point that women tend to be subordinated.[16] This can be described as a 'feminist empirical' approach, looking at the cases where international and domestic state power damage women's lives, in contrast to the theoretical approach examined later.[17]

The security of women as a group can be affected directly or indirectly. Physical violence against women, especially in the form of rape, is an obvious direct breach of their security. Male rape exists but it is comparatively rare, whereas the rape of women can be used systematically, it is contended, as a means of inducing fear among all women. In *Against Our Will*, a definitive account of female vulnerability, Susan Brownmiller argues that through rape women are transformed into mere objects, defiled by the men who 'own' them – 'rape is man's basic weapon of force against women, the ultimate test of his superior strength, used as a conscious process of intimidation.'[18] In terms of relating this to traditional security concerns, rape is often used as a weapon of warfare, against another nation and against women as a whole.[19] Rape in warfare is recognized as an international security concern by the Geneva Convention. In the recent conflict in Bosnia, rape was a tool of 'ethnic cleansing', used to terrorize the population, forcing certain ethnic groups to flee; and reports of rape camps housing at least 20,000 women victims rebut the notion of rape as a solitary, criminal act.[20] Rape is only seen as a security concern *per se* when the perpetrator is a foreign soldier. But whatever the nationality of the perpetrator, rape can be seen as a collective assertion of dominance and masculinity, objectifying women through the act itself, and further dehumanizing them as members of 'the other'; women become just another form of property claimed by the winning side.

Another common example of female-specific violence is wife-battering. This is generally treated as a domestic concern, with no place in the security arena. Broad-school theorists argue for the inclusion of human rights as a crucial component of security policy but tend to overlook the massive, transnational and violent abuse of women as a group. A thorough examination of the phenomenon can be found in Dobash and

Dobash, who see domestic violence as indicative of 'a historical hierarchy whereby men possess and control women'.[21] Violence can only be understood within its socio-cultural context, which in this instance is a patriarchal society founded on a public–private divide where the female sphere is subordinate. This can be taken as a global context, as patterns of gender subordination are common to most if not all societies (though a feminist analysis generally acknowledges the significance of cultural and historical differences, as its approach is inclusive and complex rather than monolithic). The sheer scale and frequency of domestic violence reinforce women's position *vis-à-vis* their husbands. For example, according to a 1998 report by the British Medical Association, more than one in four women experiences domestic violence at some time.[22] By being threatened with violence, women are forced to comply, and so are denied the fundamental freedom 'from personal harm motivated by hatred or fear of one's ascribed characteristics' in the same way as any persecuted ethnic minority or political dissident.[23]

As Russell points out, the preponderance of male violence is remarkable, with 90 per cent of people arrested for violent crimes in the US being male – 'if there were an ethnic group or social class responsible for this, its members would be considered pariahs.'[24] She argues that this propensity is largely due to the prevalent definition of masculinity and its associated qualities of aggression, toughness, competitiveness and the absence of what is seen as 'feminine'. The fundamental gender division associates these masculine values with the public, political sphere, treating people (particularly women) as means rather than ends. For feminists, to ignore this strongly gendered dynamic of violence is to adopt the patriarchal perspective (and its definition of masculinity as indicative of societal success) as a standard of objectivity, while ignoring its underlying relationships, which are founded on power inequalities and endemic insecurity.

Underlying direct violence against women are more subtle, indirect forces that continue the gendered dynamic of insecurity. Just as broad-security theorists look to unequal trading patterns and colonial legacies to explain poverty and ethnic unrest, so feminists argue that the sexual division of labour and the self-victimization of women result in endemic, structural insecurity. Unless these hierarchical, structural inequalities are dismantled, basic, gendered patterns of insecurity will remain.[25] Women are presented as 'natural' victims at many levels, their political and cultural autonomy limited; and with this argument, any practice that effectively reifies and dehumanizes women is one that oppresses. The most obvious is pornography. One of the clearest exponents of the view that porn is harmful to women by fetishizing and victimizing them through imagery is Andrea Dworkin (though references to the damaging impact of pornography can be found throughout feminist literature).[26] For radical feminists, pornographic imagery can be harmful not because it is necessarily a direct cause of rape, but because it is a perpetuation of polarized images, depicting relationships based on domination, control and violence. In doing so, it reinforces gendered hierarchical structures between people, and the violence and exploitation that these involve. Pornography helps perpetuate belief-systems that justify and encourage the categorization and commodification of a group of people (women), and the resulting prejudice constitutes an undercurrent of violence which can possibly manifest itself in other ways, such as active discrimination or direct violence.

Other, less glaring examples of the objectification of women are listed in Naomi Wolf's *The Beauty Myth*. Even in affluent societies women's lives and livelihoods are constrained and threatened by the socially enforced 'Rites of Beauty'. Wolf sees beauty products and fashions specifically marketed for women as very powerful in defining women's roles, and highly capable of engendering insecurity and a sense of inadequacy. In doing so, she argues, they are simply implementing male-initiated capitalist/consumerist ideas, as 'someone must have figured out that they [women] will buy more things if they are kept in the self-hating, ever-failing, hungry and sexually insecure state of being aspiring "beauties".'[27] By portraying women's physical attributes as crucial to a female sense of identity and success, the media helps to trivialize and disempower women. One of the most obvious examples of this phenomenon is in the near-epidemic level of eating disorders among American female students; the feminist argument that socio-cultural factors are significant causal elements is gaining credibility.[28] The issue is political, Wolf contends, as 'cultural fixation on female thinness is not an obsession about female beauty, but ... about female obedience ... Dieting is the most potent political sedative in women's history; a quietly mad population is a tractable one.'[29] As millions of women starve themselves out of fear and self-disgust, millions more undergo medically unnecessary surgery to conform to the role and image that society dictates.[30] Concepts of female beauty differ over time and across cultures. The Rubenesque curves of fashionable eighteenth-century European women have this century been replaced in the West by an ideal of thinness, so that 'dieting is the essence of contemporary femininity.'[31]

When any group suffers from starvation though there is enough food to go round, structural violence is operative. This holds whether the group is a victim of North–South inequality[32] or of a gendered, culturally imposed dynamic of violence. In such ways are women 'kept in their place', through sustained, insidious, structural violence reinforcing sex-role socialization. Just as starvation through poverty is a valid security issue to the broad school, avoidable through concerted political action, so the self-enforced starvation of millions in stable, wealthy societies represents an endemic dynamic of violence. While no feminist would claim that adolescent eating disorders are medically or morally equivalent to mass starvation in the South, what *is* perhaps significant is the dynamic of power that lies behind this structural violence. In both cases starvation results in powerlessness and openness to manipulation, reflecting a systemic hierarchy of power and violence.

Levels of security vary across societies. In the South, issues of environmental security such as water shortages, or sociostructural security issues such as endemic poverty and malnutrition, are far more important on an everyday level than in the North. In a gendered sense too, levels of insecurity vary. Where food is scarce, women are more likely than men to go hungry; where resources are limited, they are the most likely to be uneducated. The overall pattern of gendered power relations is that women are consistently more vulnerable, even in wealthy, liberal democracies, and unless the unequal nature of power relations is rectified, this will remain endemic. Even in the West it is seen as unsurprising that a wife earns less than her husband, that it is she who stalls her career – the primary public expression of autonomy and status – for the family, that she must dress carefully and 'appropriately' to avoid verbal and physical abuse.

In the area of birth control too, women often lack autonomy and are expected to act according to prevailing socio-cultural norms. According to Faludi, the gains made by Western women in the early 1970s in controlling family size are now threatened by increasingly virulent 'pro-life' campaigns which seek to limit women's choices. She argues that many campaigners are less concerned about the unborn child than with the profound social and economic dislocation that giving women autonomy over their bodies and reproductive capacity has brought about: 'as resentment over women's increasing levels of professional progress became mixed with anxiety over the sexual freedoms women had begun to exercise, they developed a rhetoric of puritanical outrage to castigate their opponents ... sexual independence, not murder, may have been the feminists' greater crime.'[33] By denying women that freedom and restricting access to birth control (or even, as in China and India, rigorously enforcing birth-control measures), societies and governments attempt to control women's choices and categorize them in terms of dependency and insecurity.

According to Glenn, a gendered pattern of subordination is reflected in less obviously violent patterns of everyday social relations and interaction. For example, the family tends to lock women into the roles of wives and mothers to perform domestic, service behaviour in the private sphere, which is trivialized, and these attributes are internalized and transmitted via socialization through generations.[34] In contrast, 'male' properties of independence, strength and rationality are associated with the public, 'high political' institutional needs of the state and the military.

For Enloe, as long as women support and service men, the patriarchal structure of privilege and control is perpetuated at all levels, effectively legitimizing all forms of violence. In *Bananas, Beaches and Bombs*, Enloe questions the traditional exclusion of women from IR, arguing that they are in fact crucial to it in practice and that nowhere is the state more gendered in the sense of how power is dispersed than in the security apparatus.[35] She questions whether 'national security' refers to a state's protection from external attack, arguing that it is also preoccupied with preservation of the existing male-dominated order. Despite women's crucial backroom role, they are by and large excluded from 'high' international politics.[36] Enloe questions the importance of key IR terms such as the balance of power, or weak and strong states, arguing that they have been constructed from a partial, gendered perspective. In *The Morning After: Sexual Politics at the End of the Cold War*, she calls for a recognition of the significance of lower-level politics and ordinary people's lives in international processes, thereby necessarily taking account of gender, shifting the focus away from the purely public realm to include what is often marginalized as the preserve of the private. For example, we can see the end of the Cold War as representing a change not just in inter-governmental activities but in individual minds, relationships and popular images.[37]

Thus, there are forces operative transnationally and cross-culturally that affect women's security. Sidelining women and their usual activities is symptomatic of a dualistic, patriarchal philosophy, with an either/or mind-set, reflecting the public–private divide. In addition, emotions, associated with the female realm, are dissociated from the decision-making process,[38] as is illustrated by the traditional discourse of strategy. As Cohn persuasively argues, this is highly gendered, seeks a tone of cool detachment, and simply ignores or uses euphemisms for the psychological, physical and emotional effects of warfare. The nuclear weapon that devastated Hiroshima was referred to by the Defence Establishment as a 'clean bomb', and civilian deaths were referred to as 'collateral damage'. Within this discourse, the female is used as a term of degradation and delegitimization, while state actors are generally referred to as 'he', bringing to bear a whole host of gender-specific competitive assumptions.[39]

A Feminist Understanding of Security

The literature discussed so far, while addressing matters related to the security of women as a group, has little to say about more traditional and conceptual security studies issues (with the partial exception of Enloe). This is a new field for feminist analysis, and can perhaps be categorized as 'applied' feminism – that is, using feminist principles as tools to shed light on underlying power relations and expose the resulting bias in order to offer an alternative perspective on an established discipline, examining influential factors which are usually hidden.

One of the first writers to make explicit connections between feminist scholarship and the recent, broad reading of security was J. Ann Tickner. In *Gender in International Relations*, she draws a new definition of international relations, moving away from the traditional male-dominated politics of war and *realpolitik* and the realist values of autonomy, abstraction and independence, towards a more community-based, interdependent concept, embracing views from the margins of power (women's traditional position). 'Just as realists centre their expectations on the hierarchical relations between states and Marxists on unequal class relations, feminism can bring to light gender hierarchies, embedded in the theories and practices of world politics, and allow us to see the extent to which all these systems of domination are interrelated.'[40] Thus, a feminist approach adopts the broad school's tendency to view the world as interdependent, and shifts from dichotomies of war and peace to a broad, positive peace. In addition, it systematically highlights gendered structures of power and security relations.[41] Tickner critiques the realist approach and its basic, gendered components of 'political man', 'the masculine state' and 'the international system', arguing that such views are only partial, and fail to take account of the contextual, personal, interdependent reality (which, for example, includes reproduction as well as production and the private sphere as well as the public). Traditional approaches to international relations mimic the patriarchal structure of the liberal state, adopting a dualistic approach, and using fixed, hierarchical concepts of power.[42] By convention, security studies is couched in classic, binary liberal language, based on reason and bounded concepts. Yet standard ideas, such as Just War theory, which attempt to constrain the practice of warfare according to certain set rules and principles, fail to address the unpredictable reality of warfare, and its inevitable social and emotional impact.[43]

An alternative perspective is of a bottom-up process, broadening our understanding of power relations, embracing and validating women's experiences as well as men's, and offering different models of power beyond the usual relationship of domination and submission. An alternative power paradigm would be Jaquette's power through persuasion; or Arendt's power through acting in concert; or Ruddick's 'maternal thinking', which elevates humility rather than domination as a behavioural model.[44] Tickner claims that such a view of IR is dynamic, multidimensional, and based on contextual and personal relations, as opposed to the abstract, top-down, system-level analysis of traditional IR. While idealist, it is pluralist rather than narrowly morally prescriptive – it uses key elements of female socialization, such as ideas of caring and responsibility, to build communities from the grass roots, up to the overall international system.[45]

Another broad and holistic approach is explored by Christine Sylvester, who uses a postmodern perspective to open up the study of IR and ally it with a fissiparous, multilevel form of feminism. She seeks to avoid the latent dangers of essentialism that exist in conjoining feminism with peace politics (promoting a stereotypical and limiting image of woman as nurturer, carer, etc.) by introducing the plurality of postmodernism.[46] Postmodern approaches are particularly appropriate now when old certainties have been shattered and the traditional balance of power has been disrupted by rogue states, random terrorists and the growing significance of non-state bodies.[47] Sylvester sees realist IR as highly gendered and 'stuffed and bristling with male decision-makers', failing to take account of women as agents of knowledge and theory. An alternative version of IR, based on the concept of 'empathetic co-operation', is developed instead, with the aim of forging a sense of solidarity among different groups, avoiding domination through frequent negotiation, and using and validating the subjective. In this way, a feminist approach could move beyond the nation-state egoism of realism and the self-help co-operation of neo-realism, as well as the relativist claim that there are no common interests. Where postmodernism fails to converge happily with feminism, however, is in its fundamental epistemology. Feminism is rooted in clear values and ideals concerning equality, emancipation and social justice, and is too explicitly utopian to conform with the fluidity and moral vacancy that defines postmodernism.

Non-postmodern feminist work perhaps combines more

effectively an acceptance and validation of the subjective with a clearly defined, value-based understanding of security. In *Gendered States*, V. Spike Peterson asserts that we are not abstract human actors but embodied, gendered beings and, as such, require a relational, structural analysis, rather than the traditional ahistorical, atemporal approach, which has no real meaning beyond the abstract.[48] She makes the conceptual point, key to a gender-sensitive understanding of security, that the tendency in Western philosophy and metaphysics to value the scientific and objective, and to elevate ideas of unity, stability and self-mastery (all equated with masculinity) above their opposites of body and spontaneity, creates a clearly gendered hierarchy that is fundamental to various forms of actual domination. And, as Sylvester argues, a focus on gender issues contrasts with the traditional reflection of the masculine standpoint of separateness, independence and autonomy.[49] The frequency of sexual violence towards women reflects these conceptual rankings, with women treated as 'other', providing a naturalized model of oppression for other exploitative relationships such as slavery and colonialism. Women's systemic insecurity is thus a domestic *and* an international issue. The state itself can play a role not only in direct oppression but in indirectly perpetuating a gendered dynamic of structural violence (inadequate health-care policies for women, unequal wages, non-intervention in domestic violence, etc.). Transnational patterns of women-specific violence, dehumanization and exploitation mesh with domestic practice. Similarly, Walker points out the limitations of the gendered concept of state sovereignty as the reification of rational 'man',[50] which assumes that women's and men's interests coincide and universalizes men's experiences, ignoring significant sociocultural gender distinctions.

Feminists offer alternatives to the traditional concept of peace as the 'absence of war', and security as maximum self-defence. Reardon argues that peace entails social justice and economic equality, creating situations which are less likely to break down into conflict.[51] This meshes broad-school concerns about structural violence with a strongly feminist focus on relationships, needs and empathy (rather than institutions, organizations and goal maximization).[52] Reardon also marks out two key feminist principles of security: inclusivity (that is, security as indivisible, so that only fully global security is meaningful and reasonably stable); and holism (that is, a multi-level approach, to address the various different, interconnected constituent elements of security).

Similar arguments, espoused earlier in the 1980s and somewhat less sophisticated, are found in the work of Penny Strange, who makes sweeping comments about 'male cosmology' and its tendencies toward dichotomization, domination and the quest for mastery, which provide a common thread from violence against women to arms races and the nuclear threat.[53] Such arguments can be seen as anticipating the convergence of feminism and security studies concerns that developed throughout the 1980s. This convergence reflects well-established links between women, peace and the anti-war movement dating from before the early suffragettes.[54] Yet the traditional women–peace link tended to be based on an idealization of womanhood and femininity, seeing women as innately disposed to pacifism due to their maternal, nurturing roles.[55] Such associations can be based on essentialist assumptions and arguments of biological determinism, which can easily be used in a conservative sense, to justify a status quo based on gendered inequality. Non-essentialist feminist analysis, however, does not rely on 'innate' qualities of maternal pacifism; it sees pacifism as a social construct which can be both challenged and used positively to add the gendered values, experiences and perspectives that are traditionally hidden, in order to deepen the concept of security. In this way, feminism is grounded in a strongly utopian tradition when applied to IR: it seeks to challenge the orthodoxy and instigate change. In a biologically determined world, a desire for meaningful change would be futile.

The objective of feminist analysis is clear-cut: to challenge and deconstruct patriarchal practices that oppress and demean any 'other' entity, and to create practices and processes that are egalitarian and non-hierarchical, building web-like, interrelational structures and means of decision-making. The underlying approach is holistic, embracing the parts of our identities usually omitted from public and political discourse, including the emotive and subjective. This is clearly political, as it challenges the way that power operates and how political decisions are made. Moreover, it includes the private, emotive and subjective, and see the political and personal as indivisible.

Feminism embraces human motives, relationships and behaviour in the analysis. A feminist understanding of IR is messy, and cannot be reduced to neat diagrams of game-theory decision-making. It is founded on relational links at many levels, from the individual to the international. As well as being web-like in a two-dimensional sense, connecting different issues and concerns, feminism adds a third dimension by introducing subjective, individual-level understandings. The aim is not to 'win', or achieve a bland consensus; rather, it is to avoid any objectification, the creation of an 'enemy' entity, because the complexity and depth of the relations of states, individuals, communities, regions, and so on make simplistic, black-and-white scenarios inappropriate and damaging.

For traditional realists, such an approach renders the discipline so diffuse and broad as to be meaningless: they prefer to focus on purely international actors, understanding the dynamics of the international arena only in terms of nation-states and their relative threat capabilities. A key difference between the two approaches lies in the depth and complexity of the model being used: realism relies on a sparse construction with which to explain and predict security concerns; and the feminist model is far more complex, as it recognizes the meshing of the inter-relational and the international and entails a sense of empathy, seeking to understand other perspectives rather than dominate with just one view. Decision-making is ideally seen as a shared process rather than the province of an insular, elite establishment. With a greater sense of mutual empowerment and respect, conflicts might be defused or prevented, with fears and concerns acknowledged earlier on rather than allowed to escalate.

If we use this model to address the key questions underlying this book, the answers are accordingly complex. An obvious response to 'who is being secured in a feminist understanding of security?' is 'women' – that is, our 'normal' security analysis is extended, to include the group that has traditionally been excluded from the high politics of strategy. In concrete terms that could, as a start, mean that rape as a tool of warfare is acknowledged and taken more seriously. Yet the purpose of a feminist analysis is not just to add women as a group to established concepts. Rather, it is to challenge those concepts. So, if we are looking at who is being secured, a feminist would reject the realist focus on the atomized, depersonalized state actor, operating in a field of high politics; and instead would focus on the inter-personal and inter-relational networks that sustain the state actor – thus, the private as well as the public is secured.

Equally, an obvious and simplistic retort to 'what is to be secured against, under feminism?' would be 'men'. But for all but the most radical essentialist and separatist feminists this answer is deeply flawed. In terms of building a feminist idea of security, the threat is not men as a group, but the dynamics of power and hierarchy based on violence and inequality that feminists understand as intrinsically gendered. And it is this that makes a feminist understanding of security distinctive. While ideas such as structural violence and environmental security are used elsewhere, feminism understands these forms of insecurity as following from a construction of power which is based on gendered divisions. The difference between male and female social roles, the public and private, and so on, predetermine the hierarchical and exploitative power relations which allow for an elevation of, say, scientific development over the renewal of natural resources, or 'hard' economic policies over effective social welfare (a 'soft' concern). By fully integrating the private into what is deemed political/public, a gender-aware analysis highlights the divisive nature of tradi-tional constructions of power and security. This concern with power differs significantly from the realist focus on power. As has been explored already, feminists offer alternative construc-tions of power to the traditional realist hierarchies – for example, power through acting in concert, or power as empowerment. Second, a feminist model of security does not reify power in state form – instead, exclusionary borders such as state boundaries are seen as part of the problem, in helping to construct bipolarity and division, and so perpetuate insecur-ity. Feminist security theorists do not privilege the security of the nation-state's territorial integrity; rather, the concern is with the 'low' politics of the state, translated into the security of individuals and communities, on which the state depends.

5 | The Post-Positivist Turn

Post-positivism is the label for approaches that seek to provide a different insight into the social sciences and, by extension, into IR and security studies.[1] Positivists see power inequalities as rooted in material reality, and thus taken as a given. Post-positivists see inequalities as socially constructed, and thus needing to be problematized. Belief in the social construction of knowledge is the element binding post-positivists together. Steve Smith suggests that five post-positivist perspectives can be identified: scientific realism; hermeneutics; critical theory; the feminist standpoint; and postmodernism.[2] As only the last three have something to say about security, we will focus on them, and we will add a fourth category, that of social constructivism.[3]

Yet even after narrowing the topic, grouping a variety of views under this one heading is, at best, tenuous. It is important not to underestimate the differences between postmodernists, critical theorists and feminists in trying to offer a typology that is accessible.[4] Postmodernism focuses 'on the role of rhetoric in constructing both power relations and bodies of knowledge'.[5] Critical theory uncovers underlying power structures in order to emancipate the oppressed. And not everyone includes gender perspectives under the post-positivist umbrella. Ship argues that:

> for all their initial promise, they [post-positivist approaches] have remained very much science as usual ... Thus, critical theories and postmodernist approaches, as is the case with their

mainstream counterparts, fail to confront the multiple ways in which gendered presuppositions inform and shape epistemological, ontological, and axiological assumptions underpinning theory, methodology, international practices, and political projects.[6]

The last section of this chapter returns to the differences between various post-positivist accounts along with an assessment of positivists' reactions. Before that, however, we examine the core elements of post-positivism, and the security-related arguments of post-positivist feminism, postmodernism and critical theory, and then look at the constructivist challenge.

Beyond Positivism

Post-positivism is an extremely sophisticated and complex approach to the social sciences. Often it appears abstract and obscure. Sometimes this is due to an apparent lack of clarity in the writings ('apparent' because the use and meaning of words is of extreme importance to post-positivists). More often it is due to the reader's lack of knowledge about the philosophy of the social sciences. For nearly all analysts in IR, positivism has been the default mode of training and, with little interest in the philosophy of the social sciences, they rarely question this positivism.

What is positivism? There are four linked assumptions underlying it. The first is that there is an objective truth that can be discovered. The second is that the means of discovering that truth is reason and there is only one correct form of reasoning. Third, the tool of reasoning is empiricism, which enables the analyst to test propositions. Finally, there can be a distinction between observer and observed.

Post-positivists reject all of this. Instead, reason is seen to be a tool to silence and marginalize, a means of delegitimizing difference. In place of the positivist stress on reason, the post-positivists place emphasis on the social construction of knowledge. This leads to a very different perspective. Instead of describing a world through empiricism, the post-positivists suggest that it is not possible to divide observer from observed in order to discover material 'truths'. Rather, the world is composed of knowledge constructed socially. Positivism leads us to look at evidence which is socially constructed and view it as objective reality. As Neufeld has put it:

> in short, ideas, words, and language are not mirrors that copy the 'real' or 'objective' world – as positivist conceptions of theory and knowledge would have it – but rather tools with which we cope with 'our' world. Consequently, there is a fundamental link between epistemology – the question of what counts as reliable knowledge – and politics – the problems, needs, and interests deemed important and legitimate by a given community.[7]

Compare this notion of social construction to that put forward by neo-realists Buzan, Jones and Little: 'Social "facts" may be more important than real ones in determining outcomes: the perceived power of a state, and therefore its ability to determine outcomes, may exceed (or under-state) its real capabilities.'[8] In this positivist conception there is reality, and perceptions: 'real' facts and 'perceived' facts, and the analyst may compare the two. However, for the post-positivist, there is only socially constructed knowledge; there is no 'real world' in the positivist sense. Rather, perceived facts and real facts are one and the same, for the ideational is privileged over the material.

Thus, because our reality is socially constructed, theory is a fundamental part of it, and there can be no division between theory and practice as there is no objective world to be known. Enloe and Zalewski are absolutely clear on this point: 'theory does not take place after the fact. Theories, instead, play a large part in constructing and defining what the facts are.'[9] Most work in this area inevitably makes reference to Anthony Giddens, for whom 'all forms of social life are partly constituted by actors' knowledge of them.'[10]

If knowledge is a part of reality but is socially constructed it follows that there is no objective 'truth', only socially defined truths, no single 'reason', only socially defined reason, and consequently no role for empiricism, for there can be no distinction between observer and observed, as theory and practice cannot be separated. 'Thus objectivity, understood as a "perspectiveless gaze", is impossible in a socially constructed world; rationality is not transcendental but historically specific, learned activity; and methods are necessarily contextual, and therefore shaped by culture and particular values.'[11] Post-positivism is sometimes portrayed as extremist, but these ideas have a good deal of support. Consider an example related to E.H. Carr, usually identified as an archrealist: is this actually a fair description, or is that rather the way his work has been socially constructed? Booth points out that Carr was comfortable with discussing structures and forces other than states, and in addition, *The Twenty Years' Crisis, 1919–1939* contains significant elements of the utopianism Carr supposedly condemned out of hand.[12]

For post-positivist approaches, it is not possible to examine 'security' without first examining the 'state'. The state is certainly problematic.[13] It is a social construction; it was not inevitable that humanity be organized politically in this way, nor must it always be organized in this way. This has implications for our understanding of security, for 'the meaning of security is tied to specific forms of political community.'[14] As Wæver notes, 'only to the extent that other forms of political community begin to become *thinkable* (again), does it make sense to think about *security* at other levels.'[15] In addition, this means that security must be thought about in a holistic sense. As Haas puts it, 'The *problématique* is the problem of all problems, not merely the sum of the problems of pollution, war, famine, alienation, resource depletion, urban crowding, and the exploitation of the Third World by the First. It is a systematic construct that assumes causal connections among these problems, connections that amplify the disturbance in the metasystem.'[16]

Positivism, then, is rejected for a number of reasons best summed up by Jan Aart Scholte. It 'purports that there is one truth . . .; that a clear distinction can be drawn between "logical" and "mythological" accounts; . . . that empirical observation provides the whole essential link between human consciousness and social reality; and that facts and values are discrete elements of thought, with social science incorporating the former without the latter.'[17]

One of the confusions in the debate relates to a problem of labels. When Europeans talk of critical theory, they are referring to a specific area of inquiry based on the work of Jürgen Habermas and the Frankfurt School, for whom postmodernism represents a neo-conservatism, a loss of concern for those subjugated within dominant power structures, and a turn away from political responsibility.[18] In the United States, however, the term 'critical theory' tends to be applied as an umbrella to include all post-positivists. For example, Alexander Wendt says it is 'a family of theories that includes postmodernists (Ashley, Walker), constructivists (Adler, Kratochwil, Ruggie, and now Katzenstein), neo-Marxists (Cox, Gill), feminists (Peterson, Sylvester), and others. What unites them is a concern with how world politics is "socially constructed".'[19] In this book, post-positivism is used as the umbrella term, and critical theory refers to those who work in the tradition of the Frankfurt School.

The next sections examine the means by which three forms of post-positivism – feminism, postmodernism and critical theory – use social construction to understand security.

Post-Positivist Feminism and Security

As seen in chapter 4, feminists maintain that 'security' must include structural violence. This 'refers to reduced life expectancy as a consequence of oppressive political and economic structures (e.g. greater infant mortality among poor women who are denied access to health-care services). Structural violence especially affects the lives of women and other subordinated groups. When we ignore this fact we ignore the security of the majority of the planet's occupants.'[20] Women as such are missing in the debate about security.[21] In addition, the debate is highly gendered. One of the most famous critiques of this is that made by Carol Cohn. While the defence debate is conducted in terms of abstraction, Cohn notes multiple examples of how it is actually loaded with sexual imagery.[22] Post-positivist feminists agree with all of this, and also that 'Patriarchy not only oppresses women, but instils values and behaviour in men which are a model for other forms of oppression.'[23]

Why should feminism be considered again in this chapter, since chapter 4 was on feminist approaches? One of the problems the feminists have faced is that various groups have sought to absorb them. There are 'Marxist' feminists and 'liberal' feminists. Robert Keohane sought to recruit feminists to the neo-liberal cause, while post-positivists seek to bring feminism within their orbit. There are certainly insights for feminism in these various perspectives, but there is a danger of fragmentation, one symbol of which is the division between the (broadly) positivist feminist views covered in chapter 6 and the post-positivist feminism in this chapter.

Post-positivist feminists argue that feminism offers a partic-ular insight. 'Here the distinctiveness of the feminist voice consists in extending antifoundational critiques by identifying objectivity, rationalism, and even science itself as specifically male/masculine ways of knowing (derived from male ways of being under patriarchal relations).'[24] This view would suggest that positivism itself is masculinist, and that therefore all feminists need to become post-positivist. But in addition there are particular problems that feminists especially face. As V. Spike Peterson notes, 'to the extent that masculinity remains privileged and positivism is identified with masculinity, all critics of positivism meet resistance not only to their argu-mentation per se but to the "demasculinization" of science their argument entails.'[25] Thus, post-positivist feminism is, in this sense, the ultimate heresy for the positivists.

Feminist thought therefore can be divided into two groups: positivist and post-positivist.[26] There are those feminists who base analysis on notions of essentialism. Gender is defined according to the essential nature of women and men and this seems to produce unalterable roles. This is particularly so when feminists talk about the nurturing role of women which, it is suggested, reconfirms masculinist notions of the need to 'protect' women as the 'weaker' sex. Postmodernist women go further. While 'essentialists' focus on the gender division and its implications, postmodernists criticize the whole notion of gender. A person's gendered experience varies according to a series of other factors: age, race, class and sexuality, to name a few. Thus, the category 'women' varies across time and cul-ture, and cannot be related simply to gender. All these labels – gender, class, ethnicity, sexuality – are socially constructed; that is, they may arise from physical difference, but more important is the social meaning given to them, meaning that varies according to the social environment. Thus essentialists can create a feminist security concept which is generally applicable, but for postmodernists this is impossible; all they can construct is a security relevant to some women at a particular time. While essentialists can speak of a common experience of oppression, for postmodernists women have different experiences of oppression. As Tickner puts it, 'Just as feminists more generally have criticized existing knowledge that is grounded in the experiences of white Western males, postmodernists claim that feminists themselves are in danger of essentializing the meaning of woman when they draw exclusively on the experiences of white Western women.'[27]

As Ship notes, 'as feminism constitutes the political expression of the concerns and interests of women from different regions, classes, nationalities, or ethnic and racial groups, a critical feminist international relations project recognises that feminism cannot be monolithic in its goals, issues and strategies. Gender subordination, although universal, cannot be grounded in a rigid conception of universality.'[28] This is the heart of the difference between positivist and post-positivist feminism.

Postmodernism

The concept of social construction is also at the heart of postmodernism. It is 'defined as much by its rejection of modernity as by its own internal coherence. The modern project is seen as a cultural construction that attempts to extend one particular mode of thinking – rationality – to all corners of the world, destroying diversity in the name of progress.'[29] Postmodernists deconstruct texts to demonstrate that positivist approaches do not discover pre-existing meaning; instead, they create hierarchies and boundaries that silence 'others'. David Campbell, for example, in a highly complex work, suggests that state identities can only be constructed and maintained by constructing a threat beyond the boundaries. Thus, conflict and the danger of war are inherent in the construction of the state itself.[30]

Postmodernism is sometimes criticized for being concerned with 'theory' rather than 'reality'. But for the postmodernists, positivist thought is still based on the outmoded modernist concept of rationality. Postmodernists reject the notion that there is a single rationality waiting to be discovered objectively. This modernist obsession with objective reality means that we lose sight of the 'real' influences on world politics in the search for 'rational theory'. James Der Derian, for example, suggests that Tom Clancy has had more direct impact on the practice of international relations than Kenneth Waltz; image is more important in understanding the world than objective reasoning.[31]

The postmodernists therefore argue that rationalism is not unitary and objective. This has important implications. While Banks talks about an inter-paradigm debate, for the postmodernists such a *debate* is not possible.[32] Under the important notion of incommensurability, the paradigms are constructed in terms of different values and serve different political projects and, hence, have no common measure. As will be seen later, this is where a clear difference can be drawn between postmodernists and critical theorists.

With no foundational basis for comparison between different paradigms, postmodernists are anti-foundational. This is most clearly expressed by George and Campbell, for whom postmodernism 'refuses to privilege any partisan line'.[33] Peterson agrees, saying that postmodernism 'recognizes all knowledge claims as socially (intersubjectively) constructed (not "objectively" received through a neutral method); there are no *transcendental* (decontextualized) grounds for establishing truth claims or foundational meanings'.[34] A particular, perhaps extreme, version of this is provided by writers such as Jean-François Lyotard and Jean Baudrillard.[35] Postmodernists argue that the postmodern period – and in particular the late twentieth century – is witness to the destruction of meaning on an unprecedented scale. Baudrillard, for example, argues that the human condition is characterized by *hyperreality*, in which the modern media form as well as represent social reality. As Vasquez puts it, 'the idea of representing the world is entirely overturned and replaced with the notion that only simulation is possible, because there is no reality or truth to be represented; indeed the distinction between truth and falsity is blurred.'[36] Under hyperreality, one cannot be sure what one's senses are comprehending. Was it a real crime on television, or actors replaying a role? When buttons on a keyboard are pressed, does that lead to the destruction of a computer image on the screen, or of soldiers on a battlefield?

For security studies, hyperreality becomes important with Baudrillard's examination of the Gulf War, the conditions for which, he suggests, were engendered by simulation with war-gaming utilized at every level, from the policy-making core to the battlefront.[37] Der Derian explores this further, suggesting that before the war, Iraq purchased a war game from BDM International, a US company, and the software for the planning of the invasion of Kuwait was also bought from the United States. As he continues, 'this is not to suggest that the 500,000+ troops in Kuwait were not real; rather, to point out that their being there might well have been a consequence of a "reality" constructed out of the imagined scenarios created within the computer war games.'[38] He continues by suggesting that the coalition forces did not defeat Iraq in the conventional sense, but rather as 'a cyberwar of simulations'.[39]

However, Baudrillard puts a rather different complexion on the war. Because of hyperreality, it was simply 'unreal'.[40] From this, David Lyon suggests Baudrillard argued that the Gulf War did not happen, which is certainly *not* the same as suggesting that it was unreal.[41] Baudrillard's point is, rather, that humanity 'has entered into a phase of terminal indifference where the passage to war is a non-event, something that either won't happen – as Baudrillard inclines to believe – or where happening will in any case not be noticed, since we have lost any means of distinguishing "reality" from its simulated counterpart'.[42]

Baudrillard presents a rather extreme view of postmodernist security studies but nevertheless it is of value to examine his views on how a postmodernist perspective alters perceptions of reality. Fundamentally, Baudrillard – like the other post-modernists – rejects the notion that one theory or, as they would term it, 'discourse' is superior to others, thereby arguing that those discourses that depend upon Enlightenment criteria (truth and so on) have lost all claim to persuasiveness. Incommensurability is central, based on the significance of anti-foundational thought; however, as we shall see, anti-foundationalism is not a part of the critical theorists' armoury.

Critical Theory

Critical theory is broadly in the Marxist tradition, but breaks with Marxism in several vital areas. Critical theory does not just focus on class, but broadens out to consider other notions of social exclusion. It expands the Marxist notion that production is the key determinant, and it argues that social knowledge requires a purpose, which for the critical theorist is emancipation.[43] For Robert Cox, the essential contrast is between positivism and historicism. The former sees social science rather like physics, in which subject and object can be separated so events are seen as 'caused' by actors, making 'explanation' possible. In contrast, historicism sees institutions as constructed by people as collectivities, facing a collective problematic.[44] There is an identity of object and subject in this approach, emphasizing 'understanding' over 'explanation'. Cox argues that:

> The ontologies that people work with derive from their historical experience and in turn become embedded in the world they construct. What is subjective in understanding becomes objective through action. This is the only way, for instance, in which we can understand the state as an objective reality. The state has no physical existence, like a building or a lamp-post; but it is nevertheless a real entity. It is a real entity because everyone acts as though it were; because we know that real people with guns and batons will enforce decisions attributed to this non-physical reality.[45]

Critical theory and postmodernism are, therefore, very different theoretical projects. While postmodernists identify different discourses that have no common ground, critical theory is based on the proposition that:

> theory is always *for* someone and *for* some purpose. Perspectives derive from a position in time and space, specifically social and political time and space. The world is seen from a standpoint definable in terms of nation, or social class, of dominance or subordination, of rising or declining power, of a sense of immobility or of present crisis, of past experience, and of hopes and expectations for the future.[46]

Critical theory is about identifying structures of domination and working towards destroying those structures to emancipate the disadvantaged.

Thus there are distinct types of post-positivist theory. While postmodernists can criticize paradigms, they cannot comparatively evaluate them. Critical theorists are able to make such an evaluation, based on the emancipatory potential of the theory.[47] Developing this, and drawing on Cox and Neufeld, we can postulate three versions of theory from the perspective of critical theory.[48] Two are conservative; one is emancipatory. First, problem-solving theory is concerned with explaining the world; it is otherwise known as policy-relevant study. It takes the world as it is, and develops generalizations within set parameters. However, since those parameters serve national, sectional or class interests, problem-solving theory is ideologically biased and conservative. Second, postmodernism seeks to deny that it has a political project, a particular line. It does not choose between rival paradigms and this, from a critical theory standpoint, leaves the dominant social order unchallenged; thus it is also a conservative approach. Third, and by contrast, critical theory takes an emancipatory stance and proffers a normative choice in favour of a different social order.

From the postmodernist perspective, however, there are only two forms of theory. The first claims that there are no foundations for evaluating between different discourses; for the postmodernists, this is not conservativism but rather the consequence of anti-foundationalism. The second suggests that there are foundations upon which competing claims can be judged. This category contains positivist thought and also from the postmodernist perspective critical theory, for the latter claims to be able to judge rival claims on the basis of emancipation. But emancipation for whom? As Smith points out, 'for critical theorists, emancipation means something very different from what many radical feminists mean by it.'[49] In other words, critical theory is deficient in the same ways as neo-realism; it claims a superiority for its discourse that has no foundation.

Illustrating this point, it is worth a second look at the critical theorists' condemnation of problem-solving theory. Is it necessarily conservative? Certainly so, to Cox. But this deserves more investigation. The neo-realist and neo-liberal paradigms could be categorized in this way, but is all positivist theory conservative? Peace studies, for example, or utopian writings in the inter-war period, are positivist yet argue for fundamental change in international politics. The main purposes of peace research are to define ways of resolving conflict, moving IR away from violence. Is this conservative or reformist in outlook?

What, then, does critical theory mean for security studies? As Ken Booth argues, it means recognizing that 'The sources of human (in)security are far wider than those traditionally in the purview of strategists. Whose interests are being served by keeping the other issues off the agenda? ... broadening and deepening – the task of a critical security studies – will reveal Cold War security studies as an Anglo-American, statist, masculinist and militarized ideology.'[50] In contrast, critical security studies seeks to identify the victims of social exclusion and to evaluate strategies for their emancipation.

The Constructivist Challenge

The final category that will be examined in this chapter is that of the social constructivists. Again, we have a difficulty with our terminology. Postmodernists, critical theorists and many feminists also base their analysis on the concept of 'social construction'; the constructivist school, however, disagrees with each of those other schools.

Constructivism draws implicitly upon earlier work and in particular that of the English School of international relations.[51] Adler defines constructivism as 'the view that the manner in which the material world shapes and is shaped by human action and interaction depends on dynamic normative and epistemic interpretations of the material world.'[52] Institutions and practices, for constructivists, are based on collective understandings, and constructivists seek to investigate these understandings of the material world.[53]

Constructivism in security terms has to date mostly been applied to understanding the relationship of the ideational and the material in security institutions. If the European Union has been the focus of the engagement of neo-realism and neo-liberalism, it has been the future and nature of NATO that have provided an important theme in the constructivist challenge to neo-realism. Neo-realists have argued that where there are objective threats, states will respond by forming an alliance. If that objective threat dissipates, the cohesion of that alliance will weaken. Thus, with the collapse of Soviet power, and the objective impossibility of an equal replacement, NATO must wither away.

The constructivist approach to NATO is rather different, and is perhaps best illustrated by Thomas Risse-Kappen.[54] First, constructivists reject the notion of an objective threat. As he argues, 'threat perceptions do not emerge from a quasi-objective international power structure, but actors infer external behaviour from the values and norms governing the domestic political processes that shape the identities of their partners in the international system.' Second, once functioning, alliances are shaped by shared values: 'the Western Alliance represents an institutionalization of the transatlantic security community based on common values.' Third, this institutionalization of common values is robust in the face of political change, for 'it is easier to adjust an already existing organization, which encompasses an elaborate set of rules and decision-making procedures, to new conditions than it is to create new institutions of security cooperation.'[55] Thus, international institutions are, for neo-realists, responses to real threats and to changes in the balance of power; to constructivists they can be fundamental representations of values and, as such, can be and often are constructed to play a central role in international affairs.

Constructivists, then, seek to engage with other perspectives; they do not share the postmodernists' anti-foundationalism. This reflects the different epistemological basis of the two views. The use of the terms 'positivism' and 'post-positivism' implies that there are in essence only two epistemological positions; constructivists would hold that there are three. The 'positivism/post-positivism' divide refers to the relationship between the material and the ideational. Positivism, in its behaviouralist, neo-realist or historical materialist guise, shares the assumption that IR is based on the material. Post-positivism, in its postmodernist and feminist guises, accepts the centrality of relativism, that the ideational is central to international relations. But there is a third category (confusingly for IR scholars, it is termed 'realism' in epistemological terms) that applies to the constructivists and also to the critical theorists. This position holds that there is a material base to understanding IR, but that what is important is the ideational construction of the material. Thus, the world is socially constructed in that ideational factors crucially affect outcomes, and those ideational factors are constrained by the material world. Feminism does not itself represent one particular epistemology; hence, one can find 'material' feminists, 'ideational' feminists, or feminists who focus on ideational construction, or discursive construction.

Reactions to and Problems with Post-Positivism

As all post-positivist accounts suggest, there is a great difference between traditional and 'dissident' accounts of security. Traditional positivist approaches focus on strategies for preventing great-power war and on forwarding national interests, on negotiations, on diplomatic solutions to conflicts and regime formation, and on securitizing differing areas of international activity (that is, constructing or presenting them in such a way that they are perceived as or become a security issue). Post-positivists open up the agenda by questioning epistemological and ontological assumptions and thereby provide space for a range of issues that would otherwise be ignored.

One of the central issues that has run through the debate on IR is the degree to which a theory can be developed which can or should be autonomous of other disciplines. Neo-realism can clearly be seen at one end of the spectrum in which an autonomous theory of IR is possible; at the other end are the various post-positivist approaches, for which it is not possible to develop an autonomous theory not only of IR, but in any of the social sciences. Thus, for the post-positivists, the problem with security studies is that it has been seen within narrowly constructed positivist IR traditions. As IR must be opened up to a range of different theoretical perspectives that are generally applicable to the social sciences, so must security studies. However, there are several problems with this approach to IR.

First, post-positivism is relatively new to IR (although not to the social sciences) and perhaps more vulnerable to critique than more 'mature' traditions.[56] There are, in addition, whole areas of post-positivist social and political thought not yet integrated into IR and security studies. One obvious area is queer theory,[57] which is increasingly important in sociology and political theory yet silent in IR. Second, post-positivism is a broad umbrella under which a number of approaches are placed even though they are often incompatible. Most notable is the fundamental disagreement between postmodernism and critical theory on whether there can be a foundational basis on which to evaluate competing knowledge claims. Third, the unity in the post-positivist approaches lies in what they are against – positivism – rather than in what they favour. However, 'positivism' contains an enormous range of social, political, economic and IR thought that stretches, illustratively, from Hayek to Trotsky.

For all these reasons, post-positivist approaches to IR are still largely characterized by a relatively broad brush. This is not a condemnation of post-positivist approaches, for they add to our understanding of IR and security studies. Largely as a result of post-positivism, the range of security studies in the 1990s is broader than ever.

Unfortunately, rather than revelling in theoretical diversity, the field abounds in bitterness. Neo-Marxist Fred Halliday suggests that post-positivism – like behaviouralism – privileges methodological inquiry over substantive analysis.[58] He tells us that Der Derian's postmodernist On Diplomacy uses 'The word "continental" ... to give spurious cachet to these ideas and style, rather as the term "imported beer" was pioneered in the 1970s.'[59] Postmodernist IR, he tells us, is 'pretentious, derivative and vacuous, an Anglo-Saxon mimesis of what was already, in its Parisian form, a confused and second-rate debate'.[60] Realist Kal Holsti criticizes post-positivism for having nothing to do with real world crises, such as 'ethnic cleansing, fourteen new international peacekeeping efforts, starvation in Africa, the continued shadow of the Balkans and the Middle East, and arms racing in Asia'.[61] Feminist Christine Sylvester condemns neo-institutionalist Hidemi Suganami's *The Domestic Analogy and World Order Proposals* as 'old-fashioned, one-sided, shallow. It is insensitive to domestic institutions that engulf "women" and to international applications of domestic practice that could exacerbate sexism.'[62] Postmodernist Jim George tells us that neo-realist Waltz's *'Theory of International Politics* and (to a lesser degree) *Man, the State and War* ... stand as major indictments of an IR community which, closed to critical reflective capacity for so long, has accorded such high status to works of so little substance.'[63] Realist John Mearsheimer sums up – and sweeps aside – the whole post-positivist approach with the comment that 'in fact the distinguishing feature of the critical theory literature ... is its lack of empirical content.'[64] Adrian Hyde-Price criticizes Steve Smith, because Smith found the debates between 'state-centrism versus transnationalism' and 'neo-realism and neo-liberalism' less important and interesting than those on 'constitutive versus explanatory theory' and 'foundationalism and anti-foundationalist international theory'.[65] Hyde-Price complains that 'to privilege this intellectual navel-gazing seems perverse in a world of war, ethnic cleansing and genocide.'[66] Neo-realist Stephen Walt says post-modernity has nothing of value to offer.[67] And William Wallace warns that post-positivism leads to scholasticism, a pedantic exercise where participants dispute each other's terminology and methodology without addressing common issues.[68]

Thus, the post-positivist project in security studies is controversial. Analysts are often more interested in polemics than in elaborating their own position or in accurately representing the views of other discourses. None of this helps clarify the issue of what is meant by security. But security studies is, and will remain, one of the core areas for the debate.

6 | Non-Traditional Security Threats: The Environment as a Security Issue

The political and strategic upheaval following the Cold War has dramatically altered the global security environment. Traditional threats, particularly those related to superpower competition, have been reduced or eliminated. The end of the Cold War did not, however, make the world safe or easier to understand. States continue to pursue political goals with force; in addition, a broad range of non-military challenges to stability and security has emerged. How states will perceive their security interests in this new global reality is not yet clear, but change is forcing a fundamental re-evaluation of the types of issues and factors which may jeopardize stability and security.

Many security issues which currently preoccupy policy-makers and analysts, such as nationalism and ethnic conflict, the proliferation of weapons of mass destruction, and regional political and military stability, are relatively consistent with past national security concerns and practices. Non-traditional challenges, however, command increased attention. Concerns such as environmental degradation, economic well-being, trans-state criminal organizations and the mass migration of people are of a different character from past concerns. The heightened salience of these 'new' issues invites not only a rethinking of what constitutes threats to security but a reconception of security.

These non-traditional threats to security are diverse, but have some features in common. First, for the most part they are not state-centred. Instead, they emanate from factors or actors which are sub-state or trans-state in character. As a consequence, they do not conform easily to state-centred theories and analyses. Second, these challenges have no particular geographic locus. The past focus on the danger posed by the military power of other states provided a location for efforts to contain the threat. The *sine qua non* of security was the construction and maintenance of military balances in strategic regions. Non-traditional challenges, however, represent dangers which are diffuse, multidimensional and multidirectional. Increasingly, they have to be viewed generically or sectorially, as well as territorially.[1] Third, these challenges cannot be managed by traditional defence policies alone. Defence or military organizations may have a role, especially where violent conflict is involved, but effective management requires a range of non-military approaches. Finally, the analyses delineating or elaborating these new concerns suggest that individuals as well as states are endangered.

This chapter examines the linkage between environmental change and security. The following chapter looks at other non-traditional challenges to security, including organized crime, refugee movements and economic problems. There are several reasons for devoting a chapter to environmental degradation. First, it has captured the imagination of the public and policy-makers. In part this stems from the meteoric rise in concern about the impact of human activity on the environment since the late 1980s. The discovery in 1987 of the annual massive depletion of stratospheric ozone over the Antarctic made clear that human-induced environmental change can occur far more rapidly than anyone anticipated. Another factor has been the growing understanding of the extremely complex and pervasive nature of the impact of human activity on the environment. In particular, there is a gathering appreciation that the implications of environmental degradation are likely to be far-reaching, with uncertain but potentially adverse consequences. There is increasing appreciation of the potential dangers of environmental disruption.

Second, while the security implications have received attention from academics and, to some extent, policy-makers, and although a number of states, notably the United States, have identified environmental degradation as a security concern, whether human-induced pressures on the environment should be considered a threat to *security* is still the subject of debate. The central element in this debate is how security should be defined. This chapter starts with a brief overview of the debate and then explores three main themes linking environmental degradation to security.

Conceptualizing Environmental Security

Environmental challenges did not suddenly emerge with the end of the Cold War. The development of industrialized economies depends on natural resources. Possession of, or reliable access to, important natural resources is often seen as central to the development and maintenance of state power, and thus has long been a core element of state-centred theoretical approaches such as realism. States have struggled throughout history to gain secure supplies of resources and this has often contributed to the onset of war. The emphasis for the most part, however, was on non-renewable resources, such as metallic minerals like gold, aluminium or iron ore and non-metallic minerals such as oil and coal which are critical to modern economic development. The 'oil crises' in 1973–4 and 1979 that appeared to threaten the foundations of the world's economies sparked renewed interest in the resource dimensions of security.[2]

In the same period there emerged some early articulations of broader conceptions linking the environment and security. Dennis Pirages urged that 'ecopolitics' be the new agenda for international relations.[3] Lester Brown sought to redefine national security to make the environment a security issue while others attempted to broaden the concept of security to such a degree that the environment could be included.[4] In the 1980s the first Palme Commission report on 'Common Security' mentioned such a linkage[5] and a few analysts probed the links between environmental decline and human conflict.[6] But, for the most part, links between environmental degradation and security were not followed up in any detail.

In the late 1980s, however, the environment as a security issue began to achieve heightened salience, particularly with the appearance of a number of promotional statements in 1989.[7] Since then there has been a steady proliferation of analyses and the notion has gained considerable, though hardly total, acceptance.[8]

Recent discussions depart significantly from state-centred, realist-based understandings. Many seek to link security to more broadly conceived environmental issues than strategic minerals and natural resources, issues such as greenhouse warming, atmospheric ozone depletion, acid deposition, soil erosion, deforestation, depleted fish stocks and fresh water scarcity. Many not only seek to define a connection between environmental issues and security, they use this to assert that the concept of security needs to be redefined.[9] The intent is to extend the notion of security beyond states to objects such as individuals, groups, bioregions and the globe.

Broadly speaking, recent notions of environmental security hold that human-induced environmental degradation and scarcity pose fundamental physical threats. However, there exists no agreed conception as to precisely what this entails. The range of views or approaches can be broken down into the following categories:

1 environmental scarcity as a cause of political instability and conflict;
2 environmental degradation caused by the conduct of or preparation for war;
3 environmental degradation as a threat to human health and human well-being.[10]

Another, lesser argument is that efforts to mitigate environmental degradation can infringe on sovereignty, which can also be a security issue given traditional concerns with state autonomy.[11]

These four main approaches rest on differing notions of security. The first and the fourth are largely based on sheltering the state from threats. The second and third approaches mainly focus on non-state referents. These different interpretations are not mutually exclusive but they are not interchangeable. The level of analysis in each is distinct, hence the implications are different. There are essential differences with respect to what is being secured, what it is being secured against, who provides security, and what methods can be undertaken to provide it.

The linkage between environmental degradation and security is contested. There are a number of arguments questioning the utility of a concept with multiple meanings as well as the validity of 'environmental' security *per se*. These criticisms come from a range of perspectives, including some that assign high priority to environmental problems.

What do we mean when we refer to the environment? The 'environment' consists of all living and non-living components of the planet – the lithosphere, biosphere, atmosphere and stratosphere. Thus the links between the environment and security might include the implications of terrain and vegetation for military tactics, the influence of geography on strategic thinking, or competition for and conflict over natural resources. An important aspect of thinking about environmental change, however, is that it focuses attention on novel phenomena, ones not previously associated with questions of security. Thus, in this chapter we exclude standard concerns such as inter-state competition for strategic resources and focus on issues previously not connected with security, in particular, human-induced renewable-resource scarcities like deforestation, degradation of agricultural land, overuse and pollution of water supplies, and exhaustion of fish stocks.

Environmental Change as a Cause of Conflict

The view that may have attracted the most public and government attention is that environmental scarcity contributes to competition and conflict. In the recent literature on this the focus has been not on non-renewable resources, as in state-centred conceptions, but on links between the depletion of renewable resources and the onset of conflict. The most important environmental effects cited are the degradation of agricultural land, deforestation, and overuse of water and other renewable resources. Competition over renewable resources can help incite conflict, it is argued, because these resources (1) are increasingly scarce in some regions, (2) are essential to human survival, and (3) can be physically seized or controlled.[12] Conflict over renewable resources in the past has been relatively rare, but some analysts argue it will increase in the future. Growing human utilization has increasingly strained these resources to the point where some are functionally non-renewable, transforming them into scarcities.

The best-known and most influential research investigating this is the work of Thomas Homer-Dixon.[13] Its impact stems from two factors. First, he developed an analytical framework on environmental decline and conflict which his team of experts in the Project on Environment, Population and Security at the University of Toronto sought to test with empirical evidence.[14] He reported the findings in 1994.[15] Perhaps more significant, Robert Kaplan's 1994 article 'The Coming Anarchy' set forth an apocalyptic vision of future chaos due to environmental degradation,[16] and in citing the environment as '*the* national-security issue of the early twenty-first century'[17] identified Homer-Dixon as at the forefront of relevant research. Kaplan's article got the attention of US policy-making circles, leading to Homer-Dixon being invited to Washington to brief high-level officials.[18]

Homer-Dixon is not the only person to examine the connection between environmental degradation and conflict.[19] Nor is he the only analyst to develop a conceptual framework on this.[20] But the centrality of his work and the general utility of his framework make it a useful focal point here.

The impact on state security of environmental degradation and conflict can be direct or indirect.[21] For the former, environmental change may bring a state into conflict with others for control of or access to an increasingly scarce resource, while for the latter, environmental decline may have social and political effects which generate conflicts that impact adversely on state security. Homer-Dixon hypothesized three connections. Inter-state conflicts arising from non-renewable resource scarcities are historically familiar. Homer-Dixon hypothesized in 1991 that inter-state conflict could now originate in whole or in part from renewable-resource scarcity,[22] but subsequent studies found no evidence to support this.[23] Nevertheless, it has been asserted that both fresh water and fish stocks are likely to stimulate future inter-state wars.[24]

There have been no instances in which fresh water directly provoked inter-state conflict; nevertheless, it is the renewable resource most commonly cited as a potential source of acute conflict. An adequate supply of fresh water is critical for societies, but rivers and aquifers often flow across national frontiers and one state's actions in drawing water can affect another's access.[25] Overuse by a state can limit or decrease the amount available for others. Downstream riparian states highly dependent on river water may be especially vulnerable to the activities of upstream neighbours and may fear that the water may be used as an instrument of coercion.[26] Conflict may occur when a state with an acute water shortage feels it has the military capability to redress this. Water is a likely source of conflict in very arid regions such as the Middle East, North Africa and Central Asia.[27] Many countries in these regions share river systems and require sufficient water from these common sources. Continued population and economic growth will increase the domestic demand and these states may be willing, as a last resort, to use force to secure what they need.

Maritime fisheries are another renewable resource that is being progressively depleted, inciting state competition over continued access.[28] Maritime fish stocks are a key food source in many parts of the world and may contribute significantly to a state's economy. Many stocks, such as tuna, are in international waters, but others are in localities that straddle or lie within the 200-mile economic zone of a coastal state. Disputes over control of or access to stocks could provoke acute conflicts. One example is the Anglo-Icelandic clash of 1972–3 (the so-called 'Cod War'), which resulted from the efforts of Britain and Iceland to protect their access to fish stocks.[29] In the 1990s there has been a significant increase in clashes of rival national fishing vessels and governments over fishing rights and fisheries management.[30] Other striking examples are the 1992 dispute between Canada and the European Community about overfishing of northern cod in the Grand Banks and the 1995 dispute between Canada and the European Union about the overfishing of turbot in the same region.[31] In both cases, Canada and the EU (in particular, Spain) issued diplomatic warnings and sent naval vessels to the region because of concern about the economic impact of loss of the fisheries and concern about sovereign rights to control (Canada) or have access to (Spain) these fish stocks.[32] Although both were resolved peacefully, disputes that culminate in armed ships sent to signal resolve underscore the possible role declining stocks may play in future violent conflict.[33]

The prospect for conflict seems likely to grow unless mechanisms are developed to alleviate the increasing stress renewable resources are being subjected to. States dependent on outside sources of non-renewable resources have developed elaborate mechanisms to secure supplies.[34] Although wars with non-renewable resources in mind can occur, as in the 1991 Gulf War, these mechanisms curb the resort to military force. States concerned about 'renewable-resource wars' may decide to co-operate in managing and conserving scarce renewable resources and develop regimes to regulate their management, conservation and distribution.[35] Such regimes might be bilateral, regional, or international. Such solutions may not come easily because shrinking renewable resources are often shared by several states, and thus efforts to conserve and manage by one or several countries will go for naught unless other interested parties co-operate.

Much more probable than direct scarcity-induced conflict is environmental change that is indirectly linked to conflict. The most salient environmental effects in this context are the degradation of agricultural land, deforestation, and overuse of water and other renewable resources. Homer-Dixon hypothesized two types of conflict related to resource scarcity.

First, he suggested 'that large population movements caused by environmental stress would induce "group-identity" conflicts, especially ethnic clashes'.[36] People will abandon areas when environmental disruption jeopardizes their existence or seriously erodes the quality of their lives.[37] Environmental refugees may move internally or leave their country. Attempts to resettle in new areas will intensify local competition for resources, which can result in a backlash from the indigenous people, putting severe stress on the country, particularly when there is persistent violence, and may also exacerbate inter-state conflicts.[38] The movement of Bangladeshi migrants into Assam in India, in part because of land scarcity, resulted in violent ethnic clashes and contributed to a violent insurgency there between 1980 and 1988.[39] At the heart of the 1969 Soccer War between Honduras and El Salvador were Salvadorean refugees who had fled to Honduras because of intense competition for arable land made scarce by severe environmental degradation, the skewed distribution of land and a growing population. Honduras sought to expel these refugees because they intensified pressures on its own farm-land.[40]

Second, Homer-Dixon has suggested 'that severe environ-mental scarcity would simultaneously increase economic deprivation and disrupt key social institutions, which in turn would cause "deprivation" conflicts such as civil strife and insurgency'.[41] As environmental degradation and scarce land bring economic decline, appropriate responses can adversely affect a state's capacity to act effectively while contributing to the marginalization and disaffection of its citizens, which 'aggravates popular and elite grievances, increases rivalry between elite factions, and erodes the state's legitimacy'.[42] If there is no way to express grievances satisfactorily, people may resort to violence. Some examples are the insurgency in the Philippines, the rise of the Sendero Luminoso in Peru, and intra-state violence in China.[43]

The central insight is that environmental degradation and society may interact in a complex series of feedback processes. The source of increased resource scarcity is some combination of population growth, a decrease in the quality and quantity of a renewable resource, and unequal access to it. Four main societal effects have been identified as likely to increase the probability of conflict: decreased agricultural production, eco-nomic decline, population displacement, and disruption of legitimate institutions and social relations.[44] These societal effects are often interlinked and sometimes reinforcing. The result is a weakened state, which establishes the political context for ethnic conflicts, *coup d'états* or deprivation con-flicts.[45] Appropriate responses can ameliorate environmental decline and its impact, but inappropriate ones can aggravate pressure on the environment. In most situations environmen-tal change would probably be only one of many contributing factors, even just a minor element in a tangled web of political, economic and physical conditions which generate conflict. Society's response to environmental change will depend on many physical and social factors, like available resources, political institutions and social relations, that vary from state to state, region to region. Thus the influence of environmental change is situation-dependent. Developing countries tend to be the most susceptible to the societal effects of environ-mental deterioration. They lack the material, financial and technological resources to manage environmental problems, while their political and social institutions often hinder development of co-ordinated responses to such problems and their effects.[46] Many developing states face growing pressure on the land, and resultant decreased agricultural production, economic decline, displacement of population and disruption of social institutions.[47]

Although there has been considerable investigation of all this, both the concept and the supporting research, especially that of Homer-Dixon, have been challenged on a number of grounds. A key criticism is that the analytical links between environmental degradation and security are weak. Much of the evidence is anecdotal or illustrative, making it difficult to determine each link in the causal chain rigorously.[48] This problem is especially severe with respect to indirect linkages. Environmental degradation interacts with so many non-environmental factors through so many positive and negative feedback processes that it is very difficult, if not impossible, to identify the precise role and significance that resource scarcity has. Marc Levy has argued that while current research clearly refutes the idea that environmental degradation is irrelevant, 'it is less clear what the evidence might affirmatively show.'[49] He questions, therefore, the practicality and significance of focusing on environmental causes; what is really needed is more detailed research into the general causes of conflict.

In spite of these questions some states take the problem seriously. The US has identified environmental degradation as a national security issue and the government incorporates the environment as a potential cause of instability and conflict into its analysis. The fairly diffuse nature of the roots of renewable-resource scarcities, however, makes solutions, preventive or ameliorative, difficult to develop. Approaches to preserving and restoring the environment encompass a wide range of political, social, economic and environmental solutions to be applied at the local, international and global level. In general, the primary approaches are embedded within the broad notions of environmental preservation and restoration, sustainable development, and population control. Each is contested on the basis of a multiplicity of cultural, religious, economic and political perspectives on meaning, desirability and practicality. The scale and scope of the potential problems are beyond the capacity of any one state or group of states to manage, but lack of consensus on the means and methods to use makes co-operation quite problematic. This means states will be reluctant to take major steps until environmental-induced conflicts affect their security, and then they may well react violently.

In many respects this conception of environmental security resembles issues arising out of competition and conflict for strategic and natural resources. The object of security is still the state and, as a consequence, the state and its institutions are the primary agents. However, this approach is not solely concerned about inter-state competition for scarce resources; it looks beyond the state to environmental effects for sub-state actors whose reactions can have implications for state security. Yet, in spite of the difference between this and traditional conceptions, the focus is on the security of the state, and that makes this conception relatively compatible with the realist paradigm. As a consequence, it requires only a modest redefinition of security.

The Impact of Military Activity on the Environment

The second main approach to the environment as a security issue is concerned with environmental degradation and military institutions. It focuses on the impact of military activity on the environment. There are three main sets of arguments. First, war has a direct, adverse impact on the environment. Second, military organizations in peacetime (in preparing for war) have an adverse impact on the environment. Finally, the military may have a positive impact on the environment and have, or can have, a role in addressing environmental problems, especially those that may contribute to the onset of conflict.

The first set of arguments concerns the destructive impact of war. This destruction may be unintentional, a largely unavoidable by-product of military operations, or it may be an intentional attempt to affect the environment to win the war.

Conventional war has always had some unintentional impact on the environment.[50] This has grown dramatically, however, as the destructiveness of weapons has increased,[51] and seemingly reached its apotheosis with weapons of mass destruction. One hypothesis is that extensive use of nuclear weapons would have a severe impact on the environment, including altered weather (nuclear winter) and massive depletion of stratospheric ozone, with dire consequences for human survival.[52] Chemical and biological weapons can also have a major impact; the results of their widespread use on terrestrial, avian and marine species could range from quite minor to disastrous. Chemical or biological agents could have long-term implications too, for the contamination of vegetation may poison the food chain for a long time, and bacterial or viral agents could persist indefinitely.[53] The severity and duration of the effects is uncertain, but any large-scale use of these weapons has the potential to inflict serious long-term harm.

'Environmental warfare', the deliberate destruction of the environment for military purposes, has been fairly common, though its role is usually marginal and its military effectiveness often questionable. Scorched earth policies, as practised by the Russians during Napoleon's invasion or by the Union Army during the US Civil War, have a long history, while the breaching of dikes for flooding was used by the Dutch as early as the Franco-Dutch War of 1672–8. The US military in Vietnam used defoliants to destroy forest cover and enemy food crops, and even tried 'to disturb weather patterns through cloud seeding'.[54] Soviet forces in Afghanistan and government forces in the Ethiopian civil war deliberately sought to destroy food crops and to make growing food dangerous, if not impossible, as part of their military campaigns.

Industrial facilities, such as nuclear, chemical, hydrologic and petrologic facilities, may be attacked for military purposes, with their destruction having environmental consequences. They may be attacked to reduce enemy manufacturing or to make it more difficult for the enemy to fight, or they may be attacked because the environmental/human consequences are militarily useful. The destruction of dams or dike systems,[55] or of industrial facilities like nuclear reactors,[56] chemical factories[57] or petroleum installations, could mean long-term flooding or contamination of surrounding areas. In the 1991 Gulf War Iraq threatened, and subsequently carried out, the spilling of oil into the Persian Gulf[58] and the destruction of Kuwait's oil wells, and after the war Iraq constructed a series of dams, embankments and canals to cut off the flow of water into the southern marshes where Shi'ite rebels were holding out against government forces.[59] During the Croatian offensive in Krajina in January 1993, there was a risk that Serbian forces would detonate mines they had placed in and around the Peruca dam rather than let it fall back into Croatian hands. Also in January 1993, Serbian barge captains running a UN-mandated blockade on the Danube River with oil supplies threatened to release the oil into the river if Bulgarian authorities attempted to stop them.[60] These and other cases suggest that some states in some instances may well perceive that deliberate destruction of the environment has tactical or strategic utility.

This prospect has led to the examination of ways to restrict such damage. A number of treaties or agreements already exist that either have environmental considerations or address the need to protect the environment. Some arms control treaties incorporate environmental considerations, notably the Antarctic Treaty the Partial Test Ban Treaty (signed in 1963 and now superseded by the Comprehensive Test Ban Treaty), the Outer Space Treaty and the Sea-Bed Treaty. A number of international agreements and conventions seek, in whole or part, to minimize the impact of war on the environment and restrict 'environmental warfare'.[61] The convention on the prohibition of military or other hostile use of environmental modification techniques (1977) specifically bans some forms of 'environmental warfare'.[62] Articles 55 and 56 of the Geneva Protocol I of 1977 call for combatants to 'protect the natural environment against widespread, long-term and severe damage' and to forgo attacking installations containing elements capable of doing severe damage to the environment.[63] However, these articles are more requests than enforceable prohibitions. Nevertheless, Western militaries are sensitive to causing unnecessary environmental and human damage, if only out of concern about public sentiment. The US, for example, attacked Iraq's nuclear facilities during the Gulf War, but in a manner designed to minimize chances of the release of radioactive material.

Then there is the environmental impact of peacetime military activities. One critical view, for example, contends that the development and maintenance of military institutions appropriates financial and organizational resources which could be put to productive uses such as environmental clean-up and protection. The core element of this argument is that environmental degradation is so threatening that we need to abandon the use and maintenance of military capabilities to resolve disputes.[64] Another view is that the day-to-day activities of military institutions in peacetime have serious environmental and economic consequences. First, military institutions are major polluters; second, military training does significant harm to the environment.

States are willing to sacrifice much to ensure their security from military attack. As a consequence, the pollution caused by the military during the Cold War was largely ignored as a price to be paid in order to be prepared militarily. Military organizations, in the US in particular, are frequently cited as the largest polluters in modern society,[65] due to their size, their range of activities and their dispersal around the US and the world.

Military or military-related peacetime pollution spans the spectrum in scale and significance. Small-scale pollution, such as the improper disposal of waste, may have only a localized impact, but given the enormous size of the military and its facilities, it attains significant proportions. Disposing of the daily accumulation of garbage over the stern of a modern warship may seem insignificant, but when this occurs on thousands of ships, every day for decades, the consequences mount dramatically. At the other end of the scale, modern forces, including those of the US, were less than conscientious during the Cold War in their use and disposal of toxic and other environmentally harmful material on bases, training and test facilities, and research facilities.[66] The improper handling, management and storage of the toxic materials used in developing nuclear weapons, for example, has resulted in the land around nuclear weapons production facilities being severely, and very dangerously, polluted.[67] The Soviet Union's practice of dumping toxic material and discarded nuclear reactors in Arctic waters has unknown but potentially very serious long-term implications for the environment.

Some analysts argue that military testing and training also have adverse environmental consequences which must be addressed. The use of live ammunition and explosives and the movement of large numbers of soldiers and vehicles during

training exercises damages vegetation, wildlife and water-
ways; in very sensitive ecological areas this can be
environmentally devastating. Certain military exercises, such
as when NATO pilots practice low flying, create noise pollution, which can be quite significant in heavily populated
countries such as Germany and Great Britain.

Western forces increasingly are forced to pay serious attention to the environmental consequences of their activities
because of the growth in public and governmental concern. The
US has gone so far as to establish the Office of Environmental
Security in the Department of Defense, with responsibility for
environmental clean-up of military sites and facilities, providing regulations to protect the environment during training
exercises, and addressing the health implications of environmental pollution for military personnel. Western militaries
now conduct day-to-day activities in a more environmentally
sound manner, in keeping with measures ranging from the
recycling of paper and proper waste disposal, to reducing spills
of fuel and other toxic material, to constraints on military
testing and training.[68] Western governments are also beginning
to clean up the toxic legacy of the Cold War. Such efforts are
very costly and long-term: it has been estimated that the effort
to clean up the US government's seventeen nuclear weapons
plants will cost $100 billion to $200 billion and will take thirty to
forty years,[69] while the problem of restoring similar areas in
Russia is even greater.

The first two perspectives, as we have seen, assume that the
military is part of the problem. The third view, in contrast,
emphasizes that the military can be part of the solution. Western militaries maintain large reserves of land for bases, depots
and other facilities. Large parts of these reserves are unused,
often deliberately so because the locales are of ecological
importance. The armed forces have had, and will continue to
have, an important role in conserving biodiversity and protecting ecological niches that in the civilian domain have been
destroyed.[70] Military and associated intelligence agencies can
also be tasked with monitoring, predicting and ameliorating
environmental problems, domestic and international, because
they have unique and powerful capabilities.[71] The surveillance
resources and mobility of the military far surpass those of any
other governmental department. These can be used to protect

scarce resources, respond to environmental crises and disasters, monitor and enforce international environmental regulations, gather, analyse and disseminate scientific data on the environment, develop and spin off environmental clean-up technologies, and implement environmental sustainability programmes.[72] Military personnel and facilities might also be tasked with environmental protection and restoration,[73] much as the military has been called on for disaster relief.[74]

These arguments are the converse of the first set to the effect that environmental degradation can contribute to the onset of conflict. The referent of security is often not specified or is left ambiguous, though sometimes there may be an impact on the ability of the state to defend itself. Constraints on training, for example, could adversely affect preparedness. Increased costs for environmentally sensitive procedures in the running of the military, in developing and manufacturing modern weapons, and in redressing past environmental damage may curb funds for military preparedness.[75] Should this be what the analyst fears, then the security referent is the state.

However, this seems inconsistent with the thrust of this set of arguments. They emphasize the deleterious impact of the military on the environment. The concern is to preserve the environment. This tends to transform environmental security into security for the environment *per se*, making the referent of security the environment, not the state.

Environment and Human Health and Well-Being

The last set of arguments emphasizes human health and welfare, especially environmental pollution and disease. Many types of pollution may affect human health and well-being. Localized pollutants, such as car fumes and industrial effluents, may have adverse effects, while broader ones such as intense smog over cities, from car, industrial or other emissions, may degrade air quality and bring on breathing difficulties that can be fatal to those with respiratory problems. The range of relevant environmental degradation is so vast it could encompass every type of pollution which might affect human beings.

Arguments about the security of human health do not begin to address all possible pollution problems. Most are centred on the security of the environment. As with arguments on the impact of military institutions and activities on the environment, the immediate referent of security is the environment, but the ultimate concern is that only in a healthy environment are individuals well off, and they are the true referent of security. Most immediately at risk are those who live and/or work in military facilities, especially ones in which serious pollution exists. Moreover, because many pollutants can be transported by air or by ground water if released into the environment, people living near military facilities may also be at risk.

Another environmental threat to human health and well-being can arise from disease-creating micro-organisms. Concern here stems from the recent appearance of virulent new diseases hitherto unknown, some of which are at present largely untreatable,[76] as well as from the resurgence of serious diseases, once thought eradicated or in decline, that have become resistant to drugs. Humanity has long been affected by lethal plagues.[77] In 1918, for example, an influenza plague which originated in Kansas is estimated to have resulted in 25 million dead in Europe and North America, a number which exceeded the battlefield deaths of the First World War. Today, people in the Third World often live in squalid conditions in cities, marginal areas or remote areas, where they are exposed to new or re-emergent diseases and have little access to modern medical care. The outbreak of the horrifyingly deadly ebola virus in remote areas in Africa is an example of the risks these people confront. People in the developed world are also at risk as modern transportation allows contagious diseases to spread readily around the world. Global warming may eventually result in diseases usually found in the tropics migrating into new regions. The threat is significant, especially if effective medical means are not found to combat them: 'infectious diseases are potentially the largest threat to human security lurking in the post-cold war world.'[78]

Such arguments focus on the security of the individual. The security of the state is not the concern. Of course, if a large proportion of its population suffers serious health problems, this would affect a state's economy and its military strength, but this is not a standard concern because such an extreme threat seems remote.

The Environment as a Security Issue

The proposition that environmental problems may be a security issue remains contentious. A number of arguments, though acknowledging that environmental degradation poses dangers which need to be urgently addressed, question the validity of the link between human-induced environmental disruption and security.

One concern is that to expand the concept of security to encompass environmental threats and dangers results in too all-encompassing an approach. Broadening the concept of security in this way, especially to include threats to individuals, permits inclusion of virtually anything that affects individuals adversely. Inclusion of the environment makes the concept of security so amorphous that it loses intellectual coherence and makes it difficult to find solutions to particular problems.[79]

Some academic analysts are also critical of the fact that arguments linking the environment and national security, especially early ones, tend to be polemical. They see proponents as intent on appropriating the language and symbolism of national security, hoping that this will result in more policy initiatives, greater domestic public support, and increased funding for managing environmental problems. This is seen as wrong-headed and ultimately counter-productive to finding real solutions. Critics suggest that linking the environment to security runs the risk of militarizing the environment instead of greening security. It may lead policy-makers to think increasingly about environmental problems solely in security or military terms, focusing only on those issues which have security implications at the expense of more important ones, or to think mainly of military solutions to environmental disputes. The latter is particularly worrisome, as the use of violence is likely to be inappropriate or, given the destructive nature of modern warfare, a gross overreaction to the stakes and values involved.[80] The central thesis of this body of criticism is that environmental problems should be seen as extremely important in their own right, able to command the attention and resources that traditional security has had, rather than being viewed through the prism of security.

The concept of environmental security raises questions

about what is meant by security: what is being secured (what is the referent), what is it being secured against, who provides this security, and what are the approaches to ensuring security? Each of the three approaches discussed provides somewhat different answers to these questions. The first linkage – environmental degradation as a factor in the development of conflict – emphasizes the protection of the state from an external-based threat of violence, including the use of military force, or the internal threat of domestic instability and violence. The second linkage – the impact of military activity on the environment – emphasizes the protection of the environment from military activity, and by extension, of individuals from the harmful environmental consequences of military activity. The third linkage – human health and well-being – also emphasizes the protection of individuals from dangers created by environmental change. Different conceptions of environmental security are based on different conceptions of security.

These in turn lead to diverging views on the link between environmental change and security. Those who conceive of security as protecting the state are unlikely to accept the second and third conceptions, and may only grudgingly accept the first, whereas those who conceive of security more broadly can accept all three. Yet even the first approach departs in some ways from the traditional conception of security. The threat may stem not from clashing state interests and actions which lead to violence, but from the actions of individuals or groups who, in responding to harmful environmental change, create circumstances in which either violence occurs or the legitimacy or cohesion of the state is undermined. To avert such threats rather than simply react to them, states must protect the environment from harm, striking at the root cause of the threat, or protect individuals or groups from the harmful consequences of environmental degradation. In other words, individuals must be safeguarded to protect the state.

Thus, identifying environmental degradation as a security issue raises intriguing questions about security. Environmental security suggests that individuals as well as, or even instead of, states should be the referent, that individuals need protection from more than military threats and that this requires some new methods. Not all analysts and policy-makers accept this, but some governments are forging ahead to incorporate environmental questions in their security agenda. The mandate of the Office of Environmental Security in the US Department of Defense is to develop and implement policies within each of the three conceptions of what environmental security entails. It is supposed to work with other armed forces, primarily but not exclusively in Central and Eastern Europe, on promoting awareness of the connections between security and environmental degradation and developing appropriate policy responses.[81] Environmental security may be less worrisome than military threats and may not command the attention and resources that military threats do, but the idea that the environment is important is being assimilated into government security agendas and is a legitimate topic for academic study.

7 Non-Traditional Security Threats: Economics, Crime and Migration

There is a range of other non-military challenges which are becoming a focus of attention for policy-makers and analysts. Economic well-being, transnational criminal organizations and the mass movement of peoples are increasingly identified as security challenges. This is in part due to the fact that in many parts of the world non-military challenges are perceived as more threatening than the military power of some prospective enemy state. As Stefanowicz notes, for example, 'Policy specialists in Warsaw, like the [Polish] public, perceive security risks to be more internal than external and more non-military than military. There is greater danger from "non-sovereign" actors – for example, corporations, migrating peoples and organized crime – than from any sovereign, state actor.' These issues, like environmental degradation, are very non-traditional. They arise from factors or actors which are sub-state or trans-state in character, are diffuse, are multidimensional and multidirectional, cannot necessarily be managed by traditional military means, and are often threatening to something besides the state. As a consequence, inclusion of these issues in the security agenda constitutes a broadening of security.

The literature on these three phenomena resembles that on environmental degradation. The various analyses are usually not specifically directed towards redefining security but aim at examining and evaluating the nature and dimensions of certain activities perceived as posing a serious challenge. The intent, at least in some of the earlier literature, was or is to place these issues on state security agendas. The primary concern is for the security of the state. Nevertheless, in promoting them as security challenges, or in assessing the nature of those challenges and the means to confront the danger, many analyses centre on a particular referent other than the state.

Economic well-being, transnational criminal organizations and mass movements of people are not the only non-traditional threats that may be considered. For lack of space, we have, however, confined the discussion to these three, as they are fairly representative of the ways in which non-traditional challenges are argued to constitute security threats and what these arguments suggest about the notion of security. Moreover, although each of these three deserves as much examination as environment degradation, we have limited ourselves to a brief examination of the way they are conceived of as security issues and what these conceptions imply.

Economics and Security

At the beginning of the 1990s a number of scholars argued that the world is entering an age in which the economic aspects of security will increasingly dominate traditional political and military aspects.[2] They suggested a new significance for economic factors in security. Perceptions of a link between economics (and the national economy) and security are not new.[3] Individuals seek job security and economic prosperity; questions of welfare and prosperity are the stuff of national politics; the search for national prosperity, along with traditional conceptions of security, is a matter of high politics, of diplomacy at the highest level. However, this leaves open the question of exactly how economic affairs are a security issue. There are numerous ways economics and security may intersect; the connections may be depicted as significant, and the changing nature of the individual, national and international economic systems may be taken into account.

Economics and security matters interpenetrate in nearly all human activities to some degree, and this section cannot do justice to all of them. Any properly constituted state seeks economic adequacy and national security. All states must calculate a 'guns versus butter' trade-off, allocating their limited resources between the shorter-term objective of security and the longer-term goal of economic welfare. Thus, economic considerations and security are profoundly interrelated.

The main arguments about this centre on the security of the state. There are arguments that address the question with a referent other than the state, such as those made within the field of peace studies or feminist thought, but these have already been addressed, if only in passing.[4] At the state level of analysis, there are three broad categories of links between security and economics. First, economic potential and capability are directly linked to the power, and hence the security, of the state. Second, economic well-being is part of the essential values of the state. Finally, economic means are used to achieve important ends of the state.

Economic Potential and Military Power

The first conception stresses that economic potential and power are an essential component of military power. As Friedberg has pointed out, 'Ever since Athens taxed its empire to raise a fleet against Sparta, there has been a strong connection between wealth and military power and therefore, in the most simple and direct way, between *economics* and *national security*.'[5] The economy provides the material and financial means for the military capability to protect national security. The relevant means that sustain the power of a state are: natural resources, manufactured resources, invisible or intangible resources, capital and labour.

Natural resources, such as water, energy sources, cultivable land and minerals, have long been seen as critical for national power. Writers from Alfred Thayer Mahan to Hans Morgenthau have argued that a state needed large geographical space, a large population and a well-endowed, diverse natural resource base to achieve great-power status.[6] Only with sufficiency in these resources could a state build and sustain a strong military capability. This reflects the past dominance of land as a factor of production. Control over land and peasants allowed monarchs to extract, through taxation and other means, a portion of the wealth generated. The more territory was controlled, the more wealth was extracted. Economic adequacy meant that a ruler had the means to feed, train and equip soldiers, and military strength meant additional territory could be conquered with obvious benefits for the treasury, which could be used to maintain even more soldiers, and so on. The acquisition of new land not only meant greater resources and more people to tax, it provided the protection of a larger buffer against attack. Territorial expansion thus was consistent with improving the state's economic position, and both translated into greater security.

This relatively uncomplicated relationship began to change in the nineteenth century. The capture of new territory added to economic well-being because conquered peasants usually obeyed the new ruler irrespective of who he was. The rise of popular nationalism, however, increasingly raised the prospect that conquered peoples might not obey, and this could shrink the additional revenues and supplies gained. Indeed, committing resources to manage such a newly won territory could damage the state's relative position.[7]

The changing nature of the expanding international economy in the twentieth century further altered the relationship. Land is no longer the dominant economic factor that it once was. Capital, labour and information technology have become of greater importance as factors of production.[8] Unlike land, these are mobile. Iraq found after it captured Kuwait that the money had been transferred elsewhere; North Vietnam captured South Vietnam but could not halt the massive flight of refugees, who often included the South's best-trained and most energetic workers. As capital, labour and information technology gained in significance, and as international trade (and interdependence) increased, states in the twentieth century were increasingly confronted with the choice of applying military force to expand national territory or of improving their access to factors of production and markets in other countries on a peaceful basis.[9] In 1986 Richard Rosecrance argued that the international system was poised between territorial and trading states, with evolving circumstances favouring trading states for the first time,[10] and John Mueller and Carl Kaysen subsequently argued that the changing nature of the means of generating wealth, the mobility of those factors of production and the costs of war have all contributed significantly to a decline in the utility of force as a tool of state policy.[11] At the end of the twentieth century the choice between control or access appears weighted in favour of the latter, with most states, particularly developed ones, preferring to gain access through peaceful means.

The value of employing military force for economic success may be in decline, but ensuring economic adequacy still remains a critical interest of modern states. Few are sufficiently endowed with natural resources, foods, energy or other main factors of production to sustain sufficient economic systems, and so they seek secure access to foreign markets and sources of supply. For many states, international commercial opportunities are a fundamental basis for domestic economic well-being, while for others trade, financial flows (foreign investment) and sometimes foreign aid are critical for survival and economic progress. Hence, a state's economic interests remain vital to its security interests, and military force may still be used to protect them. This may occur directly, as in the Gulf War, when the US deployed forces to defend Saudi Arabia and liberate Kuwait in part to ensure continued access to the oil on which many Western economies depend. More generally, protection of access to commodities and markets is ensured indirectly through the maintenance of international or regional stability, to avoid disruptions with significant economic repercussions.

Relying on access to external elements of national economic strength can have a cost. The foreign policies of a state can be skewed towards supporting countries it might otherwise ignore, because of the need to ensure access to key resources. The US in the late 1970s and the 1980s was unwilling to take forceful action against South Africa in spite of American opposition to its policy of apartheid, in part because of the need for certain critical minerals available from few other countries, and in part due to concern that hostile forces would gain control of the southern tip of Africa, round which tankers sailed carrying oil from the Middle East to Europe and North America. In an era of technologically sophisticated weapons systems and the international production of components, a state may not control the production of everything that goes into its armed forces[12] and this may have subtle effects on its ability to provide security. In the 1991 Gulf War the US used more than twenty weapons systems built with foreign-made transistors and microchips. It made over thirty requests to foreign governments for urgently needed parts, including urgent appeals to Japan for battery packs used in command and control computers, for video display terminals used to analyse real-time data from reconnaissance planes, and for semi-conductors and other components.[13] Should sources for critical components refuse to provide them when needed, because they object to the action undertaken or are actively involved on the other side, the ability to sustain weapons during drawn-out military operations would be seriously degraded. This is not very plausible and its implications for security are subtle, but it is not a situation a state can ignore.

At the turn of the century, economic capability remains a building block of security. The productive capacity of the state determines the quantity and quality of military resources it can afford. Maintenance and use of military forces, especially volunteer forces armed with state-of-the-art weapons and equipment, is resource-intensive and requires an appropriate balance in the 'guns versus butter' trade-off. Managing this is often difficult as it depends on a range of factors, not least being the proper identification of the state's interests and of how much and what kind of military capability is needed to protect them. Getting the balance wrong can have quite harmful results. Too many 'guns' depresses the ability of a state to provide sufficient 'butter', resulting in internal dissatisfaction, but insufficient 'guns' may leave a state vulnerable to the power of other states. The economics of national security – including issues of military procurement, the economics of war, economic relations amongst allies in peace and war (burden-sharing), and so on – is a matter of major concern, and the subject of considerable political debate.

One consequence of the 'guns versus butter' trade-off is that the economic capacity of a state, or gross domestic product per capita, is a limited indicator of military potential. This is due to four factors. First, states devote quite different shares of the GDP to defence, both across states and over time. Second, there are considerable differences across states in the efficiency of their military expenditures. This difference is now compounded by growth in the cost of sophisticated weapons, the differential in the cost of comparable weapons systems depending on their origin, destination and timing, and the difference among states in the costs of their military personnel. Third, factors such as resolve, quality of leadership, strategic and tactical capability, and other such immaterial elements influence effectiveness in using force. Finally, in a dispute between states that are unequal in economic and military strength, the results may be unpredictable because one or both may receive economic support from third parties.[14] Thus, a strong economy does not guarantee a strong military or the successful use of force.

A strong economy is itself a measure of power in the international system, and the greater a state's economic potential, the greater its military potential and its power potential. Although military power may not always be dictated by economic strength,[15] this interpretation of economics as a security issue is consistent with traditional views of security among realists/neo-realists and many liberals/neo-liberals. The referent is the state, which is to be secured from economic weakness and the power and influence of other states; the state must provide for economic security using domestic and international economic policies (and sometimes military power) to protect and improve the economy.

Economic Well-Being as a Security Issue

A second line of argument broadens the nature of the relationship between economics and security in that it adds that a strong or prosperous economy in itself is a security issue. The basis of 'economic security' is that economic or material means are an essential value to be pursued and protected. There are two elements to this. First, poor or deteriorating economic conditions can adversely affect internal political stability, with possible consequences for national security. Second, a weak economic position may result in foreign impositions on state sovereignty and action. These two elements are interrelated and difficult to disentangle. They apply most forcefully, and almost entirely, to developing or Third World states.[16]

Economic security is of considerable concern for many developing states because they have been attempting to consolidate themselves as nations. Most are artificial creations of the European colonial powers, with borders having little or no relation to populations of diverse peoples. As a consequence, each of these states on gaining independence has had to try to create a domestic political and social consensus, to forge a nation. Generating a lasting political and social consensus amongst diverse peoples with competing claims is a daunting task. The lack of consensus poses a threat to domestic security and the political viability of the state, to the regional configuration of states, especially when borders divide a people, and even to international security, for outside powers may be drawn into any conflicts that emerge.

The inherent difficulty of nation-building is frequently made even more arduous by economic weakness. A problem for weak states in nation-building is that it is difficult to develop a domestic political consensus, and to maintain an agreed institutional basis, without a reasonably effective economy, but it is equally difficult to develop a reasonably effective economy without domestic consensus and institutional structures. Broadly speaking, a weak economic position compounds the problems faced by these states in three ways: (1) it seriously restricts the resources available to manage competing claims; (2) it provides little foundation for the state to exert influence in the international system; and (3) it leaves the state vulnerable to outside influences which can exacerbate, inadvertently or deliberately, internal divisions. As a consequence, many states seek economic security either to facilitate nation-building projects or to protect the internal cohesion they have achieved.

Caroline Thomas has ably argued that for many states in the Third World, seeking economic autonomy and development is a core element of their search for security. Thomas makes clear that essential for their overall security are monetary security and fair trading systems. States import and export raw or manufactured products, and seek either to gain through exporting more than they import or to achieve an equilibrium between imports and exports. When imports exceed exports, however, states need to borrow money to balance the books and keep their economies functioning, and this exposes them to the power realities of the international economic system.[17] The lender of last resort for a state is usually the International Monetary Fund (IMF). IMF loans often come with conditions that impose particular economic and monetary policies. This is problematic for underdeveloped states such as Ghana or developing states such as Brazil, for these conditions often reflect economic orthodoxy in the advanced industrial states but may not be appropriate for other states. Weak states exert little influence on the conditions, for in the IMF decision-making power is based on financial contributions to the fund, not on how much is borrowed. To keep going, weak states have no alternative but to accept the conditions and the resulting infringements on their sovereignty and autonomy. If economically weak states are to achieve full sovereignty, they believe they must have monetary security to buffer them from the dictates of the international market.[18]

Related to the need for monetary security is that for a secure and equitable international trading system. Many Third World states see the conventions and institutions of the international trade regime as biased against them. Poor states see it as forcing them to export primary materials at cheap prices to the industrialized world, which turns them into exports to the Third World at much higher prices, thereby adversely affecting poorer states' balance of payments. This problem has been exacerbated over time as the price differential between primary and secondary products has increased, forcing poorer states to export ever more primary products to pay for the same finished products. Poorer states are also subject to the price instabilities of the market for these products, which makes forward development planning difficult and can create severe internal economic instability. An added problem for many countries is that they do not control their natural assets entirely, for these are often owned by foreign firms that exploit them for their own profit rather than to improve the domestic economy. The security issue in the perception of poor, weak states is that the inequality (perceived or real) in the international trading system restricts their ability to develop economically as they see fit.[19]

Thus, economic security can be important for states if their economic weakness leaves them vulnerable to outside forces which restrict and erode their autonomy.[20] In one sense, this is not a serious security issue; in an era of globalization in markets, production and money flows, few states, even economically strong ones, exercise complete sovereignty over their economies. However, many Third World states lack internal cohesion; their domestic political and social consensus is fragile. External forces or impositions can have adverse internal implications as their variable impact internally often increases disparities in the distribution of benefits, to the extent that substantial elements of society are economically marginalized. This invites the growth of political discontent and challenges to the legitimacy of the state, even violent challenges. The economic weakness of many states undermines their political legitimacy and may threaten their viability as political entities.

This problem may be pronounced when a developing state stakes its political legitimacy on first boosting and then continuing economic development. A state with widespread poverty that is squeezed by the international economic system can create insecurity for citizens and the government. If the state is pursuing rapid development, this can make for growing economic disparities within society that breed insecurity for certain sectors of the citizenship, while at the same time the legitimacy of the state is increasingly tied to that growth. In such a situation, a sharp disruption in economic growth can bring about serious political unrest, even revolution. In part this is what happened in 1997–8 in Indonesia, where President Suharto based his nepotistic, authoritarian-style rule on sustained economic gains through the 1980s and 1990s. Such an occurrence could happen elsewhere as well. And this is not new. The same thing happened in Germany, and in a less direct way Japan, during the depression in the 1930s.

Conceptualizing the economy as a question of security in this way means that events as diverse as oil price rises, increases in international interest rates, and even declines in resource prices on international markets threaten security. For many Third World states with weak economies, such events can have serious implications for stability and political legitimacy. As a general rule, developed states, though affected by such events, are not jeopardized by them. They have much stronger economies and are based on a strong domestic political and social consensus. Nevertheless, even governments in developed states are concerned about providing a domestic economic environment in which citizens are secure from hardship and deprivation. While this concern is mostly good governance and a desire to be re-elected, it also reflects fear that when citizens lack economic security the proper functioning and legitimacy of the state may be undermined. When deprivation is widespread and the economic aspirations of the citizens cannot be met, the consequences for the state may be severe. Edward Kolodziej argues that the collapse of the Soviet state indicates how important the economic and political structures of a state are, that the security of the Soviet Union was compromised catastrophically by its inability to satisfy the economic needs and political aspirations of the governed.[21]

The Soviet economy was stronger than those of most Third World states, but not comparable to Western economies. Nevertheless, the US appears to have adopted the broader interpretation of economic well-being as a security issue. The Clinton administration, in its first national security statement, identified the strength of the American economy as the first security interest of the US. The country is not in any danger of coming apart as did the Soviet Union or as some developing states might; the reasons for identifying the US economy as a security priority lie elsewhere. First, this is good domestic politics, for in the US the achievement of material well-being or at least an adequate standard of living is an individual and national value of great importance. Second, the Clinton administration recognized that a strong and prosperous economy underpins US influence in the international system, and economic decline, even if only relative to selected other states, would translate into a reduced influence and power.

This conception of economic well-being as a security issue overlaps with the first one. But going beyond the basic relationship between economic and military potential to encompass the relative effectiveness and strength of the economy is distinctive. In the first conception, adverse economic change is a danger to security only to the extent that it seriously affects military capability. In the second conception, anything which adversely affects the domestic economy is a security issue. The reference point is the state, with the security concern having to do with constraints and infringements on state autonomy and/or the ramifications of economic activity for domestic legitimacy and stability. The loss of autonomy need not even be the result of malign steps by other states; in the developing world states are susceptible to profit-driven international market forces, forced by circumstances to shape their economic and other policies to suit international markets to sustain economic stability and well-being. Equally, domestic instability may be created by impersonal forces at work in the international economy. A fall in the price of coffee beans due to supply outrunning demand harms the economy of coffee-producing countries, and thus can legitimately be deemed a security concern. As Giacomo Luciani points out, 'any economic event has a security implication.'[22]

Economic Instruments of State Policy

Increased reliance on transnational economic opportunities and transactions creates vulnerabilities that leave states not only subject to impersonal forces in the international economic system but vulnerable to deliberate exploitation by other states. Economic instruments are important tools states employ to further their national interests. The intentional disruption of transactions in some cases can cripple the economy of a state or at least impose serious costs. Countries that export only a few commodities (as in the developing world), that send those exports to only a few markets (trade concentration), or that rely heavily on single countries for vital goods are particularly vulnerable. Interdependence, with dependence on international economic transactions, permits a country to manipulate these transactions to change the attitudes and behaviour of another.

States may use economic instruments to reward or punish a state to induce or coerce it to behave in particular ways. Among the most common of these tools are: raising or lowering tariffs on imported goods; currency manipulations to alter terms of trade; quotas on imports from the target state; granting import and export licenses to control the exchanges of particular types of goods; freezing or expropriation of another state's assets; blacklisting of companies that conduct business with the target state; granting loans or extending credits; manipulation of foreign aid, including military aid; boycotts against another state's products; embargoes on goods sent to another state; and sanctions and blockades. The impact of these and other economic instruments will vary. Tariffs (and quotas), for example, may be manipulated upwards or downwards to provide punishment or inducement. The US extended Most

Favoured Nation (MFN) status to Poland as a reward when it showed its independence from the USSR, and then revoked this status as punishment in 1981 when the Polish government imposed martial law. Such manipulation affects the economy and hence can be an effective policy tool, but it is unlikely to pose a serious threat to a state. Sanctions, on the other hand, can pose a very serious threat to the economy and well-being of a state. For this reason, sanctions are usually reserved for punishing extremely wayward states whose behaviour is considered intolerable.

Precisely how effective economic instruments may be is uncertain. Tariffs work on a unilateral basis only if the actor possesses such a large share of the world market that it can influence the price of the particular commodity through restrictions on access to its market. Thus, the US might use tariff manipulation with some effect, whereas smaller states with smaller markets may not. Sanctions may seriously affect a state's economy but they may also, over time, stimulate local production of the embargoed commodity or result in product substitution.[23] Another limitation is that there is often a reciprocal influence, with both the initiating and target state suffering costs. Economic instruments usually work because an economic relationship already exists from which both parties benefit, and curbing this relationship often affects both states. The more significant the relationship, the greater the impact, and the larger the impact on the initiating state the more likely that adversely affected domestic interests will seek to reverse the policy. Thus, while economic instruments are commonly used to influence another state's behaviour, there is no guarantee they will produce the accommodation desired.

The economic techniques available to states can be employed independently, without the use of force. Usually they are used to adjust what are considered unfavourable or unacceptable economic transaction agreements. At the same time, however, they form part of the spectrum of instruments a state can use in pursuit of its interests. In a lengthy crisis, economic pressures can be precursors to, or parallel threats to, the use of force. In wartime, economic instruments like blacklists and blockades (enforced sanctions) are adjuncts to military operations. Economic pressures are a means of exercising state power to achieve political ends, just like force, and the more powerful a state's economy, the better able it is to exert influence on others and to resist efforts by others to influence it.

States with strong economies not only have a greater ability to maintain armed forces, they have a greater range of instruments of influence. States with relatively weak economies, on the other hand, tend to be susceptible to the blandishments of economically stronger states. This may entail a loss of security and autonomy, as weak states are forced to modify their behaviour by the pressure from strong states. The increasingly interdependent international economic system provides states with more opportunities now to use economic instruments to sway others, and a strong economy furnishes a greater capacity to wield these instruments successfully. The deliberate use of economic instruments is usually an attempt to affect a state or its regime, and hence is consistent with the traditional state-centric approach to security.

Transnational Criminal Organizations

The international system is, as was discussed earlier, based on sovereignty. States have not been the only actors in the international system but traditionally they have been the dominant one in setting the rules by which the others live. James Rosenau has argued convincingly, however, that the state-centric world is no longer dominant, that an international system is emerging that is bifurcated into two sets of actors: states, which are sovereignty bound, and transnational actors such as international organizations, multinational corporations or political interest groups, which are non-sovereignty bound. The non-sovereignty-bound actors, individually and sometimes jointly, increasingly compete, conflict, co-operate or otherwise interact with the sovereignty-bound actors and in doing so pose a challenge to the concept of sovereignty.[24] In recent years some states and analysts have identified transnational criminal organizations (TCOs) as a non-sovereignty-bound actor which poses a security risk. There are many forms of crime that are transnational in that they occur in or have connections between two or more national jurisdictions. A transnational crime that fits traditional conceptions of security is illegal trafficking in weapons or weapons-related materials and technologies, especially those connected to the development of nuclear, biological and chemical weapons. Much of the concern in the last half of the 1990s, however, focused primarily on the implications of transnational organized crime trafficking in other illicit goods such as cigarettes or alcohol, and especially on the illegal drug trade because of its enormous scale and scope.[25]

International trafficking in illegal drugs is driven by supply and demand. When supplies are greater than demand prices generally decrease, and when demand outstrips supply prices usually rise. With controlled or banned commodities that are hard to obtain, prices are high and made even higher because of the risks involved. Sub-state or trans-state organizations in the drug trade must circumvent government regulations, controls and enforcement by operating secretly and thus they are difficult to control. TCOs clearly are an increasing problem for governments and society but they do not pose an obvious military threat. They are economic rather than military organizations, are not normally an overt threat to the state, and have traditionally been perceived as a law-enforcement problem.[26] Nevertheless, TCOs 'by their very nature undermine civil society, destabilize domestic politics and undercut the rule of law'.[27]

The movement of illicit goods across borders is not new; smuggling is an ancient trade. That organized crime is involved is also not new. What is new is the scale of the problem and the growing power and capability of organized crime.

The increase in the scale of organized criminal activity is due largely to increased market demand. The growth of disposable wealth in advanced societies and the resultant increase in demand for goods and services, recreation and leisure, has created a new market for narcotics. This pattern of consumption is now emulated in less well-off states as well, so there is growing convergence in consumer tastes across disparate countries. The larger scale of TCOs is also due to changes in global politics and economics. Increasing interdependence, the speed and effortlessness of international communication and travel, the growing permeability of national borders, and the globalization of international financial networks have been particularly conducive to the growth of TCOs. These factors have greatly facilitated the capacity of criminal groups to penetrate foreign locales, increased the ease of circumventing state controls and moving illicit commodities to distant markets, and provided the means to shift illegal profits quickly about the globe.[28] The growth in markets and the ease with which they can be supplied have provided the motivation and means for TCOs to burgeon.

TCOs have also grown considerably in power due to the lucrative nature of drug trafficking. Putting a precise figure on how much money is generated is difficult, but estimates range as high as £300 billion sterling (US$ 500 billion) annually. Although the profits are distributed amongst a growing number of TCOs and used to support the vast networks of people and capabilities they need, much of the money goes directly to the core of individual TCOs. Some of the larger drug-trafficking organizations such as the Medellin and Cali cartels in Colombia have enormous material and financial resources. TCOs have been able to acquire a range of skills increasingly available for hire in the global market, buy lots of lethal weapons and people to use them, and obtain very sophisticated technology, some of it intelligence-related; all the tools once largely reserved for states.[29]

TCOs against the State

Arguments that the expansion of TCOs brings growing convergence with security issues see the danger as occurring at the levels of the state, the international system and the individual.[30] On the first of these TCOs pose a serious challenge to either their host state or others which are important conduits for drugs. First, these organizations may directly confront the state with the use of force; and second, they may erode state legitimacy.

TCOs involved in narcotics trafficking have accumulated vast resources, and can compete directly with the state in terms of the use of force. It is increasingly easy for sub-national actors to acquire lethal weapons and to train willing 'soldiers' to use them. TCOs have the means and will to develop trained forces with considerable firepower, and increasingly are doing so.

Reportedly, Pablo Escobar of the Medellin cartel sought to obtain surface-to-air missiles (SAMs) from Cuba, and tried to buy US Stinger anti-aircraft missiles.[31] The Cali cartel, for its part, apparently tried to buy 500-pound bombs to use against Escobar, and Kuhn Sa, the Thai warlord and heroin trafficker, has Russian and American SAMs in his personal arsenal.[32] Even more worrisome is the possibility that they may obtain weapons of mass destruction (WMD), such as chemical weapons like the Sarin used in the Tokyo subway. There are increasing reports that military equipment and fissile material from Russia and other members of the Commonwealth of Independent States is leaking to sub-state actors,[33] raising concern that they may acquire radioactive material which, even if not transformed into a nuclear weapon, can do great harm. The ease with which trans-state actors like TCOs procure a wide range of weapons in the global arms market has undermined the monopoly on force once held by the state. 'Once the legal monopoly of armed force, long claimed by the state, is wrested from its hands, existing distinctions between war and crime will break down ... Often crime will be disguised as war, whereas in other cases war itself will be treated as if waging it were a crime.'[34]

TCOs are not reticent about using their military capabilities. They may challenge the state. In many countries politically motivated terrorist or rebel organizations use drug trafficking to fund themselves, while in others there are links or co-operation between such groups and TCOs.[35] Profit-motivated TCOs also may threaten the state through violence. In the late 1980s, the Medellin cartel used force to try to stop the Colombian government extraditing drug lords to the US to face criminal charges and jail. The cartel embarked on a campaign of violent terrorist attacks on the agents and agencies of the government and the institutions of civil society, such as the press, media and judiciary, that resulted in thousands of dead. The campaign forced the Colombian government to end extradition, as the violence threatened to destabilize the country and undermine its legitimacy, but in the end this backfired, for the government declared narco-terrorism the principal threat to Colombian democracy and cracked down hard on the cartel.[36] Nevertheless, the cartel's campaign indicates the willingness of some TCOs to use violence for political aims, broadly consistent with Karl von Clausewitz's dictum that 'war is the continuation of policy by other means' and in a fashion that states have traditionally displayed. Such violence has not been confined to less developed states. In the 1980s the Mafia in Italy regularly killed magistrates, the police, politicians, civil servants and trade unionists in a direct political challenge to the judiciary and the rule of law.

More commonly, the armed might of TCOs is directed at one another, as they fight over territory or markets or attempt to eliminate rivals, in efforts to expand their illegal enterprise and profits. The loss of life from 'drug wars' can be substantial, with many of the people killed being innocent civilians caught up in the violence. Even when sustained over time, this violence does not pose a direct challenge to the state, but the state's inability to control internecine fighting and provide a safe environment undermines its authority, weakening a fundamental basis of civil society. In states with a weak institutional basis or a fragile domestic political consensus, such violence can corrode regime legitimacy.

The other major way TCOs may challenge the state is to undermine its legitimacy through corruption. TCOs protect their operations through 'bribes, economic penetration and legal manipulation'.[37] The Cali cartel acquired political influence and legal immunity by payments to politicians, judges and bureaucrats, to the point where the cartel sought to use 'corrupt' politicians to make changes in Colombia's penal code.[38] Drug-related corruption is also widespread in countries like Mexico, where the head of that country's anti-drug campaign accepted large sums of money from the drug organizations the government supposedly wanted to put out of business. Many TCOs invest heavily in the business sector too, both for 'laundering' illegal profits and to gain influence there. As Peter Lupsha argues:

> Penetration of the legal system and legitimate sectors by organized crime tilts the scales of justice, unbalances the economy, eliminates the rule of fairness, and tilts the playing field against ordinary citizens. In the long term, criminal impunity creates political immunity that leads to fear, intimidation, oppression, violence and tyranny as the state becomes criminal and delegitimate. The end result is the rupture of civil society and community.[39]

Corruption of the political and judicial foundations of the state is an invidious threat, difficult to deal with due to its relatively faceless nature, and unless checked it can seriously undercut the legitimacy of the state.

Organized crime may also do this via a bottom-up strategy, which means investing in the community to win support. This policy is pursued, especially amongst the poor, by investing in civic improvement programmes such as housing projects, water wells, sports facilities and even satellite TV dishes. Pablo Escobar of the Medellin cartel, for example, instituted a 'Medellin without Slums' project in the 1980s which constructed some five hundred housing units for marginalized urban dwellers. Colombian traffickers reportedly sought to win popular support in Boca Manu, Peru, by contributing money to repair local roads, docking facilities, schools and the medical clinic, and made direct cash payments to local police, teachers, politicians and other influential people to gain community approval so they could turn the town into a major collection and transhipment point for cocaine.[40] In Italy, organized crime can play a central role in the local community, even ensuring that the community is crime-free to win support. This strategy of 'system penetration and control' calls into question the ability of the government to provide for the people, especially marginalized people. If organized crime is better at contributing to the welfare of local communities than the government, people will transfer their loyalty to the organization that meets their needs.

This conception of the challenge posed by TCOs focuses, obviously, on the security of the state. The challenge is not major, for it is unlikely that a criminal organization, even a very well-armed one, could topple a state. Nevertheless, the danger is serious; as the Medellin cartel's war against the Colombian government indicates, a well-armed and determined TCO intent on confronting the regime can have a seriously destabilizing impact. The implications of widespread corruption and system penetration for state security are more insidious, for they attack the very foundations of civil society. There are no examples of drug-related corruption so deligitimizing a ruling regime that this caused the collapse of the state. Nevertheless, the potential danger of this was illustrated in Somalia. Many of the local warlords who rose to power in

Somalia after a civil war were deeply involved in the trafficking of khat,[41] and they contributed significantly to the internal instability and starvation in 1991–2 that provoked the US-led international military intervention.

International Security

The corrosive impact of TCOs on the legitimacy and authority of states can translate into challenges at the level of the international system. The general challenge to the concept of sovereignty posed by most non-sovereignty-bound actors is not great, for they operate within states only with the latter's permission and in accordance with state regulation, reaffirming the concept of sovereignty. TCOs, however, operate outside the normal rules of international behaviour as a matter of course, seeking to circumvent or suborn by clandestine means the control that states have traditionally exercised over their territories. Trafficking in illegal commodities demonstrates the permeability of state boundaries and evades state regulation, and this contributes to undermining sovereignty.

The impact of TCO activities on sovereignty can take other, roundabout ways. The United States has officially identified the international trade in narcotics as a security threat not only because of its concern about the impact of drugs in the country, but because of its economic and security interests in Central and South America. TCO activity is destabilizing in countries such as Colombia and this affects regional stability and security, which jeopardizes the spread of democracy, a major US goal. Moreover, the US fears the pernicious tendency of the drug trade to spread to other countries, such as Mexico, where the undermining of government legitimacy and stability is repeated. In the late 1980s the US declared a 'war on drugs', a critical element of which has been going after drugs where they are produced or seizing them before they reach US territory.[42] With this in mind, the US intervened in the region by providing training to local troops in anti-drug operations and putting political pressure on regional governments to take a tough stand against the drug trade and attendant political corruption. This intervention has reduced the political autonomy of states like Colombia, Peru, Bolivia and Mexico that are the US targets.[43]

Finally, not all states want to check and neutralize TCOs. Rogue or pariah states might find TCO networks attractive and arrange alliances of convenience. Once a drug-trafficking network is operating effectively it is easy to diversify the products moved, shifting from drugs to technology or components for WMD.[44] One worry about the ready availability of nuclear materials and other military equipment in the Commonwealth of Independent States is that organized crime is becoming involved, increasing the difficulty of keeping these things out of the wrong hands abroad.

Internal Violence

A third argument on the threat posed by the drug trade is that drugs endanger individual citizens. The starting point is that in a civil society individuals should be able to go about their lives in a safe environment, free from the fear of violence and intimidation. In countries ruled by oppressive regimes the state itself poses a threat of violence and intimidation to citizens. But most states offer functioning institutions, such as police forces and a judiciary, to enforce the rule of law. People and organizations in the drug trade violate the laws and mores that sustain security for individuals.

There is a strong correlation between illegal drugs and violence.[45] Three types of violent crime have been linked with the drug trade: violence by criminal organizations to protect their distribution areas and profits; crimes against people and property for money to buy drugs; and violence by individuals under the influence of drugs.[46] The problem is evident in many countries, but it is most prominent in the US. In 1988, 16 per cent of 17,971 homicides involved drugs in some way (in those 2,875 homicides, in only 12 per cent had the victims been involved with the killers in drug relationships). In 1993, of the 23,271 homicides in which the circumstances were known, 5.5 per cent were drug-related. A much greater number of people are injured in such cases every year. Ten per cent of all inmates in US prisons in 1991 were convicted for crimes committed to obtain money for drugs.[47]

The conviction that violence stemming from the drug trade is a security issue is not widely held. Nevertheless, drug-related violence against individuals is a prominent feature of the literature on transnational criminal organizations. To identify violence against individuals as a security issue is a substantial change from the traditional notion of security. State-centric paradigms would normally treat drug-related crime as a domestic law-and-order issue.

There is no question that TCOs are a serious problem, but are they a threat to security? Many governments have identified TCOs and the illicit trafficking of narcotics as a security threat. The US has gone so far as to task its armed forces with contributing to the 'war on drugs', while British Foreign Secretary Douglas Hurd told the UN General Assembly in 1994 that the drug trade and associated crime were a growing threat to everyone's security and well-being.[48] States, however, may see TCOs as threats more for the domestic costs of the drug trade than for the challenge posed to state legitimacy and international stability. Indeed, whether TCOs are a security threat depends on the referent chosen. If the referent is the individual, then the threat is the harmful consequences of drug use and the decrease in personal security. As a corollary, drug trafficking which jeopardizes state legitimacy and control is also a threat to individual security if it adversely affects personal safety. The answer is less clear if the referent is the state. Challenges to state legitimacy and control are serious, but perhaps not a security threat if they do not involve military force. However, if state legitimacy and control are treated as vital then when they are challenged it is a security threat. If so, then what security means is again muddied, for when state legitimacy is threatened at least in part by the inability of the government to control violence, its problem stems from failure to provide a secure environment for its citizens. If transnational crime is a security threat, then the use of military forces may be appropriate; if it is considered a law enforcement problem, then military forces are inappropriate; how it is labelled affects who provides security and what means are used.

Migration and Security

Mass migrations of people and flows of refugees are increasingly engaging the attention of governments. In part this stems from humanitarian concern. But it also reflects uneasiness about the implications of a big influx of people for the financial capacity, well-being, political and social stability, and integrity of their own or other countries.

Mass movements of people are not new, nor is treating them as a security issue. Attila the Hun, whose armies threatened Europe in the fifth century, was the leader of a people who had been pushed progressively westward from their homeland near Mongolia by other waves of migrants. Even the scale of such movements is not particularly new, for though there has been a general upward trend in numbers of refugees, from around 8 million in 1980 to 16 million in 1995, there were 30 million refugees just in Europe at the end of the Second World War. The new political salience of migrations seems due to the end of the Cold War and to improved awareness of the issue, plus rising appreciation of the impact migrations may have and an increased willingness in states to intervene.

What motivates masses of people to move is important for tailoring policies to fit the problem. The causes fall into four broad categories. A principal reason, particularly for refugee flows, is war and associated activities. People in the neighbourhood of a war flee for many reasons: fear of genocide/ politicide or ethnic cleansing; fear of military occupation (and potential genocide or ethnic cleansing); danger from the fighting; military seizures of food and goods.[49] In such circumstances, refugee flows can be dramatic, with hundreds of thousands crossing a border in only a few weeks. Another source of refugees is internal oppression. Sometimes people flee because they are specific targets due to the lack of civil liberties and freedom of worship, restrictions on access to basic necessities, and so on. Such refugee flows tend to stretch over a long period and, as the exodus of South Vietnamese (the Vietnamese boat people) in the late 1970s demonstrated, the cumulative numbers can be substantial. Third, refugee movements may be occasioned by natural disasters or environmental degradation.[50] Fourth, a great many people move across borders in search of a better standard of living. The movement of economic migrants from less-well-off parts of the world to the well-off regions is a slow but steady process, and over time can also result in large numbers moving (good examples are the movement of Central Americans into the southern United States and Africans into southern Europe).

Large-scale movement across borders, or within states, has been a consistent phenomenon since the Second World War. Clearly not all such movements are threats to security. Whether they are is not necessarily a function of the numbers involved, or the speed of the movement. In what ways does the movement of peoples sometimes constitute a security issue?

Myron Weiner has identified five broad categories of threat: first, refugees and migrants who work against the regime of their home state; second, migrants who pose a threat to the host state; third, immigrants as a cultural threat; fourth, refugees and migrants as social or economic threats; and fifth, the use by host countries of migrants and refugees as instruments to threaten the country of origin.[51] In these categories it is not always clear what the referent object is. It may be the state and seeing the state as threatened, and, by extension, international peace and stability (the first, second and fifth categories), or on the societal level, with the threat being to social cohesion and societal identity (the third and fourth categories).

State-Level Threat

Analysts and policy-makers have come to appreciate that large-scale population movements may have several adverse implications for states, and for international stability and peace. In some situations a mass exodus is a security challenge to the sending or receiving state. Whether a particular challenge has a trans-state or international impact is situation-dependent, and hence it is best to consider these two levels together. There are two basic types of security challenge which may arise: external political-military challenges, and internal struggles.

Providing asylum to people claiming refugee status on grounds of persecution can create or heighten antagonism between states. Accepting refugees because they have a well-founded fear of persecution is often perceived as political criticism, even condemnation, of the regime and policies of their country of origin. To acknowledge that refugee claims of persecution are legitimate is to suggest that these people have a moral right to oppose their government. This need not result in conflict. Debate in the US about offering asylum to Chinese students in the wake of the Tiananmen Square massacre was condemned by China as interference in its internal affairs. This worsened relations but did not lead to open conflict or a major security threat for either state.

Refugees and migrants may pose a quite serious challenge when they form the basis of a trans-border political and/or military challenge to the regime. Political refugees are usually hostile to the regime in their native country and may seek to oust it. Refugee and allied migrant groups may use political means, highlighting their opposition through speeches and demonstrations. It is of greater concern to the regime when a skilful refugee and migrant opposition is effective in lobbying the host and other governments or international institutions to change their policies towards the regime.

Political refugees may pose a more direct threat in actively attacking the regime militarily or through terrorism. The threat is heightened if the host country supports the effort. Refugees and migrants may be used by the host state as a tool in its opposition to the regime. Examples abound: the US, Pakistan and others arming Afghan refugees against the Soviet occupation of Afghanistan; the US arming Nicaraguans opposed to the Sandinista regime; China's support for the Khmer Rouge trying to overthrow the Vietnamese-backed government of Cambodia; and Arab support for the Palestinians against Israel.[52] The refugees can build an armed resistance for military incursions or terrorism to destabilize and overthrow the regime, or set off civil war in which military resistance is supported through refugee communities by other states. Thus, countries which produce refugees have to be concerned about how this may come back to haunt them.

The willingness of a host country to support or turn a blind eye to the military efforts of refugee and migrant groups to overthrow their home regime, however, may have serious repercussions for its own security. The Mobutu regime of Zaire provided a haven to refugee groups opposed to the regimes in

Rwanda, Uganda and Angola, and also provided considerable support for their activities. The military incursions against Rwanda by Hutu militants from refugee camps in Zaire in 1995–6 led the Rwandan government, with the support of Uganda and Angola, to assist anti-Mobutu groups, and in 1997 they not only broke up the refugee camps in Zaire but also gained control of the country (now the Democratic Republic of Congo). This is an extreme case. More common is a state launching limited attacks against dissident groups in neighbouring countries. Israel, for example, regularly retaliates for terrorist attacks by air attacks on Lebanon. Any state which hosts and supports a dissident refugee or migrant population seeking to topple the regime of another state runs the risk that the latter will counter with force.

Another risk for host countries is that political refugees can turn against their benefactors. Refugees and migrants have launched terrorist attacks within the country, worked with domestic opponents of the government engaged in drug trafficking, and in other ways posed problems, especially when that state did not support their opposition to the regime back home. Refugee or immigrant populations that have created problems for host countries include Palestinians, Sikhs, Croats, Kurds, Armenians, Sri Lankan Tamils, Algerians and Northern Irish refugees. Thus, agencies responsible for security often examine claimants to refugee status on the basis not of whether they have a legitimate fear of persecution but of whether their presence will constitute a threat.[53] The problem may be quite unlikely and largely political rather than violent in nature, but it is not one host states will simply ignore.

The movement of peoples across international boundaries does not necessarily generate security problems. There are instances, however, when it does. The dangers vary in severity and manageability, from an increase in public disorder to serious military challenges, but concern centres on the security of the state. As such, these conceptions of the risks and dangers are consistent with traditional conceptions of security, particularly of those challenges which derive from military activities. However, the dangers are produced from non-state actors, are not always of a military nature, and may occur at the domestic rather than the international level. As a consequence, while mass movements of people as a potential threat do not require a redefinition of security, they do constitute its broadening as a topic.

Society and Security

The risks and dangers in accepting large numbers of refugees or migrants may be domestic in nature, and the second main line of argument is that this often occurs. To talk about the threat to societies is to shift away from the traditional focus on the state and on state security. The difficulties may be social and economic burdens or a cultural danger.

Refugees or immigrants can impose substantial economic costs and strain the infrastructure in housing or land, education, transportation facilities, and welfare-providing institutions. In less-developed countries, refugees may illegally occupy private or state lands or intensify competition for scarce arable land; they consume scarce or limited local resources such as firewood, fresh water and food supplies, while their livestock may overgraze and degrade lands and forests. The need to provide food, medicine and shelter may be a large burden on the government. In the developed world, the welfare state usually provides services such as welfare payments, education, housing and medical care to illegal immigrants, permanent immigrants or refugees. Immigrants may increase competition for jobs, and provoke charges that they are 'taking jobs away' from the native population. These economic and social costs can breed resentment against immigrants or refugees. Resentment may be accentuated by the perception that the immigrants bring an increase in crime, delinquency or welfare dependency.

The willingness of a society to tolerate these burdens is conditioned in part by its perception of the reasons the exiles left home. Resentment is more likely when the host country or society believes that the influx is the result of a state's deliberate policy to 'dump' unwanted elements such as criminals, ethnic minorities, and surplus or unproductive populations.[54] The US welcomed Cubans who fled the communist regime in the 1960s, but not those whom the Castro regime sent from prison in the 1970s. Advanced industrialized states have become deeply concerned that less-developed states will engage in population dumping in order to transfer the burden of providing for them. As a consequence, developed states tend to be warier now about granting refugee status for fear that this will open the floodgates.

Societies are also concerned about the growth of legal and illegal immigration from the less-developed world for economic gain. These immigrants are not forced (pushed) to leave but rather are induced (pulled) to do so due to a disparity between what they can hope to achieve in a more prosperous society and what they can achieve at home. The movement of economic migrants can be small, significant only over a long period, or it can be enormous. The number of Latin Americans attempting to enter the US illegally each year is many hundreds of thousands, and the government has to commit enormous resources and take steps like building fences along crossing points, increasing border patrols and improving their equipment, and using military reconnaissance teams to locate and track illegal migrants. European states are likewise more concerned about the increasing flow of economic migrants; south European states worry about peoples across the Mediterranean, whilst states in Central Europe worry about economic migrants from the region of the former Soviet Union and from South and East Asia who transit through Central Asia. This is leading many states to tighten restrictions on legal immigration and drastically step up efforts to stop illegal immigration.

The dimensions of the danger which immigration poses to the state or society are ambiguous. Resentment and domestic discontent stem from a perception that immigrants are taking resources that could be used for other purposes while not contributing enough to the general welfare. In addition, immigrants may be seen as disreputable and contributing to social disorder. This may lead to violence directed at the immigrants, who may retaliate out of fear and anger and create a vicious cycle that contributes to a sense of growing disorder. Persistent anti-immigrant sentiment and violence is a serious social issue and may result in challenges to government policies. Groups such as the National Front in the United Kingdom and Jean Marie le Pen's Front National party in France, with overt anti-immigrant, race-oriented politics, demonstrate the political consequences that domestic resentment of immigrant groups may have. This formulation makes no real distinction between the state and society; the two are considered co-extant, with the challenge being to the economic welfare of the state and its people (economic security), to domestic and social order, and/ or to governance (state legitimacy).

The other concern is the danger for the prevailing culture.[55] This particular formulation stresses the way in which migrants may pose a threat to society. If societal security is to be discussed, we must delineate what is meant by 'society'.

The concept is nebulous, with a range of definitions and common usage, and it is not possible to arrive at a conclusive definition. The term usually refers to a group identity which permits the word 'we' to be used; that is, it refers to social identity. Following Wæver, Buzan et al., the foremost proponents of societal security, it is useful to distinguish society from social groups, with the former 'having a high degree of social inertia, a continuity often across generations and a strong infrastructure of norms, values and "institutions" in the wider sense'.[56] A further useful distinction these authors make is that society, unlike social groups, is comprehensive enough in its following, and wide enough in terms of the character of the identity it embodies, to be capable of providing a political organizational principle which rivals that furnished by the state.[57] Thus, society is greater than social groups, which rest on a host of affiliations providing a narrower sense of identity and come in a great variety of forms in society, and can be more or less co-extensive with, or even wider than, a state as an organizational principle. Wæver argues that the value of this admittedly inexact conception is that it allows for the association between society and state to be complementary, in that society can provide legitimacy for governance, and contradictory in that societal divisions may furnish the basis for questioning the government's legitimacy and authority. Based on this conception, the most significant units of concern when discussing society are politically significant ethno-national and religious identities.

What is societal security? It 'concerns the ability of a society to persist in its essential character under changing conditions and possible or actual threats. More specifically, it is about the sustainability, within acceptable conditions for evolution, of traditional patterns of language, culture, association, and religious and national identity and custom.'[58] Such a definition makes identifying particular threats to society rather difficult, for often this is not an objective assessment but a subjective one. Thus, security of a society is jeopardized when that society perceives that its identity is endangered and reacts to protect it.

Whether immigrants are perceived as such a societal threat is a complicated matter, but it hinges initially on how the host society defines itself. Societies have different norms governing who is admitted, their rights and privileges, and whether migrants are regarded as potential citizens or members. Citizenship law in some countries is based on *jus sanguinis*, where a person is a citizen of the state of his or her parents. *Jus sanguinis* is based on ties of blood descent that are more expansive than parentage or place, for it implies a broader people to whom one belongs in a subjective relationship. Citizenship based on consanguinity is thus complementary with membership in society. Germany, for example, bases citizenship solely on descent.[59] People who no longer live in Germany or speak German but who are of German descent are accorded citizenship and welcomed, but guest-workers and migrants from other cultures even if born in Germany are not accorded citizenship or perceived as being members of German society. Other states, such as Britain and the US, base citizenship on *jus soli*, with nationality derived from the 'soil' or place of birth. Countries with citizenship laws based on consanguinity welcome those of the right blood descent regardless of numbers or economic consequences, because they are part of the same identity. Such countries, however, find it difficult to accept people not of blood descent, not of the same culture, and may see an influx of aliens as posing a threat to their identity. Germany is a case in point; much of its concern about the influx of foreign peoples and of a large population of foreign guest-workers stems from fears that the presence of alien cultures, languages, mores, and so forth will affect and change German identity in unacceptable, perhaps unnatural, ways.

In this formulation, what is to be protected is not the state, but society or identity. It may be that in protecting society, the state is itself protected, because they are co-extensive. But this need not be the case, for society can be less than or greater than the state. Moreover, what society is being protected from is the invasive effect of alien influences which change or 'pollute' society in ways seen as threatening.[60] Concern about the societal impact of migrants and/or refugees does not require a radical redefinition of security, merely a broadening of its nature as traditionally conceived. Concern about their impact on its identity suggests a quite different conception. What is to be protected is society, or more directly, a society's common culture or sense of identity, and what is threatened is unacceptable change stemming from the influences of other cultures. This is not consistent with traditional conceptions of security, and rests on a reformulated notion that traditionalists find objectionable.

Non-Traditional Challenges and Security

Non-traditional challenges such as environmental degradation, economic welfare, transnational crime and mass movements of people have all become salient in both academic and policy-making circles largely in the post-Cold War era. The issues are not new; each has been around for some time and some, like economic concerns, have long been associated with security. The new recognition of these issues as having security implications stems partly from their intensification as problems more widespread than before. This is particularly true of transnational crime, environmental degradation and mass emigrations. The recognition of these problems is also one result of the end of the Cold War. The threat and use of military force remain, but during the Cold War the chances of inter-state war seemed much higher. The possibility that the superpowers with their massive nuclear arsenals would come to blows overshadowed lesser problems and preoccupied analysts and policy-makers. Now the threat of superpower nuclear war has receded, shifting attention and resources to other issues. Indeed, one could say that non-traditional issues have blossomed because analysts have had to hunt for new issues, new threats to keep themselves busy. Still, there are real issues; many governments take non-traditional challenges quite seriously, and in some cases identified them as security problems before the Cold War ended.

In any case, they are now on the security agenda and have contributed to a reassessment of the study and practice of security. In each, one view saw them linked to the onset of conflict, which is consistent with the traditional view that security is about the threat or use of force. This perspective simply broadens the questions and problems involved without substantially altering the traditional focus on the state and military issues.

Moving beyond state and military issues, a second strand of argument, especially with respect to economics, transnational crime and immigration, is that these pose a danger to the socio-political foundations of the state. The contention is that these issues can adversely affect socio-political cohesion, by either internal destabilization or delegitimization, and this can result in the failure of the state, which would clearly constitute a failure of national security. Moreover, a failed state can have severe consequences for the security of neighbouring states.

The implication is that the security of the state is not affected solely by military issues, that the foundations of state security are considerably broader. These arguments highlight the inter-play between factors and issues at different analytical levels – individual, society, state and international system. A good example of this complex interaction are some of the implications of the mass movement of people. Individuals move because they feel threatened, whether due to environmental degradation, war, oppression or economic dissatisfaction. In doing so, however, they can generate situations which, though unintended, have adverse consequences for the host society and state. Thus, security is more complex than traditional conceptions suggest, it is not compartmentalized or exclusionary in terms of the referent or the danger, and it is not divisible in terms of what is being jeopardized or by what circumstances.

This converges with the endeavour by Barry Buzan in *People, States and Fear* (1991) to develop the concept of security further. Buzan argues for a broader understanding of security, based on the contention that human collectivities are affected by factors in five sectors: military, political, economic, societal and environmental:

Generally speaking, military security concerns the two-level interplay of the armed offensive and defensive capabilities of states, and states' perceptions of each others intentions. Political security concerns the organizational stability of states, systems of government and the ideologies that give them legitimacy. Economic security concerns access to the resources, finance and markets necessary to sustain acceptable levels of welfare and state power. Societal security concerns the sustainability, within acceptable conditions for evolution, of traditional patterns of language, culture and religious and national identity and custom. Environmental security concerns the maintenance of the local and planetary biosphere as the essential support system on which all other human enterprises depend.[61]

Thus, national security cannot be fully comprehended without understanding the complex interrelationship among these sectors. Though security, especially as 'national security', usually refers to the state, there are strong connections between this level of analysis and that of the individual, the region and the system that should be integrated into our studies. This view is inherent in many of the arguments about non-traditional security concerns.

Buzan suggests that the differing levels and sectors are most useful not as self-contained realms for policy or analysis but as 'viewing platforms' that allow analysts and policy-makers to approach security from different angles. Security is integrative and a comprehensive understanding must include all levels and sectors.[62] However, Buzan always comes back to the state because he accepts the anarchic nature of the international system and the primacy of the state within that system.[63] Assertions about the danger posed by non-traditional security threats are consistent with Buzan's formulation. These threats are non-traditional but conform to the traditional emphasis on the state.

The third strand of argument about non-traditional dangers to security goes beyond broadening the range of factors which can endanger the state, to point to entities other than states which may be in jeopardy and need safeguarding. This shifts the referent to be secured to a human collectivity other than the state, which is a significant shift from traditional conceptualizations. This is even more pronounced with respect to environmental degradation and transnational crime, where a priority in security is security and welfare for individuals. This view is not universally held in the literature, but clearly implies a referent quite distinct from the state.

To take such a step requires a significant reappraisal of what is meant by security. Indeed, it requires a reappraisal of the epistemological foundations of security and IR more broadly, much as feminist and post-positivist approaches do. A difference, however, is that these latter theoretical approaches or paradigms expressly challenge traditional conceptions and theories much more directly than do arguments about the need to take non-traditional issues seriously as threats.

Conclusion: Security and Security Studies

There is great diversity in the range of perspectives on how we should think about and analyse security, reflecting the lack of agreement within the discipline of IR about the notion of security. The dominant perspective on security, the one that can be said to hold the high ground, focuses on the state as the unit to be secured and on issues relating to the threat, use and management of force and coercion in world politics. The other perspectives we have looked at either expand on or directly challenge this 'traditional' understanding of security. Indeed, many of the perspectives, such as peace studies, feminism and post-positivist theories, stand in open opposition to this particular understanding and are often couched in language attacking it, and the realist paradigm in particular. Hence, security studies has become fragmented, with different perspectives unable to engage in a meaningful dialogue with each other due to profound differences in the particular body of knowledge from which they draw their understanding of security. Not to put too fine of a point on it, often these different perspectives appear to be not so much debating with each other as talking past each other.

If this is the case, if the many different interpretations of security lack sufficient common understandings to make meaningful dialogue possible, how then are we to make sense of the growing discussion on security? Consider, as an example, the war in former Yugoslavia. Neo-realists emphasize the role of the great powers. The war began because none was particularly interested in the country, but as they began to focus on it, they did so in the light of their interests. Germany asserted its new-found diplomatic strength by compelling the EU to recognize Croatia and Bosnia, while NATO's use of force was a by-product of US–Russian relations. Neo-liberals would argue that although the war was bloody, there were important elements of co-operation; within the EU, NATO and the UN; between NATO and partner countries in Central and Eastern Europe (Hungary or Ukraine, for example); between NATO countries and Russia; and between the UN or non-governmental organizations (NGOs) and representatives of governments and factions in the region. Peace studies analysts would focus on the need for negotiation and compromise. They would also highlight not just the direct results of military force but the indirect consequences (refugees, the state of hospitals), arguing for significant investment to cope with them. Feminists would emphasize the role of patriarchy in creating the conditions for war, and the way in which wide-spread violence against women has given victims a greater identity with each other regardless of nationality than with co-nationals who perpetrated it. Post-positivists would assert that even to take up this example in this fashion is to apportion disciplinary power in a particular way, one that is most favour-able to a realist perspective, and ignores post-positivist analysis. Transnationalists would focus on the environment, which has been severely degraded; how the breakdown of civil society allowed TCOs to flourish (moving medicines, fuel and weapons between the former Yugoslavia and other states, particularly the former Soviet Union); and how refugees flee-ing the fighting caused internal problems for states such as Germany.

An obvious starting point for understanding the growing discussion on security is to have at least a basic grasp, if not a thorough knowledge, of the theoretical basis of the different viewpoints. This approach is what we have provided in this book for the main perspectives that can be identified in the study of IR. Many of these perspectives are grounded in particular theoretical bodies of knowledge on IR: these include realism, peace studies, feminism and post-positivist approa-ches. Other perspectives are intrinsic to sets of arguments oriented to examining specific non-traditional or non-military challenges to security; these analyses are policy-oriented arguments aimed, first, to advocate the nature and seriousness of the challenges these issues pose and, second, to define and design policy responses to mitigate the danger. These sets of analyses as a whole do not fit comfortably within one particular body of knowledge, even though some of the single strands of argument about these issues can be seen to derive from particular understandings of what constitutes an appropriate analytical approach to IR and hence to security. By understanding the intellectual foundations of the varied approaches, we can understand the particular perspective brought to bear, the conditionalities and value judgements assumed, the form of analysis used and the definition of security predicated. Developing such an understanding is a necessary step towards grasping why each of the contending positions defines security in the way it does and the basis for the difference between alternative definitions. Only then is it possible to evaluate the advantages and limitations of each approach, as well as assessing how they are utilized and to what ends.

The examination of security in the book has been organized according to the main approaches to analysing international relations and how these define security. We have, in other words, categorized definitions of security largely, but not entirely, according to theoretical or policy-directed conceptualizations. There is an alternative way of developing categories other than by these perspectives. Although the various theoretical approaches to understanding security may appear to be incommensurable, does that mean in fact that they have nothing in common? At bottom, they are all examining the same thing; the concept of security. David Baldwin makes a strong case to support the contention that the discourse on security is not about the concept of security *per se*.[1] What is in dispute, he argues, are the specifications made about security. We agree wholeheartedly with him on this point. Security is, to use Arnold Wolfers's characterization, 'the absence of threats to acquired values'.[2] Precisely what that means, or rather precisely how we would then define security, depends entirely on the specifications made. In other words, that there is fragmentation in the field of security studies does not mean that we cannot study security. Rather, our argument is that when studying security it is necessary to be aware of the range of perspectives contained within the field. We suggested at the outset of the book that there were four main specifications: what is being secured? What is being secured against? Who provides for security? What methods may be undertaken to provide for security? In thinking conceptually about security it is clear that the first two are the most important specifications, and are the two that we have highlighted throughout the book.

Categorizing different definitions of security according to 'what is being secured' furnishes a useful way to think about security, one based on the unit of analysis. Just as there is a spectrum of theoretical perspectives to defining security, so there is a range in the unit of analyses that we may be concerned to secure from harm. In the various approaches examined in this book, the primary level of analysis ranges from the state and the individual to such units as society and the environment. It is tempting to think of each of these different units of analysis as existing in a distinct linear relationship to each of the others, but this would be somewhat misleading. First, although in each of the perspectives we have examined the unit of analysis needs to be specified, there is a clear distinction between positivist and post-positivist approaches. Positivist perspectives – realism/neo-realism, peace studies, policy-oriented analyses and some forms of feminism – are empirically based and explicitly or implicitly specify what is the referent with which they are concerned. Each post-positivist perspective – post-positivist feminism, postmodernism, critical theory and constructivism – in its particular way seeks to uncover structures of power and domination that are hidden when analysis focuses on the state and determine what effect these structures have. The normative project – excluding postmodernism, which eschews normative ends – is to emancipate those entities affected by these structures. Post-positivist approaches are concerned that to emphasize a specific referent at the expense of others serves only to obscure structures that these perspectives desire to uncover. They therefore emphasize methodology over the empirical identification of a specific referent to be secured. Thus, positivist and post-positivist perspectives stand apart from each other, and so they need to be considered separately.

Second, even taking only positivist perspectives, the units of analysis do not exactly fit an unbroken line along which each can be specifically located in a distinct relation to the other units, for there can be a significant degree of overlap. The specification of a particular referent may focus the analysis on that unit, but often there is an implicit overlap or connection to another unit. Furnishing security for one particular unit of analysis may result in another unit of concern also gaining security as a by-product, either intentionally or unintentionally. In providing for the security of the state from military threat, for example, it is understood but usually not stated that society and individuals within that state are also provided with security from external military threat. But it is not always the case that this occurs; to use the same example, a state may be secure from the use of military force by another state because it fields a military force, but it may use that same military capability against its own citizens or selected ethnically determined groups, or a particular group such as women may hence be safe from external military force, but not secure from domestic-level violence.

Keeping in mind that positivist and post-positivist perspectives cannot be treated together, what are the main categories that can be identified by focusing on the referent to be secured? There are a great number of different levels and referents that can be emphasized: national security, international security, regional security, global security, individual security, societal security, economic security, and so on.[3] In the perspectives we have examined, four main units of analysis have been clearly identified: state, society, individual and environment. Most other levels of analysis in fact fit these basic units of analysis. National security is concerned with the security of the state; for example, regional security is concerned with the security dynamics of a region, but with the analysis focusing on the patterns of interaction amongst states, the unit of analysis is the state. Global security is concerned with much wider issues that affect everyone and hence while the focus is on the international level the primary referent is humanity, and so on. Moreover, it is immediately obvious that a number of different perspectives may designate one of these four as the primary referent of concern, yet operate on a different definition of security. Thus, the second main specification – that is, what is being secured against? – can usefully be used to delineate subdivisions within these categories.

Positivist Perspectives

State-Centric Security

Almost the entire range of perspectives on security may use the state as the referent for security. This occurs in part because the state is currently the most significant institution through which humankind organizes itself in much of the world and hence through which it seeks to provide solutions to common problems, including that of protection from harm. The significance of the state as the focus of security is also in part common because, though some perspectives may focus on an alternative referent which is to be secured, the state too may be made more secure as a consequence. Indeed, some may even argue that the state can ultimately only be made more secure if another referent is made secure first, and hence that, though the focus is on another referent, the state is considered an important referent as well. What distinguishes the various state-centric approaches, as well as their theoretical basis, is the determination of what the state is being secured against.

The key perspectives that focus on the state as the primary referent to be protected are realism/neo-realism (and the closely related neo-liberal/neo-institutional perspective) and peace studies, plus some elements of the sets of arguments about specific non-military challenges. Within this spread of perspectives on security, it is possible to derive two main divisions based on what the state as security referent is to be protected from; bounded state-centric and unbounded state-centric. Bounded state-centric approaches are those perspectives which are concerned only with the state and no other levels or units of analysis, and hence identify what the state is to be protected against quite narrowly. Perspectives that may be categorized as being bounded state-centric are realism/neo-realism and neo-liberalism/neo-institutionalism, as well as early variants of peace studies, which is rooted in idealism. Unbounded state-centric perspectives acknowledge the impact of other levels or units of analysis on the state, and hence identify what the state is to protected against more broadly. Perspectives that may be categorized as being unbounded state-centric are some later variants of peace studies and elements of policy-oriented bodies of arguments.

A constant feature of realist/neo-realist analysis is that, while it is recognized that states are not always in conflict, the nature of international politics is conflictual. Conflict arises because there is no overriding authority within the international system to mediate instances when one state's pursuit of its interests clashes with the interests of one or more other states. Thus, in the realist/neo-realist view, the source of threat stems from the interaction of states within an anarchic system, particularly when their interests conflict. The degree to which a state is threatened by other states, whether as a consequence of its own or other states' actions, resides in its ability to impose its will on others or to resist efforts by one or more other states to impose their will on it. This capacity depends significantly on the relative power, or capability, of the state with respect to others. States as the referent for security therefore need to be protected from efforts by other states to get their way at the expense of the state itself and the external interests that the state sees as important to its welfare and survival. What is meant by security, then, primarily centres on the state's capacity to protect its territorial boundaries and its sovereign ability to act as it sees best, with respect to both internal and external issues. The primary means by which one state may jeopardize the security of another is through the threat or actual application of military force. Thus, for realists/neo-realists, security is defined in terms of that of the state, and what the state needs to be protected against is the threat or use of military power or other related instruments of coercion by another state.

The neo-liberal/neo-institutionalist perspective essentially defines security in the same way for much the same reasons. The difference between these two theoretical perspectives is the degree to which they view institutions as being able to moderate the anarchic nature of the international system, and hence the behaviour of states, which are the structuring agent of the international system. What they disagree about is the degree to which states can rely on institutions to ameliorate their security concerns, and whether states can focus on absolute rather than relative gains, not about the referent for security or what it is to be protected against.

Unbounded state-centric approaches continue to emphasize the state as the primary referent to be protected, but broaden out what it is to be secured against. Peace studies, with its process of evolutionary transformation, has advanced a wider conception of what the state needs to be secured against to delineate problems other than inter-state violence that may jeopardize the state. Also within this sub-category are those arguments about the environment, economics, transnational criminal organizations, and mass movements of peoples that are concerned with the way in which these challenges affect the security of the state. Taken as a whole, unbounded state-centric approaches predicate the security of the state as being founded on being secure in five domains: military, political, economic, social and environmental.[4]

Unbounded state-centric perspectives can be usefully divided into two forms. First, there is a series of perspectives that focus on non-military challenges primarily because of the prospect that they can generate situations in which the use of force may occur. In other words, this prospect remains the critical challenge against which the state should be guarded. The difference between this interpretation and that of bounded state-centric perspectives lies primarily in the source of the violence, not in what the state is ultimately to be protected against; unbounded state-centric analyses undertake a different level of analysis of the problem. The general perspective adopted is that there are a number of components to state security, and that these components may interact in a way that gives rise to violence and the use of military force. Another difference is that though the analysis may focus on the state, such as is the case in peace studies' concern with inter-state conflict and nuclear weapons, the real concern may in fact be individuals; the state is to be protected so that individuals are protected because it is the state which controls the use of violence. One last difference is that unbounded state-centric perspectives incorporate within their notion of threat internal violence even if short of civil war, whereas bounded state-centric perspectives such as realism focus on inter-state violence. These distinctions are nuances in understanding and approach. They indicate the porous nature of the division between bounded and unbounded state-centric perspectives; this is reflected in the fact that this interpretation of wider challenges to the state is accepted by some, though not all, of those who conduct analysis within the realist paradigm.

Second, some unbounded state-centric perspectives also advance the notion that non-military challenges may jeopardize the state in other ways. Each of the different areas of security is perceived as being important in its own right to the security of the state. The five identified domains – military, political, economic, social and environmental – are the pillars on which the security of the state is founded, and hence a failure to secure one pillar weakens and may even undermine the security of the state, while a failure of several (even if the military one remains secure) may seriously jeopardize the security of the state. In essence, the argument is that the security of each of the five domains is integral to the security of the whole, the state.

A key characteristic of unbounded state-centric approaches is that the generation of a challenge to state security may occur through an interaction between the five main constituents of state security. In some instances, as noted above, problems in the non-military elements create a challenge in the military realm. In others, problems in one non-military element create challenges in one or more other non-military realms. Degradation of the environment can cause migration, with impacts in the social or military realm, or may have an impact on the economic, social and political realms, both connections which may have repercussions for state security. Economic weakness and dislocation may leave the state vulnerable to external pressure on its sovereignty or may have consequences in the political realm. Mass movements of peoples may generate external, inter-state tensions and conflict, or may create social and economic problems that impact adversely on the political realm. Transnational criminal organizations may contribute to internal military challenges to the state or may threaten state legitimacy in the political realm. Thus, though these five aspects of the state's security can be conceived as being separate, they are in fact interrelated in a synergistic way, and this synergistic interrelationship means that effects in one domain, unless managed appropriately, have effects in one or more of the others, with an ultimate impact on state security.

The central and critical distinction between bounded and unbounded state-centric perspectives is not simply a question of the nature of what the state needs to be protected against, but between whether concern about security challenges centres solely on the level of the international, external to the state, or whether they occur at both the international and domestic levels. Bounded state-centric perspectives such as the realist paradigm focus largely on the challenges that emanate from the interaction of states within the international system, and hence are primarily concerned with the international level. Unbounded state-centric perspectives in focusing on particular issues are concerned with the challenges these may create at both the international and domestic levels. Much of the analysis within the unbounded state-centric perspective, no matter in which particular issue area, emphasizes challenges to the stability of the state, because of concern that internal instability may render it vulnerable to the coercion of other states, undermine its authority and capacity to manage challenges from internal groups with aspirations for alternative forms of governance, or result in the collapse of effective governance within the state to the extent that it ceases to exist as a functioning collective entity. This concern with domestic, as well as international, sources of challenges to state security significantly broadens the security agenda for both analysts and policy-makers.

Societal Security

Society is a second referent which can be specified as needing to be secured. Many of the arguments about the challenges to society do not really distinguish between society and the state, and these particular conceptions of the challenge are ultimately concerned with the state, and hence fall into the unbounded state-centric category. An alternative conception of societal challenges directly specifies society as distinct from the state as being the referent to be protected.[5] This specification is concerned about the impact of 'foreign' influences on society. It is not so much notions of social cohesion that are emphasized as the sense of identity that individuals derive from being members of a particular society. What society in this conception is to be protected from are influences which are perceived as altering in unacceptable ways the traditional patterns of language, culture, association, and the religious and national identity and customs of society. Simply put, what society needs to be secured against are those influences which challenge the indigenous people's sense of self-identity.

Individual Security

A third referent identified as being a unit which needs to be secured is the individual. This represents a signal change from the traditional state-based formulations of security. There are, as in the case of state-centred approaches, a significant range of perspectives. The main ones are variants of peace studies and feminist theory, while there are a number of arguments that particular non-military challenges pose a specific threat to individuals.

Focusing on the individual as the referent to be made safe almost automatically enlarges the question of what is to be secured against, for individuals are jeopardized by a much wider range of issues than are the state or society. The various perspectives do take somewhat different stances on what the individual should be protected against; indeed, there are differences on this question within particular theoretical paradigms. There are some approaches which can be identified within the various perspectives which are concerned primarily to protect the individual from violence. Beyond this basic subdivision, there is no obvious way to identify clearly demarcated sub-categories. In part this problem is because some of these perspectives do not specifically identify violence as being what the individual is to be protected from, but at the same time they do not exclude violence from what they are concerned with. In part the problem stems from the fact that feminist thought analyses gender differences within society to reveal hidden structures of power that harm the individual. Feminist perspectives may be broadly categorized as seeking to emancipate the individual, but at root this applies as well to those perspectives concerned about violence towards individuals. Thus, unlike the case with state-centred perspectives on security, there is no easy way to provide clearly delineated subdivisions within this referent category.

There are a number of perspectives which are largely if not specifically concerned to protect the individual from violence. Peace studies in some of its latterday variants emphasizes the security of the individual, pointing to the impact of class and economic disparities within the international system as core issues which need to be addressed if positive peace is to be achieved. One aspect of the contention about the threat posed by transnational drug trafficking emphasizes that the efforts to distribute and purchase drugs may result in violence being committed against individuals not involved in the transaction process. One strand of feminist thought emphasizes the vulnerability of women to violence within the society. The concern is that the structure of society, that is, the cultural norms and mores of society, creates a milieu in which violence committed by men against women is, if not socially acceptable, then at least socially tolerated in ways in which violence against men is not. The structural bias against women is such that the prospect that violence may be committed against an individual woman is a common feature of all aspects of daily life, such that women live in constant knowledge of their vulnerability, of the fact that even at home there may be no safety from violence. The source or cause of violence, and the degree of exposure to violence, are quite different in these perspectives, but all are primarily concerned about the security of the individual from violence.

Other strands of feminist thought cast their net somewhat wider with respect to what the individual is to be secured against. This broader approach stems from the fact that feminist analysis generally seeks to uncover structures of power and domination that are hidden when analysis focuses on the state, and to determine what effect these structures have. Feminist analyses are primarily concerned about the impact of these hidden structures on women (but they do not necessarily exclude men from their concern). The concern is the degree to which structures of power and domination create a circumstance of pervasive inequity and injustice that have a repressive effect for one gender (and one obvious inequity is the greater degree to which women are less secure from violence than men). Thus, feminist thought founded on positivist observation focuses on securing the individual against gendered inequities and injustices, which can occur across the whole range of human activity and aspiration.

Some aspects of the arguments about the security implications of environmental degradation centre on the need to protect the health of individuals. Arguments regarding the impact of human activity on the spread and evolution of diseases are concerned with this. More subtly, arguments decrying the serious environmental pollution caused by war and the preparation of war are not simply about the damage to the environment but also, even if only implicitly, about the impact that this degradation will have on those individuals' health.

Shifting the referent to be secured from the state to the individual results in the fundamental change in what is to be protected from. Some perspectives stress that it is violence that individuals need to be protected against, whether organized violence such as that used by the state, structural violence or criminal violence. The emphasis on violence provides a link to those state-centred perspectives that focus their concern on the need to protect the state against violence. Other perspectives, however, take a broader position, arguing that the individual may be harmed by more than just violence; individuals need to be secure in their health, they need to be secure from being socially, economically and politically marginalized, they need to be secure from oppression. This broader notion, then, is that individuals to be secure must be free of artificial political, social and economic restraints.

Environmental Security

A fourth referent evident in the positivist perspectives we have examined is the environment. As noted above, some arguments about the need to protect the environment from human-induced degradation are underpinned by a concern about the impact of such damage for state security or for the health and welfare of the individual. In addition to this, however, there is a strand of thought that is concerned first and foremost with protecting the environment, not because it is important for humanity, but simply because the environment has a value in and of itself that transcends any ramifications for humanity. This particular strand of thought, which might usefully be termed 'ecological security' in order to differentiate it from other forms of 'environmental security', is only subtly different from perspectives concerned with the welfare of individuals, for to defend the environment for its own value serves to protect the individual. The difference ultimately becomes manifest in the methods taken to provide for the security of the environment; environmental security for individuals would be achieved with methods that balance their need with environmental protection, whilst ecological security would protect the ecology without reference to these needs.

Post-Positivist Perspectives

Post-positivists argue that there is no objective reality that can be discovered through reason as positivists maintain, rather that reality is a function of our knowledge of the world and this knowledge is socially constructed. They maintain theories are a central component of the social construction of reality, for these perform a central role in how we understand the world, in how we construct and define knowledge. Post-positivist perspectives argue that the positivist stress on objective reality obscures social and power relationships that form structures of inclusion and exclusion, and that it is the role of the analyst, of the theorist, to uncover these hidden structures. A central tenet common to most post-positivist perspectives is the desire not to privilege one particular referent over another, in the belief that to do so immediately creates the probability of socially defining knowledge, of obscuring structures of power and domination at one or more other levels, much as they argue that the privileging of the state has obscured such structures. Put another way, an underpinning element of post-positivist theoretical approaches is that all referents are equal, that it is not desirable, or in the end practical, to focus on one to the exclusion of others if we are to elucidate full (and hence emancipatory) understanding. A consequence of this focus on investigation to find that which is hidden by the social construction of other perspectives is that often the referent to be secured is not identified as part of delineating the parameters of the analysis to be undertaken; rather the analysis uncovers structures that affect and shape human behaviour, particularly in terms of being included or excluded, and this finding then determines the referent or referents in need of being emancipated, of being made secure. Thus, an attempt to define various categories based on a specified referent, as was possible for positivist perspectives, contradicts the methodology of many post-positivist analyses on security.

De-emphasizing the primacy of a predetermined referent to be secured in favour of a concentration on analytically exposing concealed social and power structures should not be interpreted as meaning that post-positivists do not identify particular referents. Post-positivist analysis locates structures of power and domination both amongst the patterns of state behaviour in the wider international system and amongst the patterns of social and political interaction within the state. Analyses investigating international phenomena tend to centre on the state, whereas analyses probing domestic phenomena tend to centre on the individual, for it is the action and interaction of these units that give rise to structures. As a central tenet of post-positivist analyses, however, is not to privilege one referent over others, so the analysis undertaken seeks to include all levels and units in order to expose all the structures. Thus some analyses may emphasize the international level and hence the state, whilst others may emphasize the sub-state level and hence the individual, but the examination undertaken includes more than just these units.

The effort by most post-positivist analyses to be inclusive means that, though there will be a tendency to centre the analysis on particular referents, it is not viable to categorize them with the same precision as is possible with positivist perspectives. Postmodernism is the most difficult to categorize, for by its own tenets it does not permit the identification of particular referents. Our reality is socially constructed and this means that we have no foundation for choosing between different interpretations of reality. It also implies that we have no means to choose between referents, for the very act of specifying a referent to be secured creates a social construction that privileges that referent and excludes others. This stance may appear to be a conundrum, for an obvious question is how it is possible to provide security unless that which is to be secured is known. The postmodernists' position, however, is that if we do not have the means to choose, we cannot and should not choose between alternative conceptions or normative aims. Postmodernists thus eschew engagement with policy prescription on the grounds that to engage would force a choice that cannot legitimately be made.

Other post-positivist perspectives disagree with the postmodernist contention that it is not desirable or even possible that analysis should be used to further normative objectives. For this reason, critical theorists condemn postmodernism as a conservative social movement. Post-positivist feminist thought argues that, though gender may be based on physical differences, its meaning, and hence how each gender behaves, is socially constructed. The social construction of gender creates structures of power and domination that, although they privilege masculinity, affect all individuals regardless of gender and so oppress all individuals. Critical theory calls into question the origins of the social and power relationships that serve as given frameworks for action, due to a dissatisfaction with traditional views of the state-as-actor in which security is based exclusively on citizenship. This conception provides an umbrella for a wide number of more distinct perspectives. Critical theory is designed to elucidate who or what creates the structures, their impact, and what and who are subjected to their effects, and so critical theorists do not start with a specification of a particular referent to be secured. In some instances the analyses are oriented to uncovering those structures which are hidden by focusing on the state, and in others the analyses are oriented to uncover hidden structures which affect the behaviour of states in the international system (which may or may not be one and the same). Nevertheless, in concordance with other post-positivist perspectives, critical theory argues that no one unit of analysis should be privileged, that all units and levels of analysis need to be considered. Critical theory thus is not concerned with one particular referent, but rather takes a holistic approach in order to acquire the understanding deemed necessary to achieve emancipation of all referents. But unlike postmodernism, critical theory is foundational in that it believes there are grounds – emancipatory potential – for making judgements.

Post-positivist perspectives focus on the socially constructed nature of knowledge (and hence reality) and the need to uncover the structures of power and domination created through this knowledge. Their starting point is methodological, in distinct contrast to positivist starting points of either a particular referent or empirical challenge. This distinction is most striking in postmodernism, which argues that it is not possible to choose between ends and so is constrained to analytical methodology and what it is this reveals, and no more. The other post-positivist perspectives do seek to achieve normative aims through the form of analysis they adopt, but contend that only by taking an inclusive approach can hidden structures which impact upon understanding and action be revealed. To be inclusive means not to privilege one referent over another, as this empowers that one at the expense of others. As a consequence, all levels of analysis, all referents, need to be considered equally, if the normative aim of emancipating the marginalized and excluded is to be achieved. Thus, in critical theory and constructivist analysis, though they may centre on a particular referent, the levels of analysis and the referents are intertwined and hence not separable.

Whither Security Studies?

The study of IR is dominated by the notion that theory must be positivist or post-positivist in orientation. As security studies is a sub-field of the discipline of IR, that central insight is vital to the study of security and, as such, it has been central to the approach of this book. But, as this conclusion has demonstrated, there are enormous tensions within this positivist/post-positivist dichotomy, because it is constantly necessary to conclude in different ways for postmodernism on the one hand, and for critical theory, feminism and social constructivism on the other.

The division of the sub-field into positivist and post-positivist approaches arises for three reasons. First, the epistemological basis of the two is fundamentally different, as has been examined in the chapter on post-positivism and in this conclusion. Second, it has been useful for traditionalists (positivists) to categorize all their critics under one label (post-positivist or 'critical' in its broad, non-Frankfurt-School sense) because this has helped to marginalize those perspectives, and to reassert the centrality of traditionalist studies.[6] Third, it has been useful for those who take a relativist epistemological position (i.e., postmodernists) to seek to gather supporters for their position, even though there are fundamental differences with other post-positivist perspectives.

In security studies, however, the tension in the positivist/post-positivist dichotomy is great. As we have just seen, postmodernism, unlike critical theory, feminism and social constructivism, will not allow choice between ends. Of course, this does not mean that one cannot have postmodernist security studies; but what it does mean is that the anti-foundational nature of postmodernism requires the definition of its security studies to be significantly different from critical theory security studies, feminist security studies and social constructivist security studies. To us, this implies that there is too great a difference to be able to speak about post-positivist security studies as an umbrella term. This arises because a third epistemological position has not been clearly defined within IR.

One can summarize the three epistemological positions as follows: positivism assumes that international and security phenomena are materially based and have material explanations; relativists argue that international and security phenomena are ideationally based and can only be understood through examining discourse; and epistemological realism (not to be confused with realism in its IR sense) assumes that there is a material basis to the world, but that this can only be understood through the interaction of social forces that operate on the ideational level. Thus, epistemological realism seems to be a middle way between positivism and relativism.[7] However, epistemological realism is encompassed within the post-positivism label in the security studies debate, and would include critical theory and social constructivism. The intellectual inadequacy of that categorization in the field of security studies is one of the central findings of this book.

Security and security studies at the end of the twentieth century seem disaggregated and bewildering. In part, but only in part, this apparent confusion is a product of the end of the Cold War, as traditional certainties have been brought into question. In part it is due to the intellectual vibrancy of the subfield of security studies, which now seeks to incorporate a range of issues from epistemological grounding to specific policy prescription. And in part it is due to the fragmentation of the discipline of IR. It is important to understand the implications of all three of these factors in order to gain some insight into the rich diversity that is security studies. Although this very diversity has meant that some specific perspectives could not be dealt with here, this book has sought to make a contribution to the intellectual mapping of the contemporary sub-field.

Mapping out the intellectual foundations of security studies is not only useful for making sense of the debate, but, more importantly, it also provides a starting point from which to begin to delineate possible points of commonality around which discussion and argument can progress. Two such points which we have highlighted are the specified referent of security and what it is to be protected from. An acknowledgement of a concurrence on what is to be protected opens the possibility of moving debate past arguments about which approach to security is better, to what each perspective reveals about the nature of the threat, the processes by which such threats become manifest and impact on the referent, and how best to provide solutions to avoid or redress them. Equally, if common ground exists on what is to be protected from, then it is possible to begin to move, even if there is disagreement on the referent to be protected, towards finding means of alleviating or removing the threat on the grounds that all referents will benefit. This suggestion is not to say that delineating points of commonality will end the widespread debate on security or even result in a common referent point around which debate can evolve. Each of the main perspectives holds often quite different viewpoints on the processes involved, even if they may agree on what is to be protected and/or from what it is to be protected. This points to a second direction in which it may be possible for the debate to progress; to examine the processes that link the various referents for security (or even from what they are to be protected). Taking the example of the mass movement of people, a realist perspective may focus on the state as being what needs to be protected and may thus be concerned with inter-state activities, yet the threat which occasions inter-state security activities may originate with threats to individuals whose reaction to those hazards is what generates a threat to the state. An emphasis on processes may undercover a range of connections, causal or otherwise, that have been little explored before and which may contribute to revealing linkages between the approaches adopted by different perspectives.

In the end, however, these suggestions are just that; suggestions, possible ways to move the debate forward. Whether the debate about security will progress and, if it does, in what direction, is hard to gauge. As we noted at the outset of this book, the debate about security is not a phenomenon that arose only in the 1990s; rather the debate has a long history. There is no reason to assume that, now there are more perspectives than ever before engaged in it, some form of denouement is likely in the foreseeable future. What can be expected, however, is that the nature of the debate will become more complex, with increased cross-fertilization of perspectives and ideas, and hence that our understanding of security will become much richer and more productive.

The study of security may be fragmented, but the opening up of its agenda makes it a very innovative and vibrant area of IR. The explosion of different perspectives within IR is being played out in security studies, imparting considerable energy to this sub-field in terms of rethinking how the international system functions; traditional perspectives of security are now being challenged and the actors and processes involved are changing and being redefined. Moreover, while it is possible to focus on the purely abstract aspects, the study of security is about more than just concepts. Security is about praxis; it is about the actual, grass-roots application of different concepts and approaches. More than other areas of IR, the study of security is translated into policy, whether it is to do with understanding NATO, examining the implications of weapons proliferation, determining the future of intervention, explicating the evolving nature of peacekeeping, or delineating the threats that states may pose to their own citizens, among many other questions. And one may undertake this task within any of the perspectives addressed in this book, whether neo-realist or postmodernist. There may not appear to be a sense of common direction within the many perspectives in security studies, but there is a sense of common purpose. In spite of the disagreements, we are beginning to recognize the potential embodied in the changes within the sub-field of security studies. The recognition of the limitations of old certainties and pictures of the world 'as it is', and the application of quite radical ideas of politics, agency and analysis to the concept of security and the realm of the international more broadly, make security an exciting area to study at the beginning of the twenty-first century.

Notes

Introduction

1 Barry Buzan, *People, States and Fear: An Agenda for International Security Studies in the Post-Cold War Era*, second edition, Boulder, CO: Lynne Rienner, 1991, p. 7. Buzan draws upon Gallie's 'Essentially Contested Concepts', in Max Black (ed.), *The Importance of Language*, Englewood Cliffs NJ: Prentice Hall, 1962, pp. 121–46.
2 Ibid., p. 16.
3 David A. Baldwin and Helen V. Milner, 'Economics and National Security', in Henry Bienen (ed.), *Power, Economics and Security*, Boulder CO: Westview Press, 1992, p. 29.
4 Patrick M. Morgan, 'Safeguarding Security Studies', *Arms Control*, 13 (3), December 1992, p. 466.
5 Arnold Wolfers, *Discord and Collaboration*, Baltimore: Johns Hopkins University Press, 1962, p. 149.
6 Ibid., p. 150.
7 David Baldwin, 'The Concept of Security', *Review of International Studies*, 23 (1), January 1997, pp. 5–26.
8 With respect to the debate about environmental degradation as a security issue, see Geoffrey Dabelko and P. J. Simmons, 'Environment and Security: Core Ideas and US Government Initiatives', *SAIS Review*, Winter–Spring 1997, p. 129.
9 Buzan calls for the adoption of an international security studies approach in Buzan, *People, States and Fear*. For another call for the development of a discipline of 'international security studies', see Helga Haftendorn, 'The Security Puzzle: Theory-Building and Discipline-Building in International Security', *International Studies Quarterly*, 35, 1991, pp. 2–17.
10 Edward A. Kolodziej, 'What is Security and Security Studies?', *Arms Control*, 13 (1), April 1992, pp. 1–31. Some criticize Kolodziej

for setting too high a standard for security studies. Freedman, for example, argues that prediction is beyond the grasp of not only security studies, but the whole of the social sciences. See Lawrence Freedman, 'The Political Context of Security Studies', *Arms Control*, 14 (2), August 1993, pp. 198–205.

11 On this, see Terry Terriff, 'The "Earth Summit": Are There Any Security Implications?', *Arms Control*, 13 (2), September 1992, pp. 164–8.

12 Jan Aart Scholte, *International Relations of Social Change*, Buckingham: Open University Press, 1993, p. 6.

13 Stephen M. Walt, 'The Renaissance of Security Studies', *International Studies Quarterly*, 35 (2), June 1991, p. 213.

14 Martin White, *International Theory: The Three Traditions*, Leicester: Leicester University Press, 1991; Michael Banks, 'The Inter-Paradigm Debate', in M. Light and A.J.R. Groom (eds), *International Relations: A Handbook of Current Theory*, London: Pinter, 1985, pp. 7–26.

15 For example, R. Little and M. Smith (eds), *Perspectives on World Politics*, second edition, London: Routledge, 1991; Robert Gilpin, *The Political Economy of International Relations*, Princeton NJ: Princeton University Press, 1987; and Robert Jackson, 'Is there a Classical International Theory?', in Steve Smith, Ken Booth and Marysia Zalewski (eds), *International Theory: Positivism and Beyond*, Cambridge: Cambridge University Press, 1996, pp. 203–16.

16 See the detailed examination of the problems with this approach in Marysia Zalewski and Cynthia Enloe, 'Questions about Identity in International Relations', in Ken Booth and Steve Smith (eds), *International Relations Theory Today*, Cambridge: Polity Press, 1995, pp. 279–305.

17 Steve Smith, 'The Self-Images of a Discipline: A Genealogy of International Relations Theory', in Booth and Smith, *International Relations Theory Today*, p. 17.

18 On this see, for example, Robert Axelrod and Robert O. Keohane, 'Achieving Cooperation under Anarchy: Strategies and Institutions', in David A. Baldwin (ed.), *Neo-realism and Neo-liberalism: The Contemporary Debate*, New York: Columbia University Press, 1993, pp. 85–115.

19 Ken Booth, *Strategy and Ethnocentrism*, London: Croom Helm, 1979, p. 133.

20 Lawrence Freedman, 'The Political Context of Security Studies', *Arms Control: Contemporary Security Policy*, 14 (2), August 1993, p. 203.

21 Ken Booth, 'International Relations Theory Versus the Future', in Booth and Smith, *International Relations Theory Today*, p. 333.

Chapter 1   International relations and security studies

1 Although there is debate about Carr's thinking, he is generally seen to be in the realist camp.
2 Thucydides, *History of the Peloponnesian War*, Harmondsworth: Penguin, 1980, p. 402.
3 E.H. Carr, *The Twenty Years' Crisis 1919–1939*, second edition, London: Macmillan, 1946, reissued 1964, p. 41.
4 Kal Holsti, *Peace and War: Armed Conflicts and International Order 1648–1989*, Cambridge: Cambridge University Press, 1991, p. 20.
5 Torbjörn Knutsen, *A History of International Relations Theory*, Manchester: Manchester University Press, 1992, p. 4.
6 On this, see the excellent section in David Armstrong, *Revolution and World Order*, Oxford: Clarendon Press, 1993, pp. 32–8.
7 Ken Booth, 'International Relations Theory Versus the Future', in Ken Booth and Steve Smith (eds), *International Relations Theory Today*, Cambridge: Polity Press, 1995, p. 341.
8 Der Derian continues: 'In its name, peoples have alienated their fears, rights and powers to gods, emperors, and most recently, sovereign states, all to protect themselves from the vicissitudes of nature – as well as from other gods, emperors, and sovereign states. In its name, weapons of mass destruction have been developed which have transfigured national interest into a security dilemma based on a suicide pact. And, less often noted in international relations, in its name billions have been made and millions killed while scientific knowledge has been furthered and intellectual dissent muted.' James Der Derian, 'The Value of Security: Hobbes, Marx, Nietzsche, and Baudrillard', in Ronnie D. Lipschutz (ed.), *On Security*, New York: Columbia University Press, 1995, pp. 24–5.
9 Robert Jervis, 'Models and Cases in the Study of International Conflict', in Robert L. Rothstein (ed.), *The Evolution of Theory in International Relations*, Columbia SC: University of South Carolina Press, 1991, p. 80. Emphasis added.
10 Michael Mann, 'Authoritarian and Liberal Militarism: A Contribution from Comparative and Historical Sociology', in Steve Smith, Ken Booth and Marysia Zalewski (eds), *International Theory: Positivism and Beyond*, Cambridge: Cambridge University Press, 1996, p. 221.
11 Peter Bachrach and Morton Baratz, 'The Two Faces of Power', *American Political Science Review*, 56, 1962, pp. 947–52.
12 On this, see, for example, Grant T. Hammond, *Plowshares into Swords*, Columbia SC: University of South Carolina Press, 1993, p. 241–67; see also Barry M. Blechman and Stephen S. Kaplan, *Force without War: US Armed Forces as a Political Instrument*, Washington DC: Brookings, 1978.

13 Lawrence Freedman, 'Strategic Studies and the Problem of Power', in Lawrence Freedman, Paul Hayes and Robert O'Neill (eds), *War, Strategy and International Politics*, Oxford: Clarendon Press, 1992, p. 291.

14 Hans Morgenthau, *Politics Among Nations: The Struggle for Power and Peace*, fifth edition, New York: Knopf, 1973.

15 Martin Wight, 'Why Is There No International Theory?', in H. Butterfield and M. Wight, *Diplomatic Investigations*, Cambridge MA: Harvard University Press, 1968, pp. 17–35.

16 See, for example, Fred Halliday, *Rethinking International Relations*, Basingstoke: Macmillan, 1994.

17 On the so-called 'Great Debate' see the chapters in Klaus Knorr and James Rosenau, *Contending Approaches to International Politics*, Princeton NJ: Princeton University Press, 1969; see also the Northedge–Rosenau debate in *Millennium*, 5 (1), 1976.

18 Ole Wæver usefully distinguishes between the third debate (which is that of the structuralists that Banks includes) and the fourth debate (which brings in the post-positivists). See Ole Wæver, 'The Rise and Fall of the Inter-Paradigm Debate', in Smith et al., *International Theory*, pp. 155–7.

19 Barry Buzan, Charles Jones and Richard Little, *The Logic of Anarchy: Neorealism to Structural Realism*, New York: Columbia University Press, 1993, p. 1.

20 For example, see David A. Baldwin (ed.), *Neorealism and Neoliberalism: The Contemporary Debate*, New York: Columbia University Press, 1993.

21 For a further elaboration, see Joseph M. Grieco, 'Anarchy and the Limits of Cooperation', in Baldwin, *Neorealism and Neoliberalism*, pp. 116–42.

22 Wæver, 'The Rise and Fall of the Inter-Paradigm Debate'.

23 Immanuel Wallerstein, 'The Inter-State Structure of the Modern World System', in Smith et al., *International Theory*, where the view is explicitly offered as a typical version of globalist thinking. On dependency theory see, in a classical variant, Theotonio Dos Santos, 'The Structure of Dependence', *American Economic Review*, 1 (60), 1970, pp. 231–6. On neo-Marxist versions, see Halliday, *Rethinking International Relations*, and Justin Rosenberg, *The Empire of Civil Society*, London: Verso, 1994.

24 Fred Halliday, 'The End of the Cold War and International Relations: Some Analytic and Theoretical Conclusions', in Booth and Smith, *International Relations Theory Today*, p. 51.

25 Michael Banks, 'The Inter-Paradigm Debate', in M. Light and A.J.R. Groom (eds), *International Relations: A Handbook of Current Theory*, London: Pinter, 1985.

26 Yosef Lapid, 'The Third Debate: On the Prospects of International Theory in a Post-Positivist Era', *International Studies Quarterly*, 33

(3), September 1989.

27 For an exception to this rule, see John Mearsheimer, 'The False Promise of International Institutions', *International Security*, 19 (3), pp. 5–49.

28 Donald Puchala, 'Woe to the Orphans of the Scientific Revolution', in Rothstein, *Evolution of Theory*, p. 45.

29 Richard Smoke and Willis Harman, *Paths to Peace: Exploring the Feasibility of Sustainable Peace*, Boulder, CO: Westview Press, 1987, p. 76.

30 Alexander Wendt, 'Anarchy is What States Make of It: The Social Construction of Power Politics', *International Organization*, 46 (2), Spring 1992, pp. 391–425.

31 J. Ann Tickner, *Gender in International Relations: Feminist Perspectives on Achieving Global Security*, New York: Columbia University Press, 1992, p. 19.

32 Cynthia Enloe, *Bananas, Beaches and Bombs: Making Feminist Sense of International Politics*, Berkeley CA: University of California Press, 1990, pp. 197–8.

33 Kenneth Waltz, *Man, the State, and War*, New York: Columbia University Press, 1959.

34 Kenneth W. Thompson, *Masters of International Thought*, Baton Rouge: Louisiana State University Press, 1980; Kenneth W. Thompson, *Fathers of International Thought*, Baton Rouge: Louisiana State University Press, 1994.

35 Tickner, *Gender in International Relations*, p. 58.

36 See, in particular, Christine Sylvester, *Feminist Theory and International Relations in a Postmodern Era*, Cambridge: Cambridge University Press, 1994.

37 Jack S. Levy, 'The Causes of War', in Philip E. Tetlock (ed.), *Behaviour, Society and Nuclear War*, Vol. 1, New York: Oxford University Press, pp. 209–333, cited in K.J. Holsti, 'International Theory and War in the Third World', in Brian L. Job (ed.), *The Insecurity Dilemma: National Security of Third World States*, Boulder CO: Lynne Rienner, 1992, p. 39.

38 Barry Buzan, *People, States and Fear: An Agenda for International Security Studies in the Post-Cold War Era*, second edition, Boulder CO: Lynne Rienner, 1991, p. 65.

39 Mohammed Ayoob, *The Third World Security Predicament: State Making, Regional Conflict, and the International System*, Boulder CO: Lynne Rienner, 1995, p. 9.

40 Mohammed Ayoob, 'The Security Predicament of the Third World State: Reflections on State Making in a Comparative Perspective', in Job, *The Insecurity Dilemma*, p. 65.

41 See, for example, Augustus Richard Norton, 'The Security Legacy of the 1980s and the Third World', in Thomas G. Weiss and Meryl A. Kessler (eds), *Third World Security in the Post-Cold War Era*,

Boulder CO: Lynne Rienner, 1991, pp. 19–34.

42 On this, see, for example, Nicole Ball, *Security and Economy in the Third World*, Princeton NJ: Princeton University Press, 1988.

43 Ole Wæver, 'Societal Security: The Concept', in Ole Wæver, Barry Buzan, Morten Kelstrup and Pierre Lemaitre, *Identity, Migration and the New Security Agenda in Europe*, Centre for Peace and Conflict Research Copenhagen, London: Pinter, 1993, pp. 17–40. For an example of a security focus on society, see Leonid Kistersky and Serhii Pirozhkov, 'Ukraine: Policy Analysis and Options', in Richard Smoke (ed.), *Perceptions of Security: Public Opinion and Expert Assessments in Europe's New Democracies*, Manchester: Manchester University Press, 1996, pp. 215–16.

44 Edward A. Kolodziej, 'What is Security and Security Studies?', *Arms Control*, 13 (1), April 1992, p. 12.

45 Ken Booth, 'Security and Emancipation', *Review of International Studies*, 17 (4), October 1991, p. 324.

46 Tickner, *Gender in International Relations*, p. 129.

47 Susan Strange, *States and Markets*, London: Pinter, 1988, ch. 3 'The Security Structure', pp. 45–61.

48 Booth, 'Security and Emancipation', p. 319.

49 Brian L. Job, 'The Insecurity Dilemma: National, Regime, and State Securities in the Third World', in Job, *The Insecurity Dilemma*, p. 15.

50 Thomas Hobbes, *Leviathan*, reproduced in Howard Williams, Moorhead Wright and Tony Evans (eds), *A Reader in International Relations and Political Theory*, Buckingham: Open University Press, 1993, p. 93.

51 This is the heart of the neo-realist analysis as well. As Art and Jervis put it, 'anarchy is the fundamental fact of international relations.' Robert Art and Robert Jervis, *International Politics*, second edition, Boston: Little Brown, 1986, p. 7. See also Kenneth Waltz, *Theory of International Politics*, Reading MA: Addison-Wesley, 1979, p. 88.

52 Clausewitz, *On War*, in Williams et al., *Reader in International Relations and Political Theory*, p. 140.

53 Robert Gilpin, 'The Economic Dimension of International Security', in Henry Bienen (ed.), *Power, Economics and Security*, Boulder CO: Westview Press, 1992, p. 52.

54 Buzan, *People, States and Fear*, p. 19.

55 Richard H. Ullman, 'Redefining Security', *International Security*, 8, Summer 1983, p. 133.

56 Emanuel Adler, 'Seasons of Peace: Progress in Postwar International Security', in Emanuel Adler and Beverly Crawford (eds), *Progress in Postwar International Relations*, New York: Columbia University Press, 1991, p. 132.

57 Caroline Thomas, *In Search of Security: The Third World in Inter-*

national Relations, Boulder CO: Lynne Rienner, 1987, p. 1.

58 *North–South: A Programme for Survival*, Report of the Independent Commission on International Development Issues, Cambridge MA: MIT Press, 1980, p. 6.

59 Ian Clark, *The Hierarchy of States: Reform and Resistance in the International Order*, Cambridge: Cambridge University Press, 1989, p. 64.

60 On this see, for example, David Dunn, 'Peace Research Versus Strategic Studies', in Ken Booth (ed.), *New Thinking about Strategy and International Security*, London: Harper Collins, 1991, pp. 56–72.

61 Ronnie D. Lipschutz, *On Security*, in Lipschutz (ed.), *On Security*, New York: Columbia University Press, 1995, p. 14.

62 Ken Booth, 'Dare Not To Know: International Relations Theory Versus the Future', in Booth and Smith, *International Relations Theory Today*, p. 344.

63 Carr, *Twenty Years Crisis*, 1964, p. 109.

64 Hedley Bull, *The Anarchical Society*, Basingstoke: Macmillan, 1977, p. 187.

65 Halliday, *Rethinking International Relations*, p. 66.

66 Waltz, *Theory of International Politics*, pp. 163, 169–70.

67 See Robert Gilpin, *War and Change in World Politics*, Cambridge: Cambridge University Press, 1981, esp. pp. 13–15.

68 Charles W. Kegley Jr and Gregory A. Raymond, *When Trust Breaks Down: Alliance Norms and World Politics*, Columbia SC: University of South Carolina, 1990, p. 120. See also Joshua S. Goldstein, *Long Cycles: Prosperity and War in the Modern Age*, New Haven CT: Yale University Press, 1988.

69 John G. Stoessinger, *Why Nations Go to War*, fifth edition, New York: St. Martins Press, p. 205.

70 Jan Aart Scholte, *International Relations of Social Change*, Buckingham: Open University Press, 1993, p. 148, n. 5. Scholte cites a number of authors here, including M.R. Davie, *The Evolution of War: A Study of its Role in Early Societies*, New Haven CT: Yale University Press, 1968, original 1929, and Q. Wright, *A Study of War*, Chicago: University of Chicago Press, 1942.

71 Neta C. Crawford, 'Cooperation Among Iroquois Nations', *International Organization*, 48 (3), 1994, pp. 345–85.

72 Lynn H. Miller, *Global Order: Values and Power in International Politics*, second edition, Boulder CO: Westview Press, 1990, p. 251.

73 Immanuel Kant, *Perpetual Peace*, is reproduced in Williams et al., *Reader in International Relations and Political Theory*, pp. 112–21.

74 See, for example, Grenville Clark and Louis B. Sohn, *World Peace through World Law*, third edition, Cambridge MA: Harvard University Press, 1966.

75 See Silviu Brucan, 'The Establishment of a World Authority: Working Hypotheses', *Alternatives*, 8, Fall 1982, pp. 209–332.

76 James Mayall, *Nationalism and International Society*, Cambridge: Cambridge University Press, 1990, p. 75.

77 Norman Angell, *The Great Illusion*, New York: Putnams, 1933.

78 Francis Fukuyama, *The End of History and the Last Man*, London: Penguin, 1992.

79 Michael Mann, 'Authoritarian and Liberal Militarism: A Contribution from Comparative and Historical Sociology', in Smith et al., *International Theory*, pp. 221–39. This is based on his *The Sources of Social Power. Vol. 2: The Rise of Classes and Nation-States, 1760–1914*, Cambridge: Cambridge University Press, 1993.

80 M. Doyle, 'Kant, Liberal Legacies and Foreign Affairs', Parts 1 and 2, *Philosophy and Public Affairs*, 12 (3), pp. 205–35, and 12 (4), pp. 323–53.

81 John W. Burton, *International Relations: A General Theory*, Cambridge: Cambridge University Press, 1965, pp. 6–7.

82 Charles A. Kupchan and Clifford A. Kupchan, 'The Promise of Collective Security', *International Security*, 20 (1), Summer 1995, pp. 52–3.

83 As defined by Leon Gordenker and Thomas G. Weiss, 'The Collective Security Idea and Changing World Politics', in Weiss (ed.), *Collective Security in a Changing World*, Boulder CO: Lynne Rienner, 1993, p. 3.

84 This point is most clearly explored in Inis Claude, *Power and International Relations*, New York: Random House, 1962.

85 Jean-Jacques Rousseau, *Extract of the Abbé de Saint-Pierre's Project for Perpetual Peace*, in Williams et al., *Reader in International Relations and Political Theory*, p. 101.

86 This is because for Rousseau humans are only *potentially* rational; but this potential is corrupted by the nature of society, which produces an alienation in which individuals lose sight of their best interests. See Knutsen, *History of International Relations Theory*, pp. 113–22.

87 Karl W. Deutsch, *Political Community in the North Atlantic Area*, Princeton NJ: Princeton University Press, 1957.

88 Robert Axelrod, *The Evolution of Cooperation*, New York: Basic Books, 1984, p. 12, cited in Joseph M. Grieco, *Cooperation among Nations*, Ithaca NY: Cornell University Press, 1990, p. 38.

89 R. Keohane, *After Hegemony: Cooperation and Discord in the World Political Economy*, Princeton NJ: Princeton University Press, 1984; see esp. pp. 51–2.

90 Robert Jervis, 'Security Regimes', in Stephen D. Krasner (ed.), *International Regimes*, Ithaca NY: Cornell University Press, 1983, p. 173.

91 See Ole Wæver, 'Securitization and Desecuritization', in Ronnie

D. Lipschutz (ed.), *On Security*, New York: Columbia University Press, 1995.

92 Barry Buzan, 'Response to Kolodziej', *Arms Control*, 13 (3), December 1992, p. 485.

Chapter 2   Traditional views of security in international politics

1 Hans Morgenthau, *Politics Among Nations: The Struggle for Power and Peace*, New York: Knopf, 1948, since reissued in many, somewhat revised, editions; Henry Kissinger, *A World Restored: Castlereagh, Metternich, and the Problem of Peace, 1812–1822*, Boston: Houghton Mifflin, 1957. Another prominent, and important, writer on 'realism' who wrote before the Second World War is E.H. Carr. See E.H. Carr, *The Twenty Years' Crisis, 1919–1939*, London: Macmillan, 1939.

2 See John J. Mearsheimer, 'The False Promise of International Institutions', *International Security*, 19 (3), Winter 1994–5, pp. 5–49.

3 'Structural realism' is sometimes viewed as being the same as neo-realism; however, some claim that the term encompasses a form of theorizing based on structures that is related to but different from what is commonly called 'neo-realism'. See, for example, Barry Buzan, Charles Jones and Richard Little, *The Logic of Anarchy: Neo-realism to Structural Realism*, New York: Columbia University Press, 1993.

4 While it would be impossible to list even a goodly portion of the realist/neo-realist works that can be consulted to pursue this line of analysis, the following would be helpful: Michael E. Brown, Sean Lynn-Jones and Steven E. Miller (eds), *The Perils of Anarchy: Contemporary Realism and International Security*, Cambridge MA: MIT Press, 1995; Barry Buzan, *People, States and Fear: The National Security Problem in International Relations*, Chapel Hill NC: University of North Carolina Press, 1983; Robert Gilpin, 'The Richness of the Tradition of Political Realism', *International Organization*, 38 (2), Spring 1984, pp. 287–304; Gilpin, *War and Change in World Politics*, Cambridge: Cambridge University Press, 1981; Paul M. Kennedy, *The Rise and Fall of the Great Powers: Economic Change and Military Conflict From 1500 to 2000*, New York: Random House, 1987; Christopher Layne, 'The Unipolar Illusion: Why New Great Powers Will Rise', *International Security*, 17 (4), Spring 1993, pp. 5–51; Michael Mandelbaum, *The Fate of Nations: The Search for Security in the Nineteenth and Twentieth Centuries*, New York: Cambridge University Press, 1988; John Mearsheimer, 'Back to the Future: Instability in Europe After the Cold War', *International*

Security, 15 (1), Summer 1990, pp. 5–55; Mearsheimer, 'False Promise of International Institutions', pp. 5–49; Hans Morgenthau, *Scientific Man vs. Power Politics*, Chicago: University of Chicago Press, 1946; Stephen Walt, *The Origins of Alliance*, Ithaca NY: Cornell University Press, 1987; Kenneth Waltz, *Theory of International Politics*, Reading MA: Addison-Wesley, 1979; Waltz, 'The Origins of War in Neo-realist Theory', in Robert I. Rotberg and Theodore K. Rabb (eds), *The Origin and Prevention of Major Wars*, Cambridge: Cambridge University Press, 1989, pp. 39–52; Waltz, 'The Spread of Nuclear Weapons: More May Be Better', *Adelphi Papers No. 171*, London: International Institute for Strategic Studies, 1981; Waltz, 'The Emerging Structure of International Politics', *International Security*, 18 (2), Fall 1993, pp. 44–79; and Arnold Wolfers, *Discord and Collaboration: Essays on International Politics*, Baltimore MD: Johns Hopkins University Press, 1962.
5 Morgenthau, *Politics Among Nations*, p. 5.
6 Thomas Hobbes, ed. C.B. Macpherson, *Leviathan*, Harmondsworth: Penguin, 1968, p. 188.
7 Joseph M. Grieco, 'Understanding the Problem of International Cooperation: The Limits of Neo-liberal Institutionalism and the Future of Realist Theory', in David A. Baldwin (ed.), *Neorealism and Neoliberalism: The Contemporary Debate*, New York: Columbia University Press, 1993, p. 315.
8 Mearsheimer, 'Back to the Future', pp. 5–6.
9 Waltz, *Theory of International Politics*, p. 131.
10 We recognize that the term 'statesman' is not an ideal choice, as it serves to underline the intrinsically gendered nature of the subject, but it is difficult to determine an alternative that does not sound awkward.
11 Waltz, *Theory of International Politics*, p. 117.
12 Ibid.
13 Robert Stausz-Hupe and Stefan T. Possony, *International Relations*, New York: McGraw-Hill, 1954, pp. 5–6.
14 Frederick Schuman, *International Politics*, fourth edition, New York: McGraw-Hill, 1969, p. 271.
15 Morgenthau, *Politics Among Nations*, pp. 25–6.
16 See Waltz, *Theory of International Politics*, ch. 5, esp. pp. 100–1.
17 Ibid., pp. 93–7.
18 Ibid., pp. 97–9.
19 See n. 4.
20 Waltz, *Theory of International Politics*, p. 102.
21 Mearsheimer, 'False Promise of International Institutions', p. 9.
22 Gilpin, 'Richness of the Tradition of Political Realism', in Robert Keohane (ed.), *Neorealism and its Critics*, New York: Columbia University Press, 1986, pp. 304–5.
23 The key distinction is that realists argue that states are motivated

by power, neo-realists that they are motivated by security.
24 Layne, 'Unipolar Illusion', pp. 50–1.
25 Waltz, *Theory of International Politics*, p. 126.
26 Stephen M. Walt, 'The Renaissance of Security Studies', *International Studies Quarterly*, 35 (2), June 1991, p. 212.
27 Morgenthau, *Politics Among Nations*, p. 29.
28 For an examination of these three categories from the perspective of political philosophers, see Kenneth Waltz, *Man, the State, and War*, New York: Columbia University Press, 1959.
29 Bruce Russett, *Grasping the Democratic Peace: Principles for a Post-Cold War World*, Princeton NJ: Princeton University Press, 1993, esp. ch. 7.
30 Christopher Layne, 'Kant or Cant: The Myth of the Democratic Peace', *International Security*, 19 (2), Fall 1994, pp. 10–12.
31 Hobbes, *Leviathan*, ch. 11.
32 On the idea of states as a social construct and the implications of this, see ch. 5.
33 Waltz, *Theory of International Politics*, p. 194.
34 Waltz, *Man, the State, and War*, pp. 80–123.
35 Robert Axelrod and Robert O. Keohane, 'Achieving Cooperation Under Anarchy: Strategies and Institutions', *World Politics*, 38 (1), 1985, pp. 226–54.
36 Ibid., pp. 247–53.
37 For a good overview of some of the more important arguments in this debate, see Baldwin, *Neorealism and Neoliberalism*.
38 Arthur Stein, 'Coordination and Collaboration: Regimes in an Anarchic World', *International Organization*, 36, Spring 1982, pp. 295–230.
39 See Mearsheimer, 'False Promise of International Institutions', p. 8.
40 Steven D. Krasner (ed.), *International Regimes, Special Issue of International Organization*, 36 (2), Spring 1982, p. 186. See also Robert O. Keohane, *After Hegemony: Cooperation and Discord in the World Political Economy*, Princeton NJ: Princeton University Press, 1984, pp. 57–8.
41 Charles Lipson, 'Is the Future of Collective Security Like the Past?', in George W. Downs (ed.), *Collective Security Beyond the Cold War*, Ann Arbor: University of Michigan Press, p. 114.
42 For more on the misleading nature of these terms, see both David A. Baldwin, 'Neoliberalism, Neorealism and World Politics', and Robert O. Keohane, 'Institutional Theory and the Realist Challenge After the Cold War', in Baldwin, *Neorealism and Neoliberalism*, pp. 9–10, 272. For an examination of idealism or utopianism, see ch. 3.
43 James A. Caporaso, 'International Relations Theory and Multilateralism: The Search for Foundations', *International Organizations*,

46 (3), Summer 1992, p. 605.
44 See Ole Wæver, 'The Rise and Fall of the Inter-Paradigm Debate', in Steve Smith, Ken Booth and Marysi Zalewski (eds), *International Theory: Positivism and Beyond*, Cambridge: Cambridge University Press, 1996, esp. pp. 161–70.
45 Robert O. Keohane and Joseph Nye, *Power and Interdependence*, New York: HarperCollins, 1989, p. 11
46 Robert O. Keohane and Lisa L. Martin, 'The Promise of Institutionalist Theory', *International Security*, 20 (1), Summer 1995, p. 39.
47 See Baldwin, 'Neoliberalism, Neorealism and World Politics', pp. 4–8.
48 See Keohane, 'Institutional Theory', pp. 272, 271.
49 Ibid., p. 292.
50 Ibid., p. 296.
51 Mearsheimer, 'False Promise of International Institutions', p. 12.
52 Ibid., p. 10.
53 See Charles Lipson, 'International Cooperation in International Economic and Security Affairs', *World Politics*, 37 (1), October 1984, pp. 4–18; Axelrod and Keohane, 'Achieving Cooperation Under Anarchy', pp. 248–50.
54 Lipson, 'International Cooperation', p. 5.
55 See, for example, Lisa. L. Martin, 'Institutions and Cooperation: Sanctions During the Falkland Islands Crisis', *International Security*, 16 (4), Spring 1992, pp. 143–78.
56 Keohane, *After Hegemony*, pp. 89–92.
57 Joseph M. Grieco, 'Anarchy and the Limits of Cooperation: A Realist Critique of the Newest Liberal Institutionalism', in Baldwin, *Neorealism and Neoliberalism*, p. 118.
58 Even neo-liberal institutionalists recognize that co-operation is much harder when military and security issues are at stake. See, for example, Lipson, 'International Cooperation', pp. 12–18; Axelrod and Keohane, 'Achieving Cooperation Under Anarchy', pp. 232–3.
59 Mearsheimer, 'False Promise of International Institutions', p. 12.
60 See, for example, Grieco, 'Anarchy and the Limits of Cooperation' pp. 116–40.
61 Duncan Snidal, 'Relative Gains and the Pattern of International Cooperation', in Baldwin, *Neorealism and Neoliberalism*, pp. 170–208.
62 Robert Powell, 'Absolute and Relative Gains in International Relations', in Baldwin, *Neorealism and Neoliberalism*, pp. 209–33.
63 Mearsheimer, 'False Promise of International Institutions', pp. 23–4.
64 Of particular salience here is the idea of reciprocity, which was discussed above with regard to the problem of cheating. See Keohane and Martin, 'Promise of Institutionalist Theory', pp. 44–6.

65 Michael Mastunado in a study of US–Japanese relations has argued that for a period of time the US was not concerned about relative gains being made by Japan. However, he further argued that in the 1980s the US, or at least certain policy actors within the US government, became increasingly concerned about relative gains considerations and attempted to redress perceived imbalances. See Mastunado, 'Do Relative Gains Matter? America's Response to Japanese Industrial Policy', in Baldwin, *Neorealism and Neoliberalism*, pp. 251–66.

66 Keohane and Martin, 'Promise of Institutionalist Theory', p. 50.

67 See, for example, Charles W. Kegley Jr and Gregory Raymond, *A Multipolar Peace?: Great-Power Politics in the Twenty-First Century*, New York: St Martin's Press, 1994; Karl W. Deutsch and J. David Singer, 'Multipolar Power Systems and International Stability', *World Politics*, 16, April 1964, pp. 390–406; Ted Hopf, 'Polarity and International Stability', *American Political Science Review*, 87, March 1993, pp. 177–80; Richard N. Rosecrance, 'Bipolarity, Multipolarity, and the Future', *Journal of Conflict Resolution*, 10 (3), September 1966, pp. 314–27; Kenneth N. Waltz, 'The Stability of a Bipolar World', *Daedalus*, 93 (3), Summer 1964, pp. 881–909; Ted Hopf, 'Polarity, the Offense–Defense Balance, and War', *American Political Science Review*, 81 (3), June 1991, pp. 475–94; Manus Midlarsky, 'Polarity and International Stability', *American Political Science Review*, 87, March 1993, pp. 173–7; Alan Ned Sabrosky (ed.), *Polarity and War*, Boulder CO: Westview Press, 1985.

68 See Ernst B. Haas, 'The Balance of Power: Prescription, Concept or Propaganda?', *World Politics*, 5 (4), July 1953, pp. 442–77.

69 This and the following paragraphs are derived from: ibid.; Alfred Vagts, 'The Balance of Power: Growth of an Idea', *World Politics*, 1 (1), October 1948, pp. 82–101; Ernst B. Haas, 'The Balance of Power as Guide to Policy-Making', *Journal of Politics*, 15 (3), August 1953, pp. 370–98; Edward V. Gulick, *Europe's Classical Balance of Power*, Ithaca NY: Cornell University Press, 1955; Inis L. Claude Jr, *Power and International Relations*, New York: Random House, 1962.

70 For a traditional realist, such as Morgenthau, the search for security more properly would be the search for power.

71 Belief that nuclear weapons had this effect for the major states led some analysts and governments to suggest that nuclear proliferation is inevitable and beneficial in international politics.

72 The general realist view was, at the outset of the nuclear age, critical of nuclear deterrence. Later, realists tended to be very attracted to it but also to analyses that suggested it was fragile or potentially unstable. Among neo-realists, Kenneth Waltz is well known for the argument that nuclear deterrence is not fragile, is profoundly stable, and that nuclear proliferation can add greatly to the stability of international politics. Most realists/neo-realists

disagree, arguing that nuclear-armed states should resist nuclear proliferation not just out of considerations of national power but because proliferation will make nuclear deterrence more unstable and international politics more insecure.

73 See ch. 1.
74 Wolfers, *Discord and Collaboration*, p. 103.
75 Patrick M. Morgan, 'Safeguarding Security Studies', *Arms Control*, 13 (3), December 1992, p. 466.

Chapter 3 Peace studies

1 Peter Lawler, 'New Directions in Peace Research', in Hugh V. Emy and Andrew Linklater (eds), *New Horizons in Politics: Essays with an Australian Focus*, Sydney: Allen and Unwin, 1990, p. 110.
2 Francis Beer, 'The Reduction of War and the Creation of Peace', in Paul Smoker, Ruth Davies and B. Munske (eds), *A Reader in Peace Studies*, Oxford: Pergamon Press, 1990, p. 15.
3 Betty Reardon, 'Feminist Concepts of Peace and Security', in Smoker et al., *Reader in Peace Studies*, p. 137.
4 Leonard Woolf, *International Government*, New York: Brentanos, 1916.
5 Ghanshyam Pardesi, 'Editor's Introduction', in Pardesi (ed.), *Contemporary Peace Research*, Brighton: Harvester Press, 1982, p. 2.
6 David J. Dunn, 'Peace Research versus Strategic Studies', in Ken Booth (ed.), *New Thinking about Strategy and International Security*, London: HarperCollins Academic, 1991, p. 59.
7 Peter Lawler, 'Peace Research and International Relations: From Divergence to Convergence', *Millennium*, 15 (3), Winter 1986, pp. 370–1.
8 Beer, 'Reduction of War and the Creation of Peace', pp. 15–16.
9 See E.H. Carr, *The Twenty Years' Crisis, 1919–1939*, London: Macmillan, 1939; Hans Morgenthau, *Politics Among Nations: The Struggle for Power and Peace*, New York: Knopf, 1965.
10 Lawler, 'New Directions in Peace Research', p. 112.
11 Quincy Wright, *A Study of War*, Chicago: University of Chicago Press, 1965.
12 Pardesi, 'Editor's Introduction', pp. 13–14.
13 Lawler, 'Peace Research and International Relations', p. 372.
14 Lawler, 'New Directions in Peace Research', p. 114.
15 Dunn, 'Peace Research versus Strategic Studies', p. 63.
16 Lawler, 'New Directions in Peace Research', pp. 115–16.
17 Johan Galtung, 'An Editorial', *Journal of Peace Research*, 1 (1), 1964, pp. 1–4.
18 Lawler, 'New Directions in Peace Research', p. 115.
19 For example, see André Gunter Frank, *Capitalism and Under-*

development in Latin America, New York: Monthly Review Press, 1967; Immanuel Wallerstein, *The Modern World-System*, San Diego: Academy Press, 1974.

20 See Lars Dencik, *International Peace Research Association Proceedings*, Third General Conference, 1, 1970, pp. 74–91; André Gunter Frank, *Capitalism and Underdevelopment*; E. Krippendorff, 'The State as a Focus of Peace Research', *Peace Research Society Paper*, XVI, The Rome Conference, 1970, pp. 47–60.

21 Lars Dencik, 'Peace Research: Pacification or Revolution', in Pardesi, *Contemporary Peace Research*, pp. 25–7.

22 A. Hoogvelt, 'Capitalism and Global Integration', in Smoker et al., *Reader in Peace Studies*, p. 37.

23 Susan George, 'The Third World Debt Crisis', in Smoker et al., *Reader in Peace Studies*, pp. 127–9.

24 April Carter, 'Nonviolence as a Strategy for Change', in Smoker et al., *Reader in Peace Studies*, p. 210.

25 Johan Galtung, 'Violence, Peace and Peace Research', *Journal of Peace Research*, 6, 1969, pp. 167–91.

26 Lawler, 'Peace Research and International Relations', pp. 374–5.

27 Anthony Arblaster, 'Structural Violence', in William Outhwaite and Tom Bottomore (eds), *The Blackwell Dictionary of Twentieth Century Social Thought*, Oxford: Blackwell, 1993, pp. 700–1.

28 Kenneth Boulding, 'Peace Theory', in Smoker et al., *Reader in Peace Studies*, p. 4.

29 Johan Galtung, 'Violence and Peace', in Smoker et al., *Reader in Peace Studies*, pp. 9–11.

30 Ibid., p. 9.

31 Johan Galtung, *Essays in Peace Research, Vol. 1: Peace: Research, Education, Action*, Oslo: Prio Monographic International Peace Research Institute, 1975, p. 25.

32 Johan Galtung, 'Violence, Peace and Peace Research', in Pardesi, *Contemporary Peace Research*, p. 122.

33 Dunn, 'Peace Research versus Strategic Studies', pp. 65–6.

34 Galtung, *Essays in Peace Research. Vol. 1*, p. 103.

35 Peter Lawler, *A Question of Values: Johan Galtung's Peace Research*, Boulder/London: Lynne Rienner, 1995, p. 81. The argument – that a dynamic of violence within a state, for example via government discrimination and oppression of a particular minority, leads to insecurity and a lack of peace – is also developed in more contemporary ideas of societal security. See Barry Buzan, *People, States and Fear: An Agenda for Security Studies in the Post-Cold War Era*, London: Harvester Wheatsheaf, 1991; and Ken Booth, 'Conclusion', in Booth, *New Thinking*.

36 Galtung, *Essays in Peace Research. Vol. 1*, pp. 252–4.

37 Lawler, 'New Directions in Peace Research', p. 119.

38 Jonathan Dean, *Meeting Gorbachev's Challenges*, London: Macmil-

lan, 1989, p. 5.
39 Dunn, 'Peace Research versus Strategic Studies', pp. 56–7.
40 Booth, 'Conclusion', p. 342.
41 Ibid., pp. 352–7.
42 Johan Galtung, *There Are Alternatives! Four Roads to Peace and Security*, Nottingham: Spokesman, 1984, p. 20. For much of the 1980s many in the peace movement or peace research were tarred as communist sympathizers. Considering the piecemeal, *ad hoc*, cheerfully amateurish approach of many peace organizations, the response of some Western governments verged on the hysterical. A classic example is Pat Jacobs, *Operation Peace Studies*, Melbourne: Rose Research and Publications, 1985, a vituperative account of the 'subversive' and 'dangerous' activities of those who opposed nuclear defence policies.
43 Galtung, *There are Alternatives!*, pp. 21–4; see also below, on critical approaches to peace and security.
44 See Alternative Defence Commission, *Defence without the Bomb*, London: Taylor and Francis, 1983; Alternative Defence Commission, *Without the Bomb – Non-Nuclear Defence Politics for Britain*, London: Paladin, 1985; Alternative Defence Commission, *The Politics of Alternative Defence*, London: Paladin, 1987.
45 Dan Smith, 'Non-Nuclear Defence', in Smoker et al., *Reader in Peace Research*, p. 93.
46 Michael Clarke, 'Alternative Defence: The New Reality', in Booth, *New Thinking*, pp. 202–5.
47 Booth, 'Conclusion', p. 339.
48 Galtung, *There are Alternatives!*, p. 162.
49 Dunn, 'Peace Research versus Strategic Studies', p. 66.
50 Booth, 'Conclusion', p. 334.
51 For example, Caroline Thomas, 'New Directions in Thinking about Security in the Third World', in Booth, *New Thinking*, pp. 267–90.
52 See chs 4 and 6 respectively for further references.
53 Lawler, 'New Directions in Peace Research', pp. 120–2.
54 Reardon, 'Feminist Concepts of Peace and Security', p. 138.
55 Lawler, *A Question of Values*, p. 237.
56 Galtung, *There Are Alternatives!*, p. 13.

Chapter 4   The impact of gender on security

1 For a usefully succinct introduction to these areas, see Dale Spender (ed.), *Men's Studies Modified: The Impact of Feminism on the Academic Disciplines*, Oxford: Pergamon Press, 1981.
2 Ibid.
3 Fred Halliday, *Rethinking International Relations*, Basingstoke:

Macmillan, 1994, p. 47.

4 See Barry Buzan, *People, States and Fear: An Agenda for International Security Studies in the Post-Cold War Era*, second edition, London: Harvester Wheatsheaf, 1991; Caroline Thomas, *In Search of Security: The Third World in International Relations*, Brighton: Wheatsheaf, 1987; Thomas, 'New Directions in Thinking about Security in the Third World', in Ken Booth (ed.), *New Thinking about Strategy and International Security*, London: HarperCollins Academic, 1991, pp. 267–90.

5 See David J. Dunn, 'Peace Research versus Strategic Studies', in Booth, *New Thinking*; Andrew Hurrell, 'International Political Theory and the Global Environment', in Ken Booth and Steve Smith (eds), *International Relations Theory Today*, Cambridge: Polity Press, 1995; E.J. Mortimer, 'New Fault Lines: Is a North–South Confrontation Inevitable in Security Terms?', *Adelphi Paper 266*, London: International Institute of Strategic Studies, 1991–2, pp. 74–86; John Ravenhill, 'North–South Balance of Power', *International Affairs*, 1990, pp. 731–48.

6 Argued by Thomas, 'New Directions'; see also Ken Booth, 'Security and Emancipation', *Review of International Studies*, 17, 1991, pp. 313–26.

7 Booth, 'Security and Emancipation', p. 318.

8 Ibid., pp. 322–3; Marysia Zalewski and Cynthia Enloe, 'Questions about Identity in International Relations', in Booth and Smith, *International Relations Theory Today*, pp. 300–1.

9 Mary Kaldor, *The Baroque Arsenal*, London: Deutsch, 1982, p. 230.

10 Thomas, *In Search of Security*, p. 104.

11 See *Millennium*, 17 (3), Winter 1988, for: S. Brown, 'Feminism, International Theory and International Relations of Gender Inequality', pp. 461–75; Fred Halliday, 'Hidden from International Relations: Women and the International Arena', pp. 419–28.

12 Anthony Arblaster in William Outhwaite and Tom Bottomore (eds), *The Blackwell Dictionary of Twentieth Century Social Thought*, Oxford: Blackwell, 1993, pp. 700–1.

13 See Ken Booth, 'Steps Towards Stable Peace in Europe', *International Affairs*, January 1990, pp. 17–45; Booth, 'Security in Anarchy: Utopian Realism in Theory and Practice', *International Affairs*, July 1991, pp. 527–45; Ken Booth and John Baylis, *Britain, NATO and Nuclear Weapons*, London: Macmillan, 1989, p. 47, for the contention that gender theory has tended to focus on interpersonal affairs, and that IR as an academic discipline is too insecure to take gender on board.

14 Booth, 'Security and Emancipation', p. 324; see also Margot Light and Fred Halliday, 'Gender and International Relations', in A.J.R. Groom and Margot Light (eds), *Contemporary International Rela-*

tions, London: Pinter, 1994.

15 Martin Kettle, 'A Woman's Place is in the Despatch Box', *Guardian*, 15 April 1995.

16 G. Lerner, *The Creation of Patriarchy*, Oxford/New York: Oxford University Press, 1986, p. 220.

17 Cynthia Weber, 'Good Girls, Little Girls and Bad Girls: Male Paranoia in Robert Keohane's Critique of Feminist International Relations', *Millennium*, 23 (2), 1994, pp. 337–49.

18 Susan Brownmiller, *Against Our Will*, London: Secker and Warburg, 1975, pp. 14–15.

19 Catharine MacKinnon, *Toward a Feminist Theory of the State*, Cambridge MA: Harvard University Press, 1989, p. 172.

20 The 20,000 figure is from an EC mission; Muslim and Croat sources claim the true figure is nearer 50,000: *Guardian*, Section 2, 20 January 1993, pp. 2–3.

21 R.E. Dobash and R. Dobash, *Violence Against Wives*, London: Open Books, 1979, p. ix.

22 British Medical Association, 'Domestic Violence: A Health Care Issue?', 30 June 1998; reported in the *Guardian*, 1 July 1998, p. 3. For further studies, see Dobash and Dobash, *Violence Against Wives*.

23 C.J. Sheffield, 'Sexual Terrorism: The Social Control of Women', in B.B. Hess and M.M. Ferree (eds), *Analysing Gender*, Newbury Park/London: Sage, 1987, p. 171.

24 In Diana Russell (ed.), *Exposing Nuclear Phallacies*, New York/Oxford: Pergamon Press, 1989, p. 65.

25 J. Ann Tickner, 'Re-visioning Security', in Booth and Smith, *International Relations Theory Today*, pp. 194–5.

26 See: Sandra L. Bartky, *Femininity and Domination: Studies in the Phenomenology of Oppression*, New York/London: Routledge, 1990; Brownmiller, *Against Our Will*; Andrea Dworkin, *Pornography: Men Possessing Women*, London: Women's Press, 1984; L. Lemoncheck, *Dehumanizing Women: Treating Persons as Sex Objects*, Totowa NJ: Rowan and Allanheld, 1985; Lynne Segal, *Is the Future Female?*, London: Virago, 1991.

27 Naomi Wolf, *The Beauty Myth*, London: Vintage, 1990, p. 66.

28 See J.J. Brumberg, *Fasting Girls: The Emergence of Anorexia Nervosa as a Modern Disease*, MA: Harvard University Press, 1988; S. Cline, *Just Desserts: Women and Food*, London: André Deutsch, 1990; Susie Orbach, *Hunger Strike: The Anorectic's Struggle as a Metaphor for Our Age*, London: Faber and Faber, 1986; Wolf, *Beauty Myth*.

29 Wolf, *Beauty Myth*, p. 187.

30 Ibid., p. 215; see also *Standard and Poors' Industry Surveys*, New York: Standard and Poors, 1988.

31 Wolf, *Beauty Myth*, p. 200.

32 See Johan Galtung, *Essays in Peace Research. Vols I and II*, Oslo: International Peace Research Institute, 1975; Galtung, *There Are*

Alternatives! Four Roads to Peace and Security, Nottingham: Spokesman, 1984; Thomas, *In Search of Security*.

33 Susan Faludi, *Backlash: The Undeclared War against Women*, London: Vintage, 1992, p. 439.

34 E.N. Glenn, 'Gender and the Family', in Hess and Ferree, *Analysing Gender*, p. 357.

35 See Cynthia Enloe, *Bananas, Beaches and Bombs: Making Feminist Sense of International Politics*, Berkeley CA: University of California Press, 1990; Enloe, *Does Khaki Become You? The Militarisation of Women's Lives*, London: Pandora Press, 1988, for a thorough examination of the full extent of militarization of women's lives, and the dependence of the military structures on women conforming to traditional notions of passivity and compliance.

36 Georgina Ashworth, 'An Elf Among the Gnomes: A Feminist in North–South Relations', *Millennium*, 17 (3), Winter 1988, pp. 419–28.

37 Cynthia Enloe, *The Morning After: Sexual Politics at the End of the Cold War*, Berkeley CA/London: University of California Press, 1993.

38 Maria Mies, *Patriarchy and Accumulation on a World Scale*, London: Zed Books, 1986, pp. 169–70.

39 Carol Cohn, 'Sex and Death in the Rational World of Defence Intellectuals', *Signs: Journal of Women in Culture and Society*, 12 (4), 1987, p. 693.

40 J. Ann Tickner, *Gender in International Relations: Feminist Perspectives on Achieving Global Security*, New York: Columbia University Press, 1992, p. 19.

41 This is an area the broad school typically overlooks; for a briefer, similar argument, see J.B. Elshtain, 'The Problem with Peace', *Millennium*, 17 (3), Winter 1988, pp. 441–9.

42 Lisa C.O. Brandes, 'The Liberal State, War and Feminist Theory', paper presented at International Studies Association conference in Chicago, 22–6 February 1995.

43 For a feminist critique of Just War theory, see Sarah Ruddick, 'Notes toward a Feminist Reformulation', in M. Cooke and A. Woollacott (eds), *Gendering War Talk*, Princeton NJ: Princeton University Press, 1993.

44 J.A. Tickner, 'Hans Morgenthau's Principles of Political Realism: A Feminist Reformulation', *Millennium*, 17 (3), Winter 1988, p. 434.

45 Tickner, *Gender in International Relations*, pp. 134–5. It is worth noting that this argument can be seen to overlap with Ken Booth's broad security ideas of operationalizing communitarian values within a cosmopolitan framework – see Ken Booth, 'Dare to Know – International Relations Theory versus the Future', in Booth and Smith, *International Relations Theory Today*, pp. 342–4.

46 Christine Sylvester, 'Some Dangers in Merging Feminist and Peace Projects', *Alternatives*, 12, 1987, pp. 493–509.

47 Christine Sylvester, *Feminist Theory and International Relations in a Postmodern Era*, Cambridge: Cambridge University Press, 1994.

48 V. Spike Peterson (ed.), *Gendered States: Feminist (Re)Visions of International Relations Theory*, Boulder CO: Lynne Rienner, 1992; see also Sandra Whitworth, 'Gender in the Inter-Paradigm Debate', *Millennium*, 18 (2), Summer 1989, pp. 245–53.

49 Christine Sylvester, 'Feminists and Realists View Autonomy and Obligation in International Relations', in Peterson, *Gendered States*, p. 157. However, it is worth noting two honourable exceptions to this masculine tendency: John Burton, *World Society*, Cambridge: Cambridge University Press, 1972, where he seeks to break down the divisive barriers erected by states to demonstrate common interests; and Ken Booth, *Strategy and Ethnocentrism*, London: Croom Helm, 1979, where he attacks the common tendency of societies to place themselves at the centre of the world, judging others solely within their own terms of reference (and usually as inferior). With this ethnocentric perspective, others' arguments and problems are never considered, as the international actor is seen as acting in isolation; and through lack of empathy or knowledge of the other actors involved, inaccurate forecasts are made and fears heightened, as demonstrated in Cold War power politics.

50 R.B.J. Walker, 'Gender and Critique in the Theory of International Relations', in Peterson, *Gendered States*, p. 191.

51 Betty Reardon, 'Feminist Concepts of Peace and Security', in Paul Smoker, Ruth Davies and B. Munske (eds), *A Reader in Peace Studies*, Oxford: Pergamon Press, 1990, p. 138.

52 See Brigit Brock-Utne, *Educating for Peace: A Feminist Perspective*, New York/Oxford: Pergamon Press, 1981; also in Smoker et al., *Reader in Peace Studies*, pp. 144–50.

53 Penny Strange, *It'll Make a Man of You*, Nottingham: Mushroom Books, 1983.

54 See M.S. Florence, C. Marshall and C.K. Ogden, M. Kamester and J. Vellacott (eds), *Militarism versus Feminism*, London: Virago, 1987.

55 A. Harris and Ynestra King (eds), *Rocking the Ship of State: Towards a Feminist Peace Politics*, Boulder CO: Westview Press, 1989.

Chapter 5   The post-positivist turn

1 For a general critique of the problems posed by positivism for security studies in particular and the social sciences more generally, see Richard K. Ashley, 'The Poverty of Neorealism', in

Robert O. Keohane (ed.), *Neorealism and its Critics*, New York: Columbia University Press, 1986, pp. 280–6.

2 Steve Smith, 'Positivism and Beyond', in Smith, Ken Booth and Marysia Zalewski (eds), *International Theory: Positivism and Beyond*, Cambridge: Cambridge University Press, 1996, pp. 11–38.

3 Some would not include social constructivism here, but like deconstruction, it is a theory or paradigm not an analytical technique.

4 Sylvester notes a variety of forms of feminism: Marxist, radical, socialist, empiricist, standpoint, postmodernist. See Christine Sylvester, 'The Contributions of Feminist Theory to International Relations', in Smith et al., *International Theory*, pp. 257–8.

5 Tony Porter, 'Postmodern Political Realism and International Relations Theory's Third Debate', in Claire Turenne Sjolander and Wayne S. Cox (eds), *Beyond Positivism: Critical Reflections on International Relations*, Boulder CO: Lynne Rienner, 1994, p. 105.

6 Susan Judith Ship, 'And What About Gender? Feminism and International Relations Theory's Third Debate', in Sjolander and Cox, *Beyond Positivism*, p. 146.

7 Mark Neufeld, 'Reflexivity and International Relations Theory', in Sjolander and Cox, *Beyond Positivism*, p. 15.

8 Barry Buzan, Charles Jones and Richard Little, *The Logic of Anarchy: Neorealism to Structural Realism*, New York: Columbia University Press, 1993, p. 68.

9 Marysia Zalewski and Cynthia Enloe, 'Questions about Identity in International Relations', in Ken Booth and Steve Smith (eds), *International Relations Theory Today*, Cambridge: Polity Press, 1995, p. 299.

10 Anthony Giddens, *The Consequences of Modernity*, Cambridge: Polity Press, 1990, p. 38.

11 V. Spike Peterson, 'Introduction', in Peterson (ed.), *Gendered States: Feminist (Re)Visions of International Relations Theory*, Boulder CO: Lynne Rienner, 1992, p. 12.

12 On Carr as a 'utopian realist', see Ken Booth, 'Security in Anarchy: Utopian Realism in Theory and Practice', *International Affairs*, 67 (3), 1991, pp. 527–45.

13 See, for example, E. Fuat Keyman, 'Problematizing the State in International Relations Theory', in Sjolander and Cox, *Beyond Positivism*, pp. 153–81.

14 R.B.J. Walker, 'Security, Sovereignty and the Challenge of World Politics', *Alternatives*, 15 (1), 1990, p. 5.

15 Ole Wæver, 'Securitisation and Desecuritisation', in Ronnie D. Lipschutz (ed.), *On Security*, New York: Columbia University Press, 1995, p. 78.

16 Ernst B. Haas, 'Words Can Hurt You; Or, Who Said What to Whom about Regimes', in Stephen D. Krasner (ed.), *International*

Regimes, Ithaca NY: Cornell University Press, 1983, p. 39.

17 Jan Aart Scholte, *International Relations of Social Change*, Buckingham: Open University Press, 1993, p. 134.

18 See David Lyon, *Postmodernity*, Minneapolis: University of Minnesota Press, 1994, pp. 78–80.

19 Alexander Wendt, 'Constructing International Politics', *International Security*, 20 (1), Summer 1995, p. 71.

20 V. Spike Peterson and Anne Sisson Runyan, *Global Gender Issues*, Boulder CO: Lynne Rienner, 1993, p. 36.

21 For example, Caroline Thomas mentions gender only once in *In Search of Security: The Third World in International Relations*, Brighton: Wheatsheaf, 1987, and that is to note that there is a general tendency to discriminate against women when food resources are scarce: p. 104.

22 Thanks to Joanna Spear for originally pointing this out. See Carol Cohn, 'Sex and Death in the Rational World of Defense Intellectuals', *Signs: Journal of Women in Culture and Society*, 12 (4), 1987, pp. 687–718.

23 Lucy James, 'Greenham Common: The Development of Feminist Security Ideas in Britain in the 1980s', PhD thesis, University of Birmingham, 1996, p. 343.

24 V. Spike Peterson, 'Introduction', in Peterson, *Gendered States*, p. 12.

25 Ibid., p. 13.

26 On this, see, for example, V. Spike Peterson, 'Transgressing Boundaries: Theories of Knowledge, Gender, and International Relations', *Millennium*, Summer 1992, pp. 183–206; and Peterson and Runyan, *Global Gender Issues*, pp. 120–2. Christine Sylvester divides the literature into three: feminist empiricism, which seeks to reduce masculinist bias in science to provide space for women; feminist standpoint, which seeks to develop women's characteristic activities into epistemological standpoints; and postmodern approaches. See Christine Sylvester, *Feminist Theory and International Relations in a Postmodern Era*, Cambridge: Cambridge University Press, 1994, pp. 10–11, 30–67. However, as Sylvester herself notes, feminist empiricism and more traditional standpoint approaches appear essentialist, while the line between later standpoint and postmodernist thinking is increasingly blurred (pp. 66–7); see also Sylvester, 'The Contributions of Feminist Theory to International Relations', in Smith et al., *International Theory*, p. 269. Yet some feminists may see the categorization presented here in terms of the male tendency to dichotomize.

27 J. Ann Tickner, *Gender in International Relations: Feminist Perspectives on Achieving Global Security*, New York: Columbia University Press, 1992, p. 16.

28 Ship, 'And What About Gender?', p. 150.

29 Tony Porter, 'Postmodern Political Realism and International Relations Theory's Third Debate', in Sjolander and Cox, *Beyond Positivism*, p. 108.

30 David Campbell, *Writing Security: United States Foreign Policy and the Politics of Identity*, Minneapolis: University of Minnesota Press, 1992.

31 James Der Derian, 'Spy Versus Spy: The Intertextual Power of International Intrigue', in Der Derian and M.J. Shapiro (eds), *International/Intertextual Relations*, Lexington MA: Lexington Books, 1989.

32 Again, Ole Wæver is particularly sophisticated on this point. He suggests that there were elements of incommensurability which went along with what he calls the 'neo-neo' synthesis (between neo-realism and neo-liberalism). Wæver, 'The Rise and Fall of the Inter-Paradigm Debate', in Smith et al., *International Theory*, pp. 161–70.

33 J. George and D. Campbell, 'Patterns of Dissent and the Celebration of Difference: Critical Social Theory and International Relations', *International Studies Quarterly*, 34 (3), September 1990, p. 281.

34 Emphasis in the original. In this section, Peterson mentions 'post-positivism', but it is argued here that this is used as a label for 'postmodernism'. Peterson, 'Introduction', p. 61, n. 27.

35 On this see John A. Vasquez, 'The Post-Positivist Debate: Reconstructing Scientific Enquiry and International Relations Theory After Enlightenment's Fall', in Booth and Smith, *International Relations Theory Today*, p. 218.

36 Ibid., p. 224.

37 Jean Baudrillard, 'La Guerre de Golfe n'a pas eu lieu', *Libération*, 29 March 1991; and Baudrillard, 'The Reality Gulf', *Guardian*, 11 January 1991.

38 James Der Derian, 'The Value of Security', in Lipschutz, *On Security*, pp. 39, 45.

39 Ibid., p. 40.

40 Thanks to Jeremy Jennings for his help in understanding Baudrillard.

41 Lyon, *Postmodernity*, pp. 52, 93–4.

42 Christopher Norris, *Uncritical Theory: Postmodernism, Intellectuals and the Gulf War*, London: Lawrence and Wishart, 1992, p. 12.

43 See Andrew Linklater, 'The Achievements of Critical Theory', in Smith et al., *International Theory*, pp. 279–98.

44 See Robert W. Cox, 'Social Forces, States and World Orders: Beyond International Relations Theory', in Keohane, *Neorealism and its Critics*, pp. 242–4.

45 Robert W. Cox, 'Towards a Post-Hegemonic Conceptualization of World Order: Reflections on the Relevancy of Ibn Khaldun', in

James N. Rosenau and Ernst-Otto Czempiel (eds), *Governance Without Government: Order and Change in World Politics*, Cambridge: Cambridge University Press, 1992, p. 133.

46 Robert Cox, 'Social Forces, States and World Orders: Beyond International Relations Theory', *Millennium*, 10 (2), reproduced in Howard Williams, Moorhead Wright and Tony Evans (eds), *A Reader in International Relations and Political Theory*, Buckingham: Open University Press, 1993, p. 276.

47 On this, see N. Rengger and M. Hoffman, 'Modernity, Postmodernism and International Relations', in J. Doherty, E. Graham and M. Malek (eds), *Postmodernism in the Social Sciences*, Basingstoke: Macmillan, 1992, pp. 127–46. Rengger and Hoffman characterize the positions as those of critical interpretative theory and radical interpretivism.

48 Cox contrasts problem-solving theory with critical theory; Neufeld contrasts postmodernism with critical theory. See Cox, 'Social Forces', and Mark Neufeld, 'Reflexivity and International Relations Theory', in Sjolander and Cox, *Beyond Positivism*, pp. 11–35.

49 Steve Smith, 'The Self-Images of a Discipline: A Genealogy of International Relations Theory', in Booth and Smith, *International Relations Theory Today*, pp. 29–30.

50 Ken Booth, '75 Years On: Rewriting the Subject's Past – Reinventing its Future', in Smith et al., *International Theory*, pp. 334–5.

51 On the constructivist–English School linkage, see Timothy Dunne, 'The Social Construction of International Society', *European Journal of International Relations*, 1 (3), 1995, pp. 367–89.

52 Emanuel Adler, 'Seizing the Middle Ground', *European Journal of International Relations*, 3 (3), September 1997, p. 322.

53 See Wendt, 'Constructing International Politics'.

54 Thomas Risse-Kappen, 'Identity in a Democratic Security Community: The Case of NATO', in Peter Katzenstein (ed.), *The Culture of National Security*, New York: Columbia University Press, 1996, pp. 359–99.

55 Ibid., pp. 367, 395, 396.

56 It is not that the literature on, say, postmodernism *per se* is slight, for it is enormous; rather, this is to say that the specifically IR-oriented postmodernist literature is not extensive.

57 See Steven Seidman (ed.), *Queer Theory*, Oxford: Blackwell, 1996.

58 Fred Halliday, 'The Future of International Relations: Fears and Hopes', in Smith et al., *International Theory*, p. 320.

59 Fred Halliday, *Rethinking International Relations*, Basingstoke: Macmillan, 1994, pp. 39–40.

60 Ibid., p. 40.

61 Kal Holsti, 'International Relations at the End of the Millennium', *Review of International Studies*, 19 (4), 1993, p. 407.

62 Sylvester, *Feminist Theory*, p. 130.

63 J. George, 'Of Incarceration and Closure: Neorealism and the New/Old World Orders', *Millennium*, 22 (2), p. 207.

64 John J. Mearsheimer, 'A Realist Reply', *International Security*, 20 (1), Summer 1995, p. 92. 'Critical theory' is here used to mean 'post-positivism'.

65 Smith, 'Self-Images of a Discipline', pp. 1–38.

66 Adrian Hyde-Price, *The International Politics of East Central Europe*, Manchester: Manchester University Press, 1996, p. 9, n. 13.

67 See, for example, Stephen Walt, 'The Renaissance of Security Studies', *International Studies Quarterly*, 35 (2), 1991, pp. 211–40.

68 William Wallace, 'Truth and Power, Monks and Technocrats: Theory and Practice in International Relations', *Review of International Studies*, 22 (3), July 1996, p. 311. Wallace continued his warning that post-positivism could lead IR to collapse in upon itself in the way that sociology and social anthropology did in the 1970s and 1980s.

Chapter 6   Non-traditional security threats: the environment as a security issue

1 John Chipman, 'The Future of Strategic Studies: Beyond Even Grand Strategy', *Survival*, 34 (1), Spring 1992, pp. 114–15.

2 See C.L. Schultz, 'The Economic Content of Security Policy', *Foreign Affairs*, 51 (3), 1973, pp. 522–40; Steven Krasner, *Defending the National Interest: Raw Materials Investments and U.S. Foreign Policy*, Princeton NJ: Princeton University Press, 1978; David Haglund, 'The New Geopolitics of Minerals: An Inquiry into the Changing Significance of Strategic Minerals', *Political Geography Quarterly*, 5 (3), 1986, pp. 221–40; Ronnie Lipschutz, *When Nations Clash: Raw Materials, Ideology and Foreign Policy*, Princeton NJ: Princeton University Press, 1989.

3 Dennis Pirages, *The New Context for International Relations*, North Scituate MA: Duxbury Press, 1978.

4 Lester Brown, *Redefining National Security*, Worldwatch Paper No. 14, Washington DC: Worldwatch Institute, 1977; Lester Brown, 'Redefining National Security', in Lester Brown (ed.), *State of the World 1986*, New York: Norton, 1986; G. Mische and P. Mische, *Toward a Human World Order: Beyond the National Security Straitjacket*, New York: Paulist Press, 1977.

5 Independent Commission on Disarmament and Security Issues, *Common Security: A Programme of Disarmament*, London: Pan, 1982.

6 See Arthur H. Westing (ed.), *Global Resources and International Conflict: Environmental Factors in Strategic Policy and Action*, New York: Oxford University Press, 1986; Norman Myers, 'The Envi-

ronmental Dimension to Security Issues', *Environmentalist*, 6, 1986, pp. 251–7; Lloyd Timberlake and Jon Tinker, 'The Environmental Origins of Political Conflict', *Socialist Review*, 15 (6), November/ December 1985, pp. 57–75.

7 Jessica Tuchman Matthews, 'Redefining Security', *Foreign Affairs*, 68, Spring 1989, pp. 162–77; Norman Myers, 'Environment and Security', *Foreign Policy*, 74, Spring 1989, pp. 23–41; David Wirth, 'Climate Chaos', *Foreign Policy*, 74, Spring 1989, pp. 3–22; Neville Brown, 'Climate, Ecology and International Security', *Survival*, 31, November/December 1989, pp. 519–32.

8 Critics identifying the environment as a security issue have appeared. See Daniel Deudney, 'The Case Against Linking Environmental Degradation and National Security', *Millennium*, 19 (3), Winter 1990, pp. 461–76; Deudney, 'Environment and Security: Muddled Thinking', *Bulletin of the Atomic Scientists*, April 1991; Stephen Walt, 'The Renaissance of Security Studies', *International Studies Quarterly*, 35 (2), 1991, p. 213; Marc A. Levy, 'Is the Environment a National Security Issue?', *International Security*, 20 (2), Fall 1995, pp. 35–62.

9 Jessica Tuchman Matthews makes this point in a widely cited *Foreign Affairs* article. See Matthews, 'Redefining Security'.

10 See Terry Terriff, 'The Environment and Security', unpublished paper presented to the National Security Studies Review Conference: Curriculum for a New Century, sponsored by Columbia University's International Security Policy Program, Fletcher School of Law and Diplomacy's International Studies Program, and National Strategy Information Center, Warren, Vermont, 8–14 July 1991; W. Harriet Critchley and Terry Terriff, 'The Environment and Security', in Richard H. Shultz, Roy Godson and Ted Greenwood (eds), *Security Studies for the 1990s: A Curriculum Guide*, Boulder CO: Westview Press, 1993, pp. 327–48; Terry Terriff, 'Environmental Degradation and Security', in Richard H. Shultz, Roy Godson and George H. Quester (eds), *Security Studies for the 21st Century*, Washington DC/London: Brassey's, 1997, pp. 254–5.

11 See, for example, Terry Terriff, 'The "Earth Summit": Are There Any Security Implications?', *Arms Control*, 13 (2), September 1992, pp. 163–90.

12 Thomas F. Homer-Dixon, 'On the Threshold: Environmental Changes as Causes of Acute Conflict', *International Security*, 16 (2), Fall 1991, p. 107.

13 See Homer-Dixon, 'On the Threshold', pp. 76–116; Homer-Dixon, *Environmental Change and Human Security*, Toronto: Canadian Institute of International Affairs, 1991; Homer-Dixon, Jeffrey H. Boutwell and George W. Rathjens, 'Environmental Change and Violent Conflict', *Scientific American*, 268 (2), February 1993.

14 Homer-Dixon, 'On the Threshold'.
15 Thomas F. Homer-Dixon, 'Environmental Scarcities and Violent Conflict: Evidence from Cases', *International Security*, 19 (1), Summer 1994, pp. 5–40.
16 Robert Kaplan, 'The Coming Anarchy', *Atlantic Monthly*, February 1994, pp. 45–76.
17 Ibid., p. 58. Italics in original.
18 Geoffrey Dabelko and P. J. Simmons, 'Environment and Security: Core Ideas and US Government Initiatives', *SAIS Review*, Winter–Spring 1997, p. 135.
19 See William H. Durham, *Scarcity and Survival in Central America: Ecological Origins of the Soccer War*, Stanford CA: Stanford University Press, 1979; Ted Robert Gurr, 'On the Political Consequences of Scarcity and Economic Decline', *International Studies Quarterly*, 29, 1985, pp. 70–1; Westing, *Global Resources and International Conflict*; Peter Gleick, 'Environment and Security: The Clear Connection', *Bulletin of Atomic Scientists*, April 1991, pp. 17–21; Norman Myers, *Ultimate Security: The Environmental Basis of Political Stability*, New York and London: Norton, 1993; Reidulf K. Molvaer, 'Environmentally Induced Conflicts?: A Discussion Based on Studies from the Horn of Africa', *Bulletin of Peace Proposals*, 22, 1991, pp. 175–88.
20 For other works that provide analytical frameworks for examining the relationship between resource scarcity and conflict, see Robert C. North, 'Toward a Framework for the Analysis of Scarcity and Conflict', *International Studies Quarterly*, 21 (4), December 1977, pp. 569–91; Robert Mandel, *Conflict Over the World's Resources: Background, Trends, Case Studies, and Considerations for the Future*, Westport CI: Greenwood Press, 1988; Ronnie D. Lipschutz, *When Nations Clash: Materials Ideology and Foreign Policy*: Ballinger, 1989.
21 See Terriff, 'Environmental Degradation and Security', pp. 257–62; Critchley and Terriff, 'The Environment and Security', pp. 329–35.
22 Homer-Dixon, 'On the Threshold', pp. 106–8.
23 Homer-Dixon, 'Environmental Scarcities and Violent Conflict', pp. 18–19.
24 Homer-Dixon suggested that fresh water might stimulate interstate war but did not comment on fish stocks. Ibid.
25 For a good general discussion of water as a strategic resource, see Malin Falkenmark, 'Fresh Waters as a Factor in Strategic Policy and Action', in Westing, *Global Resources and International Conflict*, pp. 85–113.
26 See Natasha Beschorner, *Water and Instability in the Middle East*, Adelphi Paper 273, London: International Institute for Strategic Studies, 1992, pp. 27–44; 'Ozal Says Next Regional War May be

Over Water', TA200222381 Ankara ANATOLIA in English, 1440 GMT 18 February 1991, in *FBIS Western Europe*, 91–035, 21 February 1992, p. 38.

27 See, for example, Gleick, 'Environment and Security', pp. 19–20; Miriam R. Lowi, *Water and Power: The Politics of a Scarce Resource in the Jordan River Basin*, Cambridge: Cambridge University Press, 1993; Peter H. Gleick, 'Water and Conflict: Fresh Water Resources and International Security', *International Security*, 18 (1), Summer 1993, pp. 79–112; Miriam R. Lowi, 'Bridging the Divide: Transboundary Resources Disputes and the Case of West Bank Water', *International Security*, 18 (1), Summer 1993, pp. 113–38; Stephen Lonergan, *Climate Warming, Water Resources and Geopolitical Conflict: A Study of Nations Dependent on the Nile, Litani and Jordan River Systems*, ORAE Extra Mural Paper No. 55, Ottawa: Operational Research and Analysis Establishment, Canadian Department of National Defence, March 1991; Malin Falkenmark, 'Rapid Population Growth and Water Scarcity: The Predicament of Tomorrow's Africa', in Kingsley Davis and Mikhail S. Bernstam (eds), *Resources, Environment, and Population: Present Knowledge, Future Options*, New York/Oxford: Oxford University Press, 1991, pp. 81–94; Peter H. Gleick, 'The Implications of Global Climatic Changes for International Security', *Climatic Change*, 15 (1/2), October 1989, pp. 314–17; 'Central Asia: The Silk Road Catches Fire', *The Economist*, 26 December 1992/8 January 1993, pp. 44–6; Murray Feschbach and Alfred Friendly Jr, *Ecocide in the USSR: Health and Nature Under Siege*, New York: Basic Books, 1992, pp. 75–88.

28 See 'Global Fish Stocks in Steep Decline – Report', *Calgary Herald*, 24 July 1994.

29 See B. Mitchell, 'Politics, Fish and International Resources Management: The British–Icelandic Cod War', *Geographical Review*, 66 (2), April 1976, pp. 127–38; Benno Wasserman, 'The Cod War', *Contemporary Review*, 225, July 1974, pp. 7–13.

30 There are a number of areas where such clashes are occurring, including the west coast of India, Honduras, the Bering Sea, Scotland, Senegal, Patagonia, the Falklands, the Mediterranean (Italy and Greece), the North Atlantic (France and Spain), Norway, the Indian Ocean, and Grand Banks (Canada). See 'Fighting for Fish', *Guardian Weekly*, 14 August 1994. See also Owen Bowcott and Louise Jury, 'Navy Seizes Trawler in Row Over Nets', *Guardian Weekly*, 14 August 1994; John Vidal, 'Overfishing Is At the Heart of the Conflict', *Guardian Weekly*, 14 August 1994; Owen Bowcott and Adela Gooch, 'Anger Boils Over in the Bay of Biscay', *Guardian Weekly*, 14 August 1994.

31 See, for example, Kevin Cox, 'Fishing "Pirates" Beware', *Globe and Mail*, 11 May 1994, pp. A1–A2; anon. 'Crosbie Raises Use of "Big Stick" on Overfishing', *Globe and Mail*, 4 April 1992. For an

overview of the 1992 dispute, see Terriff, '"Earth Summit"', pp. 179–84.
32 See Terriff, '"Earth Summit"', pp. 179–184.
33 In the 1992 dispute, for example, the Canadian federal minister for fisheries, John Crosbie, at one point warned that Canada would use all the means at its disposal to resolve the conflict, a veiled diplomatic threat.
34 See Ronnie D. Lipschutz and John P. Holdren, 'Crossing Borders: Resource Flows, the Global Environment, and International Security', *Bulletin of Peace Proposals*, 21 (2), 1990, pp. 121–6; Jock A. Finlayson and David G. Hagland, 'Whatever Happened to the Resource War?', *Survival*, 29 (5), September/October 1987, pp. 403–15; Bruce Russett, 'Security and the Resources Scramble: Will 1984 be like 1914?', *International Affairs*, 58 (1), Winter 1981/2, pp. 42–58.
35 See, for example, Mandel, *Conflict Over the World's Resources*, pp. 112–18; Ruth W. Arad and Uzi B. Arad et al., *Sharing Global Resources*, New York: McGraw-Hill, 1979. For a general examination of the effectiveness of, and ways to improve, international environmental institutions, see Robert O. Keohane, Peter M. Haas and Marc A. Levy, 'Effectiveness of International Environmental Institutions', in Peter M. Haas, Robert O. Keohane and Marc A. Levy (eds), *Institutions for the Earth: Sources of Effective International Environmental Protection*, Cambridge MA: MIT Press, 1993, pp. 3–24; Marc A. Levy, Robert O. Keohane and Peter M. Haas, 'Improving the Effectiveness of International Environmental Institutions', in Haas et al., *Institutions for the Earth*, pp. 397–426.
36 Homer-Dixon, 'Environmental Scarcities and Violent Conflict', p. 7.
37 Jody Jacobson distinguishes three categories of environmental refugees: 'those displaced temporarily because of a local disruption such as avalanche or earthquake; those who migrate because environmental degradation has undermined their livelihood or poses unacceptable risks to health; and those who resettle because land degradation has resulted in desertification or because of other permanent and untenable changes in their habitat'. Jodi L. Jacobson, *Environmental Refugees: A Yardstick of Habitability*, Worldwatch Paper No. 86, Washington DC: Worldwatch Institute, 1988, pp. 37–8. There are also those who migrate because an enemy destroys their food crops or denies them access to food crops as a deliberate tactic of war.
38 See Astri Suhrke, 'Pressure Points: Environmental Degradation, Migration and Conflict', Occasional Paper No. 3, Project on Environmental Change and Acute Conflict, March 1993, pp. 3–43.
39 See Sanjoy Hazarika, 'Bangladesh and Assam: Land Pressures, Migration and Ethnic Conflict', Occasional Paper No. 3, Project on

Environmental Change and Acute Conflict, March 1993, pp. 45–65.

40 See, for example, Durham, *Scarcity and Survival in Central America*; and Myers, *Ultimate Security*, pp. 122–38.

41 Homer-Dixon, 'Environmental Scarcities and Violent Conflict', p. 7.

42 Ibid., p. 25.

43 Other factors such as inequitable distribution of land, inappropriate development policies, bureaucratic inertia and corruption also have a role in generating peasant discontent. See Myers, 'Environment and Security', pp. 25–7; Gary Hawes, 'Theories of Peasant Revolution: A Critique and Contribution from the Philippines', *World Politics*, 42, January 1990, pp. 261–98; Myers, *Ultimate Security*, pp. 85–100.

44 See Homer-Dixon, 'On the Threshold', pp. 90–8.

45 Homer-Dixon, 'Environmental Scarcities and Violent Conflict', pp. 31–5.

46 Gurr, 'On the Political Consequences of Scarcity and Economic Decline', pp. 70–1.

47 For brief, if popularly presented, surveys of sub-Saharan Africa, the Indian subcontinent, Central America and Mexico, see Myers, *Ultimate Security*, pp. 70–84, 101–48. For a survey of South Asia, see Shaukat Hassan, 'Environmental Issues and Security in South Asia', Adelphi Paper 262, London: International Institute for Strategic Studies, Autumn 1991. For a survey of Southeast Asia, see Steve Lonergan, 'Environmental Change and Regional Security in Southeast Asia', Project Report No. PR 659, Operational Research and Analysis, Directorate of Strategic Analysis, Department of National Defence, Canada, March 1994. For Northeast Asia, see Vaclav Smil, 'Potential Environmental Conflicts Involving Countries of the North Pacific', NPCSD Working Paper, North Pacific Cooperative Security Dialogue Research Programme, York University, North York, Ontario, February 1992. For examinations of China, see Vaclav Smil, 'Environmental Change as a Source of Conflict and Economic Losses in China', and Jack A. Goldstone, 'Imminent Political Conflicts Arising from China's Environmental Crisis', both in Occasional Paper No. 2, Project on Environmental Change and Acute Conflict, December 1992. For an examination of environmental problems in Central and East Europe and the former Soviet Union, see, for example, Feschbach and Friendly, *Ecocide in the USSR*; Joseph Alcamo (ed.), *Coping with Crisis in Eastern Europe's Environment*, Pearl River NY: Parthenon, 1992; Barbara Jancar-Webster (ed.), *Environmental Action in Eastern Europe: Responses to Crisis*, Armonk NY: M.E. Sharpe, 1993.

48 See Levy, 'Is the Environment a National Security Issue?'; and Deudney, 'Case Against Linking Environmental Degradation and

National Security',

49 Levy, 'Is the Environment a National Security Issue?', p. 56.

50 For a partial list of wars, with a précis of the environmental impact, see Arthur H. Westing, *Warfare in a Fragile World: Military Impact on the Human Environment*, London: Taylor and Francis, for SIPRI, 1980, pp. 14–19.

51 See, for example, Susan D. Lanier-Graham, *The Ecology of War: Environmental Impacts of Weaponry and War*, New York: Walker, 1993, pp. 11–51.

52 See, for example, R.P. Turco, O.B. Toon, T.P. Ackerman, J.B. Pollack and Carl Sagan, 'Nuclear Winter: Global Consequences of Multiple Nuclear Explosions', *Science*, 222, 1983; Paul R. Erhlich, Carl Sagan, Donald Kennedy, and Walter Orr Roberts, *The Cold and the Dark: The World After Nuclear War*, New York: Norton, 1984; United Nations, *Study on the Climatic and Other Effects of Nuclear War*, UN Report A/43/351; 'Nuclear War and the Environment', Special Issue, *Ambio*, 18 (7), 1989.

53 See, for example, Arthur H. Westing, *Weapons of Mass Destruction and the Environment*, London: Taylor and Francis, for SIPRI, 1977, pp. 31–48.

54 Arthur Westing, 'Warfare in a Fragile World: Conventional, Nuclear and Environmental Weapons', *Bulletin of Peace Proposals*, 17 (3, 4), 1986, p. 360; Westing, 'Environmental Consequences of the Second Indochina War: A Case Study', *Ambio*, 4 (5–6), 1975, pp. 216–20; Westing, *Ecological Consequences of the Second Indochina War*, London: Taylor and Francis, for SIPRI, 1976. See also Arthur H. Westing (ed.), *Herbicides in War: The Long-Term Ecological and Human Consequences*, London/Philadelphia: Taylor and Francis, for SIPRI, 1984; Westing, *Warfare in a Fragile World*; Westing, *Weapons of Mass Destruction*.

55 One analyst suggested that the coalition forces utilize Turkish dam and water diversion systems to reduce the flow of the Euphrates and Tigris rivers into Iraq as part of the overall embargo. Peter Schweizer, 'The Spigot Strategy', *New York Times*, 11 November 1990, p. E-17.

56 See Bennett Ramberg, 'Targeting Nuclear Energy', in Desmond Ball and Jeffrey Richelson (eds), *Strategic Nuclear Targeting*, Ithaca NY/London: Cornell University Press, 1986, pp. 250–66.

57 The accident in Bhopal, India, in which the accidental release of industrial chemicals killed over 2,000 people and injured or maimed tens of thousands more, provides a vivid and horrifying demonstration of the potential consequences of attacks against chemical installations.

58 The oil spill in the Persian Gulf during the war was in part intentionally created by Iraq, but it was equally the result of coalition attacks against Iraqi oil tankers and shore installations.

See Douglas Kellner, *The Persian Gulf TV War*, Boulder CO: Westview Press, 1992, pp. 208–27.

59 See Jessica Matthews, 'Acts of War and the Environment', *Washington Post National Weekly Edition*, 15–21 April 1991, p. 27.

60 See John Darton, 'Croats and Serbs Broaden Battle; U.N. Pessimistic', *New York Times*, 28 January 1993; Darton, 'Battle for Dam in Croatia Grows, Ousting U.N. Force', *New York Times*, 29 January 1993; anon., 'Serbian Barges Refuse to Halt', *Globe and Mail*, 27 January 1993.

61 See Fred Roots, 'International Agreements to Prohibit or Control Modification of the Environment for Military Purposes: An Historical Overview and Comments on Current Issues', in H. Bruno Schiefer (ed.), *Verifying Obligations Respecting Arms Control and the Environment: A Post Gulf War Assessment*, Ottawa: Arms Control and Disarmament Division, External Affairs and International Trade, Canada, August 1992, pp. 13–34.

62 See Juda Lawrence, 'Negotiating a Treaty on Environmental Modification Warfare: The Convention on Environmental Warfare and its Impact Upon Arms Control Negotiations', *International Organization*, 32 (3), Summer 1978, pp. 975–91.

63 See 'Appendix 3: Geneva Protocol I of 1977', in Arthur Westing (ed.), *Environmental Warfare: A Technical, Legal and Policy Appraisal*, London: Taylor & Francis, 1984, p. 101.

64 See, for example, Michael Renner, *National Security: The Economic and Environmental Dimensions*, Worldwatch Paper No. 89, Washington DC: Worldwatch Institute, 1989.

65 See 'Report Calls Military Nation's Worst Polluter', *New York Times*, 17 March 1991; Tom Spears, 'Canadian Military Under the Gun Over Pollution', *Ottawa Citizen*, 15 September 1991; Annie McIlroy, 'World's Armed Forces are Worst Polluters, Canadian Group Says', *Montreal Gazette*, 18 March 1992; Ernie Regeher, 'Military Outranks All Other Polluters', *Tornado Star*, 10 April 1992; Bruce van Voorst, 'A Thousand Points of Blight', *Time*, 9 November 1992.

66 See, for example, Michael Renner, 'Cleaning Up After the Arms Race', in Lester R. Brown (ed.), *The State of the World, 1994*, New York: Norton, 1994, pp. 137–55; Lanier-Graham, *Ecology of War*, pp. 80–6, 92–122; Seth Shulman, *The Threat at Home: Confronting the Toxic Legacy of the U.S. Military*, Boston: Beacon Press, 1992.

67 See Jennifer Lewington, 'Deadly Legacies Haunt Nuclear Arms Plant', *Globe and Mail*, 17 October 1989.

68 Terriff, 'Environmental Degradation and Security', p. 264.

69 See Marvin Resnikoff, 'The Generation Time Bomb: Radioactive and Chemical Wastes', in Anne H. Ehrlich and John W. Birks (eds), *Hidden Dangers: Environmental Consequences of Preparing for War*, San Francisco: Sierra Club Books, 1990, pp. 18–34.

70 See Kent Hughes Butts, 'Why the Military is Good for the Environment', in Jyrki Kakönen (ed.), *Green Security or Militarized Environment?*, Aldershot: Dartmouth Publishing, 1994, pp. 83–109; Bruce A. Byers, 'Armed Forces and the Conservation of Biological Diversity', in Kakönen, *Green Security or Militarized Environment?*, pp. 111–30.

71 See, for example, David D. Dabelko and Geoffrey D. Dabelko, 'The International Environment and the U.S. Intelligence Community', *International Journal of Intelligence and Counterintelligence*, 6 (1), Spring 1993, pp. 21–41; Jeffrey T. Richelson, 'The Future of Space Reconnaissance', *Scientific American*, January 1991, p. 42.

72 Dabelko and Simmons, 'Environment and Security', p. 137.

73 Senator Sam Nunn's Strategic Environmental Research and Development Program is a step in this direction. See US, House, *National Defense Authorization Act for Fiscal Year 1991; Conference Report to Accompany H.R. 4739*, 101st Cong., 2nd sess, 23 October 1990.

74 For example, US military personnel and equipment may increasingly be used in relief efforts in the aftermath of climatic catastrophes, such as in Bangladesh in 1991 or in Central America (especially Honduras) in the aftermath of Hurricane Mitch in 1998. See 'Bangladesh Braces for New Cyclone', *Globe and Mail*, 13 May 1991, p. A-7; 'U.S. Troops Help with Life After "Mitch"', *CNN Interactive*, 28 November 1998, http:cnn.com/WORLD/americas/9811/28/us.mitch.01/index.html.

75 Terriff, 'Environmental Degradation and Security', p. 264.

76 Laurie Garrett, *The Coming Plague: Newly Emerging Diseases in a World Out of Balance*, New York: Farrer, Straus and Giroux, 1994. For a popularized account of the near-breakout of the ebola virus near Washington DC see Richard Preston, *The Hot Zone*, New York: Random House, 1994.

77 See William H. McNeill, *Plagues and Peoples*, New York: Doubleday, 1976.

78 Dennis Pirages, 'Microsecurity: Disease Organisms and Human Well-Being', *Washington Quarterly*, 18 (4), 1995, p. 11.

79 See Walt, 'Renaissance of Security Studies', p. 213.

80 See Deudney, 'The Case Against Linking Environmental Degradation and National Security', pp. 461–76; Deudney, 'Environment and Security: Muddled Thinking'.

81 See Sherri Wasserman Goodman, Deputy Undersecretary of Defense (Environmental Security), 'The Environment and National Security', remarks delivered at the National Defense University, 8 August 1996.

Chapter 7   Non-traditional security threats: economics, crime and migration

1 Janusz Stefanowicz, 'Poland', in Richard Smoke (ed.), *Perceptions of Security: Public Opinion and Expert Assessments in Europe's New Democracies*, Manchester: Manchester University Press, 1996, p. 113.
2 See, for example, Edward Luttwak, 'From Geo-politics to Geo-economics', *National Interest*, 20, Summer 1990, pp. 17–23; Robert D. Hormats, 'The Roots of American Power', *Foreign Affairs*, 70 (3), Summer 1992, pp. 74–90.
3 See, for example, Klaus Knorr and Frank N. Trager (eds), *Economic Issues and National Security*, Lawrence KS: University of Kansas Press, 1977.
4 See chs 3 and 4 in this volume.
5 Aaron L. Friedberg, 'The Changing Relationship Between Economics and National Security', in Henry Bienen (ed.), *Power, Economics and Security*, Boulder CO: Westview Press, 1992, p. 134 Italics in orginal.
6 See Alfred Thayer Mahan, *The Influence of Sea Power on History, 1660–1783*, Boston, 1890, pp. 29–87; Hans J. Morgenthau, *Politics Among Nations: The Struggle for Power and Peace*, fifth edition, New York: Knopf, 1978, pp. 117–33.
7 Richard Rosecrance, 'Economics and National Security: The Evolutionary Process', in Richard H. Shultz Jr, Roy Godson and George H. Quester (eds), *Security Studies for the 21st Century*, Washington DC/London: Brassey's, 1997, pp. 210–11.
8 See, for example, Jeffrey A. Frieden, 'Invested Interest – the Politics of National Economic Policy in a World of Global Finance', *International Organization*, 45, 1991, pp. 425–51; Robert Reich, *The Work of Nations: Preparing Ourselves for 21st-Century Capitalism*, New York: Knopf, 1991.
9 See Samuel P. Huntington, 'Transnational Organizations in World Politics', *World Politics*, 25, 1974, pp. 333–68.
10 Richard Rosecrance, *The Rise of the Trading State: Commerce and Conquest in the Modern World*, New York: Basic Books, 1986.
11 John Mueller, *Retreat from Doomsday: The Obsolescence of Major War*, New York: Basic Books, 1989; Carl Kaysen, 'Is War Obsolete? A Review Essay', *International Security*, 14 (4), Spring 1990, pp. 42–64.
12 See Theodore H. Moran, 'The Globalization of America's Defence Industries: Managing the Threat of Foreign Dependence', *International Security*, 15 (1), Summer 1990, pp. 57–99.
13 Joseph J. Romm, *Defining National Security: The Non-Military Aspects*, New York: Council on Foreign Relations Press, 1993, p. 60.

14 See Gavin Kennedy, *Defense Economics*, New York: St Martin's Press, 1983, esp. ch. 3.
15 Klaus Knorr, 'Military Strength: Economic and Non-Economic Bases', in Knorr and Trager, *Economic Issues and National Security*, pp. 183–99.
16 Much of the following discussion relies on Caroline Thomas, *In Search of Security: The Third World in International Relations*, Brighton: Wheatsheaf, 1987.
17 See Janet Kelly, 'International Monetary Systems and National Security', in Knorr and Trager, *Economic Issues and National Security*, pp. 231–58.
18 See Thomas, *In Search of Security*, pp. 39–63.
19 Ibid., pp. 64–91. See also Ronald I. Meltzer, 'Contemporary Security Implications of International Trade Relations', in Knorr and Trager, *Economic Issues and National Security*, pp. 200–30.
20 See Clark A. Murdock, 'Economic Factors of Security: Economics, Security and Vulnerability', in Knorr and Trager, *Economic Issues and National Security*, pp. 67–98.
21 Edward A. Kolodziej, 'What is Security and Security Studies?', *Arms Control*, 13 (1), April 1992, pp. 1–31.
22 Giacomo Luciani, 'The Economic Content of Security', *Journal of Public Policy*, 8 (2), p. 156.
23 On the effectiveness of sanctions, see David A. Baldwin, *Economic Statecraft*, Princeton NJ: Princeton University Press, 1985; Bruce W. Jentleson, *Pipeline Politics: The Complex Political Economy for East–West Energy Trade*, Ithaca, NY: Cornell University Press, 1986; Gary Hufbauer, Jeffrey Schott and Kimberly Elliot, *Economic Sanctions Reconsidered*, Washington, DC: Institute for International Economics, 1990; Lisa L. Martin, *Coercive Cooperation: Explaining Multilateral Economic Sanctions*, Princeton NJ: Princeton University Press, 1992.
24 James N. Rosenau, *Turbulence in World Politics: A Theory of Change and Continuity*, London: Harvester Wheatsheaf, 1990.
25 See Phil Williams and Stephen Black, 'Transnational Threats: Drug Trafficking and Weapons Proliferation', *Contemporary Security Policy*, 15 (1), April 1994, pp. 127–51.
26 See Phil Williams, 'Transnational Criminal Organizations and International Security', *Survival*, 36 (1), Spring 1994, p. 96.
27 Ibid., p. 109.
28 Ibid., pp. 96–9.
29 Peter A. Lupsha, 'Transnational Organized Crime Versus the Nation-State', *Transnational Organized Crime*, 2 (1), Spring 1996, p. 29.
30 See Williams, 'Transnational Criminal Organizations and International Security'.
31 Patrick L. Clawson and Rensselaer W. Lee III, *The Andean Cocaine*

Industry, New York: St Martin's Press, 1996, p. 53.

32 Lupsha, 'Transnational Organized Crime Versus the Nation-State', p. 30.

33 See, for example, Paul N. Woessner, 'Chronology of Radioactive and Nuclear Material Smuggling Incidents: July 1991–June 1997', *Transnational Organized Crime*, 3 (1), Spring 1997, pp. 114–209; Renseselaer Lee, 'Recent Trends in Nuclear Smuggling', *Transnational Organized Crime*, 2 (2/3), Summer/Autumn 1996, pp. 109–21.

34 Martin van Creveld, *The Transformation of War*, New York: Free Press, 1991, p. 204.

35 See Alex P. Schmid, 'The Links between Transnational Organized Crime and Terrorist Crimes', *Transnational Organized Crime*, 2 (4), Winter 1996, pp. 40–82.

36 See Clawson and Lee, *The Andean Cocaine Industry*, pp. 50–4.

37 Ibid., p. 59.

38 Ibid., p. 60.

39 Lupsha, 'Transnational Organized Crime Versus the Nation-State', pp. 43–4.

40 Clawson and Lee, *The Andean Cocaine Industry*, pp. 166–7.

41 Khat is a mild euphoric with addictive properties.

42 See Max G. Manwaring, 'National Security Implications of Drug Trafficking for the USA and Colombia', *Small Wars and Insurgencies*, 5 (3), Winter 1994, esp. pp. 384–9.

43 See, for example, Louise I. Shelley, 'Transnational Organized Crime: An Imminent Threat to the Nation-State?', *Journal of International Affairs*, 48 (2), Winter 1995, pp. 479–80.

44 Williams, 'Transnational Criminal Organisations and International Security', p. 110.

45 See, for example, Jeffrey A. Roth, *Psychoactive Substances and Violence*, Washington DC: National Academy Press, 1994; Mario De La Rosa, Elizabeth Y. Lambert and Bernard Gropper (eds), *Drugs and Violence: Causes, Correlations and Consequences*, Washington DC: US Department of Health and Human Services, 1990.

46 See Roth, *Psychoactive Substances and Violence*.

47 US Bureau of Justice, *Drugs and Crime Facts, 1994: Assessment of Drug Data Published in 1994*, Washington DC: US Bureau of Justice Statistics, 1994, http:www.calyx.com/ ~ ~ schaeffer/GOVPUBS/fax1994.html.

48 See *Drug Trafficking, Crime, Environment*, http:www.fco.gov.uyk/un/un5.html.

49 See Myron Weiner, 'Bad Neighbors, Bad Neighborhoods: An Inquiry into the Causes of Refugee Flows', *International Security*, 21 (1), Summer 1996, pp. 5–42; Barry R. Posen, 'Military Responses to Refugee Disasters', *International Security*, 21 (1), Summer 1996, pp. 73–7.

50 See ch. 6 in this volume.
51 Myron Weiner, 'Security, Stability, and International Migration', *International Security*, 17 (3), Winter 1992/3, pp. 91–126.
52 Ibid., pp. 106–8.
53 Ibid., pp. 109–10.
54 Ibid., pp. 114–17
55 Ibid., pp. 110–14.
56 Ole Wæver, 'Societal Security: The Concept', in Ole Wæver, Barry Buzan, Morten Kelstrup and Pierre Lemaitre, *Identity, Migration and the New Security Agenda in Europe*, London: Pinter, 1993, p. 21.
57 Ibid., p. 23.
58 Ibid.
59 Germany changed its citizenship laws to *jus soli* in the first part of 1999.
60 This particular conception of societal security intersects with conceptions of ethnic conflict. As noted earlier, ethno-national groups are one of two primary units of analysis when examining societal security. Much of the ethnic conflict which has resulted in horrifying atrocities in various parts of the world is not the result of the mass movement of peoples. One or more of the groups involved may have been, at some point, migrants to the area but this movement occurred long ago. The conflicts have been between different ethnic or societal groups which have co-existed for hundreds of years with varying degrees of conflict and harmony. Even in instances when two or more societies co-existed in an uneasy relationship, conflict between them seldom reached the level of savagery which occurred in the former Yugoslavia and Rwanda and horrified the world. The wars in these two states stemmed directly from the desire of one ethnic group to create an homogeneous ethno-national state of its own. Less clear is the degree to which the perceived threat posed by the other ethnic or societal group arose naturally and the degree to which it was invoked and created simply to further political ends. We do not want to stretch the conceptual connection between migration, as a threat to societal security, and ethnic conflict by contending that the latter is a special case of the former, but feel that both feature some common notions of societal security and that this similarity should be acknowledged.
61 Barry Buzan, *People, States and Fear: An Agenda for International Security Studies in the Post-Cold War Era*, second edition, Boulder CO: Lynne Rienner, 1991, pp. 19–20.
62 Ibid., pp. 328–9, 367–8.
63 Ibid., pp. 371–2.

Conclusion: security and security studies

1 David Baldwin, 'The Concept of Security', *Review of International Studies*, 23 (1), January 1997, pp. 5–26.
2 Arnold Wolfers, *Discord and Collaboration*, Baltimore: Johns Hopkins University Press, 1962, p. 150.
3 For an examination of the distinctions between 'national security', 'international security' and 'global security', see Helga Haftendorn, 'The Security Puzzle: Theory-Building and Discipline-Building in International Security', *International Studies Quarterly*, 35, 1991, pp. 2–17.
4 For two perspectives that analyse security based on these five realms, see Barry Buzan, Ole Wæver and Jaap de Wilde, *Security: A New Framework for Analysis*, Boulder CO/London: Lynne Rienner, 1998; Barry Buzan, *People, States and Fear: An Agenda for International Security Studies in the Post-Cold War Era*, second edition, Boulder, CO: Lynne Rienner, 1991.
5 See, in particular, Ole Wæver, Barry Buzan, Morten Kelstrup and Pierre Lemaitre, *Identity, Migration and the New Security Agenda in Europe*, London: Pinter, 1993, pp. 17–40.
6 See, for an example of this, John J. Mearsheimer, 'The False Promise of International Institutions', *International Security*, 19 (3), Winter 1994–5, pp. 5–49.
7 On this, see Emanuel Adler, 'Seizing the Middle Ground: Constructivism in World Politics', *European Journal of International Relations*, 3 (3), 1997, pp. 319–62.

Index